Here in a new and revised edition is the epic story of the Pike's Peak Gold Rush of 1859 and of the founding of the city of Denver and of Colorado's first boom-towns—now deserted ghost hamlets.

It was then that the "Argonauts of '59" raced across the high plains toward their goal in the "shining mountains" — their covered wagons bearing the slogan "Pike's Peak or Bust" emblazoned across their tops. It was a slogan often changed to "Busted, by God!" by those who lacked the necessary energy and stamina and so fled in panic back to the States —there to spread their tales of the "Pike's Peak hoax."

Yet still they came—a motley throng from every part of the country and from every walk of life: America at its best—and worst.

Here too is the story of H. A. W. Tabor, the ex-Vermont stonecutter who made and lost, in the space of twenty years, one of the greatest of American fortunes, and of his wives: Augusta and Elizabeth, the fabulous "Baby Doe" who only a few years ago froze to death in a miserable mountain shack; and his children, Elizabeth Bonduel Lillie ("Golden Eagle") and Rose Mary Echo Silver Dollar ("Honeymaid"). Theirs is surely one of the most fantastic and colorful of all American sagas.

The old frontier is a thing of the past. Yet in these lively pages much of the adventure and bold spirit and vivid color of those days when there was still a continent to be won has been recaptured.

Illustrated with 17 full pages of rare prints and photographs—endpaper maps.

HERE THEY DUG THE GOLD

Road to the Mines

GEORGE F. WILLISON

HERE THEY
DUG THE GOLD

Here was the glint of blossom rock,
Here Colorado dug the gold
For a sealskin vest and a rope of pearl
And a garter jewel from Amsterdam
And a house of stone with a jig-saw porch . . .

—from "Ghost Town," BY THOMAS HORNSBY FERRIL

REYNAL & HITCHCOCK, NEW YORK

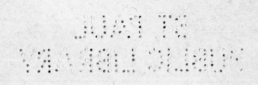

FOREWORD

From one source or the other, historical or fictional, perhaps rather more from the latter than the former, each of us has his own conception of the almost incredible hardships, the wild excitements, and even the more prosaic concerns of pioneer life in the early West. Some no doubt have been moved by curiosity to speculate upon the correspondence, if any, between the actualities of that life and their conceptions of it. Out of such curiosity has grown this volume which, for want of a better term, may be called a chronicle of early days in the Pike's Peak country—more particularly, of the great Pike's Peak Gold Rush of '59 and of the manner of life that prevailed in the larger mining camps which boomed there before the passing of the Frontier some thirty years later.

This chronicle could not, nor does it, pretend to be an exhaustive social history of early Colorado. But it may fairly claim, I hope, to represent the life and spirit of the time and place in not only significant but authentic detail. Although I have not burdened these pages with the usual scholarly apparatus, nothing has been presented as fact except upon good authority. Nowhere have I wittingly colored what was, by my own literary or dramatic notions of what should have been. Undoubtedly I have slipped into error here and there— but not, I trust, into the kind of literary "romance" that has bedeviled most literature about the West from the beginning. I have faithfully followed the record, for, to me at least, the truth here is stranger than fiction. Whenever I have had occasion to relate anything as a "story," it has been so indicated.

My goal has been to portray a whole society by presenting a group of persons whose lives were all more or less related but of very different kinds. So far as possible, these have been allowed to tell their own stories.

A background for these main characters I have attempted to re-create with materials drawn from many sources—published memoirs, public and private collections of manuscripts and letters, newspaper files, and talking with a number of old pioneers who lived through those eventful years.

With pleasure and gratitude I desire here to acknowledge the kindness of all whose advice, criticism, encouragement, and actual manual labor assisted me in the making of this book. More especially am I indebted to Mr. George Frisbie of Leadville for invaluable aid in imaginatively recreating the old camp as it once was; to the Honorable H. M. Butler, editor of the Leadville *Herald-Democrat,* for placing the files of the old Leadville newspapers at my disposal; to Miss Helen Teats, Mrs. G. H. Ferrall, and Mr. Walden Sweet of Denver for granting me access to books, papers, letters, and original manuscripts in their possession; to Mr. E. W. Milligan of Denver for many old photographs and cuts; to the Colorado Historical Society for both photographs and manuscript material; and to Mr. Thomas Hornsby Ferril of Denver and the New York *Herald-Tribune Books* for permission to quote from "Ghost Town," from which came the title of this book.

G. F. W.

Croton-on-Hudson
New York
September 15, 1931

PREFACE TO
ENLARGED THIRD EDITION

The text, though substantially unchanged, has been revised throughout and extended to include relevant developments of the story since 1931—notably, the restoration of the old Central City Opera House and its now annual play festival, and the tragic death of "Baby" Doe, the second Mrs. Tabor, rounding out one of the great sagas of the West, one of the most bizarre and dramatic stories in our history.

The Notes, the Selective Bibliography, and the Index are new, as well as the end-paper maps and many of the illustrations.

My thanks go to many with deep appreciation of their courtesies and invaluable help—to Dr. LeRoy R. Hafen, of the Colorado State Historical Society; to Mr. Malcolm G. Wyer and Ina T. Aulls, of the Denver Public Library; to Mr. James S. Holme, of the Central City Opera House Association; to the prints and maps division of the Library of Congress; to Brandt & Brandt for permission to quote the opening lines of the late Stephen Vincent Benét's unfinished masterpiece, *Western Star;* to the Scripps-Howard Newspaper Alliance for the quotation from Ernie Pyle on page 296; and to my old friend and fellow scrivener, the Swamp Angel, who knows more about "them thar hills" than any of us.

GEORGE F. WILLISON

Washington, D. C.
April 15, 1946

The text, though substantially unchanged, has been revised throughout and extended to include relevant developments of the past year...

(remaining text illegible due to show-through)

RAY A. WILSON

Washington, D.C.

CONTENTS

ILLUSTRATIONS

HERE THEY DUG THE GOLD

Americans are always moving on.

It's an old Spanish custom gone astray,

A sort of English fever, I believe,

Or just a mere desire to take French leave,

I couldn't say. I couldn't really say.

But, when the whistle blows, they go away.

Sometimes there never was a whistle blown,

But they don't care, for they can blow their own

Whistles of willow-stick and rabbit-bone,

Quail-calling through the rain

A dozen tunes but only one refrain,

"We don't know where we're going, but we're

on our way!"

—from *Western Star*,

BY STEPHEN VINCENT BENÉT

Pike's Peak

William Green Russell

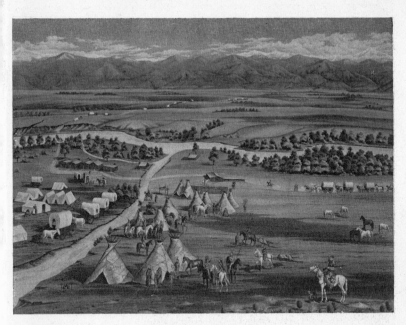

Auraria-Denver City, '59

Gregory Gulch, '59

Lynching from Larimer Street Bridge, Denver

Arrest in a Denver Saloon

Execution of the Reynolds Gang

Lieutenant-Governor H. A. W. Tabor

Mrs. Augusta Tabor, '80

High Road near Leadville

Over the Mosquitoes, '79

State Street, Leadville, 1941

"A Saw-dust Sleep in a Billiard Saloon," Leadville, '79

Dance House in the "Wonderful Mining Town of Leadville," '79

Fryer Hill, Leadville, '80

Chestnut Street, Leadville, '81

Mrs. Elizabeth McCourt ("Baby Doe") Tabor, c. 1885

Eureka Street, Central City, 1942

Ghost Towns—Ashcroft (above)
and Eureka (below), 1941

I

THE SHINING MOUNTAINS

". . . would be found to contain more riches than those of In-dostan and Malabar, or the golden coast of Guinea, or the mines of Peru."

FOR centuries England envied Spain her golden loot from Aztec and Inca temples, her vast stores of bullion from deep mines in Mexico and Peru. Always the English cherished the hope that their own less favored colonies on the cold North Atlantic might somewhere—some day—pour forth native gold in fabulous amounts. No search of theirs, however, came to more than Captain John Smith's near Jamestown, where he and his gentlemen adventurers, like millions of greenhorns before them and since, spent weeks frantically digging "fool's gold"—iron pyrites.

But in 1799, less than twenty years after Independence had been won and the last British Redcoat had departed, a twelve-year-old boy wading a creek on his father's farm in the North Carolina mountains stumbled upon a strange heavy stone, picked it up, and carried it home. There it excited sufficient curiosity to be kept and used as a doorstop until sold several years later to an itinerant goldsmith for $3.50. Other similar stones, including a legendary "twenty-eight pound lump," were found from time to time in the vicinity, but without inspiring any general excitement.

Thirty years passed before a North Carolina Negro known only as Charley, while journeying south on foot along the Appalachians, picked up gold on the banks of Dukes Creek, in northern

1

Georgia. From this lead, veins of gold-bearing quartz were soon traced back along the mountains into the Carolinas and across northern Georgia into Alabama.

A gold rush developed, the first in the United States and as boisterous as any.[1] The richest diggings, it was discovered, lay in Georgia on Indian lands belonging to the Cherokee, many of whom had already been transported across the Mississippi into Indian Territory (Oklahoma). With the advent of the gold rush, the remaining Cherokee were quickly dispossessed in the usual quite ruthless and barbarous fashion.

From the Georgia fields came the first large quantities of gold to be mined in the United States. Here, at Dahlonega, a branch mint was established in 1838, for the Georgia diggings remained the richest in the country until Tom Marshall, in far-off California, chanced to note a yellow glint in a mill pond and fished out the nugget which, far from enriching his friend and employer, Colonel John Augustus Sutter, brought him swiftly to utter ruin. For the nugget, like the bottle of the Genie, worked magic and conjured up a mighty human flood that swept Sutter away and forever shattered an immense and almost independent empire built up by long years of patient toil and loving care.[2]

The first experienced miner to reach the famous mill race on Sutter's Creek and prove the whole area rich in gold was Isaac Humphrey, an old Georgia digger. It was he, more than any other, who precipitated the great California Gold Rush of '49.

It was likewise an old Georgia digger, William Green Russell, whose discoveries along the base of the Rockies inspired the great Pike's Peak Gold Rush ten years later—as colorful and exciting an adventure, and as brave and significant, as any in our history. It was the last great westward surge. When it had run its course, we had completed the conquest of the Frontier begun so long before and under such trying circumstances at Jamestown and Plymouth.

Green Russell had joined the rush to California, journeying there with two brothers, Levi and Oliver, the former a doctor. In California the Russells appear to have done rather well. Dr. Levi, in fact, is said to have made $60,000 in the gold fields, which may well be doubted. In any case, they soon exhausted their claims and certainly were not rich upon their return to Georgia in '52.

Meantime, in 1850, another band of Cherokee, led by two Ralston brothers, formerly of Georgia and known to the Russells, had set out for California from their homes in Indian Territory, for these were Western Cherokee so-called. This party, it appears, had not entirely followed the main roads on its long trek to the gold fields. The Ralstons and their friends first joined the crowds of gold-hunters hurrying west along the old Santa Fe Trail.[3] But at Cimarron Crossing where the main trail bore off toward the southwest, they left the traveled road and pushed on alone up the Arkansas River.

Striking the Rockies near Pike's Peak, they turned north to follow along their base to old Fort Laramie and the Oregon-California Trail.[4] Panning for gold in every stream they crossed, they first "raised color" along the South Fork of the Platte, at the mouth of a small sandy creek lined with choke cherries—the renowned Cherry Creek of later years. They then moved up the Vasquez Fork (Clear Creek), and again their pans showed color along one of its tributaries, a sparkling mountain stream named Ralston Creek for the leaders of the party. But in neither instance were the colors bright enough to stay them or divert them from their goal.

Few other adventurers California-bound turned aside from the main roads, as the Ralston party did, to explore the intervening plain and mountain country. When the rush passed, consequently, there remained between the Santa Fe and Oregon-California trails a great island of virgin territory. Or semi-virgin, rather—for the Spanish had known it, the French had known it,

American traders and trappers had long since pried into every nook and corner of it.

But what all of these had learned they kept rather well to themselves for reasons of their own.

Into this island between the Platte and Arkansas rivers, Coronado had early penetrated in search of fabulous Quivera, where all plate was of solid gold and the king napped every afternoon under a great tree hung with little golden bells that lulled him to sleep with their tinkling.[5] More than a half century later—but still many years before Captain John Smith set sail with his gentlemen adventurers for Virginia—Leiva Bouilla and Juan de Humana came north from Mexico in another ill-fated search for Quivera. Then, a decade before the Pilgrims landed at Plymouth, Santa Fe was founded to become the capital of New Mexico and of all the plain and mountain country. Expedition after expedition was dispatched to the northward in search of gold and silver treasure, for the legend of Quivera was deeply rooted in men's minds and was slow in dying.[6]

The French had early heard of it. In their explorations westward from Quebec in the 1670's, Jolliet and Marquette were under instructions not merely to find passage "to the sea of China by the river which discharges into the Vermilion or California Sea," but to verify "what has for some time been said of the two Kingdoms of Thequaio. And Quivera, which borders on Canada, and in which numerous gold mines are reported to exist."

Soon the French were pushing westward across the prairies from Vincennes, Kaskaskia, and New Orleans. By 1750 bold *coureurs de bois* had penetrated to the Rocky Mountains up every large tributary of the Mississippi. Within a few years, however, the French flag was seen no more in the West as New France fell to Britain and Spain as spoils of war. The British advanced their outposts to the Mississippi from the east, the Spanish from the southwest.

Shortly, the British had to haul down their flag along the Father of Waters, and up went another—the new Stars and Stripes—along the eastern bank.

Then, less than thirty years later, came Spain's turn to retreat. With Napoleon at her throat, she had to disgorge Louisiana Territory and with many misgivings saw it sold two years later, in 1803, to the aggressive young Americans who each year came surging westward in greater and greater numbers.

Most Americans had not the slightest conception of the bargain masterfully struck by President Thomas Jefferson in buying a colossal empire for $15,000,000. But their eyes were already on the distant prairies and mountains, and they had their own notions about the site and nature of Quivera.

"These mountains are supposed to contain minerals, precious stones, and gold and silver ore," reads a book of the day. "It is but of late that they have taken the name *Rocky Mountains;* by all old travelers they are called the Shining Mountains, from an infinite number of crystal stones of an amazing size with which they are covered and which, when the sun shines full upon them, sparkle so as to be seen at a great distance. These same early travelers gave it as their opinion that in the future these mountains would be found to contain more riches than those of Indostan and Malabar, or the golden coast of Guinea, or the mines of Peru."

Lieutenant Zebulon Pike was the first to be sent on an official mission to inspect the Shining Mountains. He reached them late in 1806 to make an unsuccessful attempt to climb what he mistakenly called the "Highest Peak"—famous Pike's Peak. Pike then wandered mysteriously about the mountains with no apparent aim unless, as seems likely, he was involved in Aaron Burr's treasonable conspiracy to found an independent empire in the Southwest. Seized by the Spanish as a trespasser on their domain, he was carried a prisoner to Santa Fe and in time released.[7]

After Pike came other official exploring parties—notably, that of Major Stephen H. Long, in 1820,[8] and the five expeditions rather better publicized than led by the "Pathfinder," John Charles Frémont, the last of them in 1853.[9]

The vogue of the white beaver hat among milords of London and Paris, and the dandies of New York, had meantime sent forth hundreds of trappers and traders into the Rocky Mountain West in search of peltry. Many a romantic name is associated with this curious trade—Kit Carson, Jim Bridger, Jim Beckwourth, Uncle Dick Wootton, Tom Fitzpatrick, Bill and Andrew Sublette, Louis Vasquez, Ceran St. Vrain and his partner—perhaps greatest of all—Colonel William Bent, son of Silas Bent who had led the "Indians" at the Boston Tea Party. With three brothers, Bent had been on the Plains since 1823, building one fort after another up and down the Arkansas. That there was gold in the mountains, these trappers and traders had long known from the Indians. But the latter, according to Bent, always protested "against this knowledge being made known to the whites, for they were afraid and we believe with good grounds that this, their last and best home and hunting-grounds, will be appropriated by the white man, and they themselves be finally exterminated."

Traders and trappers, for their part, did not wish to see the country settled and guarded the Indians' secret well.

Reports of gold in the mountains began to multiply nevertheless. One circulated in '33, another in '45, a third in '46, still another in '49. Stories became less vague and circumstantial with the spread of news about the traces of gold found by the Ralston party in '50. Then, in '57, another band of Western Cherokee known to the Ralstons, who had married into the tribe, came north from Indian Territory in search primarily of good buffalo country in which to settle. But as all knew something of mining, they had an eye for gold as well. The Cherokee succeeded in penetrating as far as the mountains and raised a few colors along the tributaries of the South Platte before they were driven back home by the Arapaho and their fiercer cousins, the Cheyenne.

Through the Ralstons, or perhaps through his Cherokee wife, Green Russell learned of this Indian expedition and was soon in communication with the Western Cherokee. A joint party was agreed to, and early in '58 the three Russells and sixteen of their miner friends set out from Georgia for the rendezvous in Kansas Territory. Two months later, having been joined by some thirty men from Missouri and almost sixty Cherokee, the party, now more than a hundred strong, was slowly plodding up the Santa Fe Trail, pushing on up the Arkansas to the mountains. Here it turned north up the Fontaine qui Bouille, crossed to the head-waters of Black Squirrel Creek and at last, late in May, came rolling down the sandy banks of Cherry Creek to the South Platte —"camping that first night in a large grove of cottonwoods that three years afterward began to bear fruit with boots on."

Fording the Platte next morning after some difficulty with their heavy wagons, the party rolled on some ten miles to the north-west, to Ralston Creek, where all the men went to work in great excitement—but to little profit. Within a day or two many began to grumble and complain. Within two weeks half of the company hitched up and turned toward home, including all of the Chero-kee, who had lived in constant dread of an Arapaho attack. Those who remained now went in scattered groups to prospect neigh-boring creeks. All soon returned empty-handed and discouraged, and the party moved back to Cherry Creek, to establish a base there in the cottonwood grove at the junction of the creek and the Platte.

The sands in the vicinity were also disappointing, which pre-cipitated a second crisis, with muttered threats of violence against Green Russell. Gentle in speech and manner, tall and rather hand-some, perhaps even a little vain of his comparative elegance and neatly-braided whiskers, Russell calmly faced the mutineers and sought to quiet them by pointing out what they had sacrificed to come here, arguing that it was sheer folly to have come so far to accomplish so little.

"I have faith in this country," he declared, "and I will remain until I satisfy myself that there is no gold here if only one man will stay with me. Who will stay with me?"

A mere dozen among some fifty men chose to remain. All were Georgians and at Russell's suggestion broke camp immediately to pan their way slowly up the Platte. Loitering behind one day, a youngster began to "strip" a sand bar to bedrock. Green Russell happened to pass by, judged the sand bar likely, filled a pan with dirt, and knelt by the stream to wash it. With the water and coarser gravels disposed of, he examined the "crease" for pay-dirt. He quickly washed a second panful, and a third, before raising a great shout that brought all the Georgians running. As they fingered the pay-dirt carefully to satisfy themselves, they glanced at one another with shining eyes. They smiled—and laughed—and were soon shouting, dancing wildly.

"Our fortune!" echoed the cry, "Our fortune is made!"

Their fortunes were not made, unhappily, as they were the first to realize. Here they washed out less than $100 of "dust," but they were encouraged to go on. Working their way up the Platte, they found a richer gold pocket on Dry Creek and then another close by. But these, too, were soon washed out, and Russell called a general council. This free gold on the Plains, he argued, must have been washed down from outcropping veins in the mountains. If they would be rich, they had to find the source of the gold.

All agreed, and the party set out to trace the Platte to its headwaters in South Park, which was dangerous territory, for the Mountain Ute jealously guarded it as their one good hunting ground.[10] Finding nothing, they turned back and prospected north along the mountains some two hundred miles, almost to Fort Laramie. It was now September, and snow soon began to fly, as it does early in this high country, and the party hastened back to safety at Cherry Creek, little the wiser for their travels and exertions.

As days grew shorter and colder, a few scattered cabins began to go up in the cottonwood grove along the creek—the beginnings of a primitive settlement called Auraria by the Russells for a village of that name near their home in Georgia. Here, some seven hundred miles from the nearest settlements along the Missouri, the Georgians hurriedly made ready for the winter, anticipating months and even years of isolation.

After all, as the result of their long journey and a summer of exhausting toil and hardship, they had less than $800 of gold to be divided among thirteen of them.

Certainly, they were not rich—save in hope, every gold-hunter's one certain treasure.

II

ARGONAUTS, INC.

". . . masters of the popular Anglo-American art of town-making, understanding to perfection how to turn little or nothing into real or supposed fortunes."

MEANWHILE, unknown to the Georgians still absent in the mountains, a half dozen prairie schooners had drawn up and stopped at the Dry Creek diggings recently abandoned by Green Russell and his men. This was John Easter's party from Lawrence, Kansas, launched upon adventure by Delaware Indians, for they had never heard of the operations of the Georgians and the Cherokee until they reached the mountains.

Late in '57 Chiefs Little Beaver and Fall Leaf led a band of Delaware into Lawrence to excite the town by displaying a quill or two of gold dust. When asked its source, the Indians pointed vaguely toward the sunset. This apparently satisfied John Easter, local butcher, who began to organize a small party. Thirty or more adventurers from neighboring towns joined up before it set out the following spring. Chief Fall Leaf, one of Frémont's guides, had agreed to lead the party but on the eve of departure so injured himself in a drunken frolic that he could not go.

Without him, on almost the very day the Georgians first pitched camp along Cherry Creek, eleven prairie schooners rolled out of Lawrence and were soon lost in clouds of dust as they headed toward the Santa Fe Trail. The party was joined by two men and a woman at one remote prairie settlement, and at another gained three more men and a second woman, with a babe in arms.

10

fore, he had amassed a considerable fortune in western Pennsylvania from operation of Conestoga wagon lines and wholesale groceries, promotion of real estate developments, and investments in railroads and coal mines—an affluent career crowned with appointment as Major General of Militia. Bankrupted by the financial panic of '54 and almost frantically eager to regain an influential and respectable station in life, Larimer came west to found La Platte City on the Nebraska prairie, an ambitious but soon abandoned settlement. Retreating to Omaha, he served a term in the Nebraska territorial legislature before hastily transferring his allegiance to Leavenworth, Kansas, when that town began to boom.

As a speculator in lands and land warrants, the General naturally objected to the free and easy ways of squatters who were peopling the frontier. And as he raced toward the mountains, he only hoped that they had not yet had time to preempt all choice sites.

The Larimers had other anxieties as they slowly plodded up the Santa Fe Trail in their single covered wagon, traveling from fifteen to twenty miles a day. Before them, and to either side, stretched the apparently endless prairie, gently rolling away to the far horizon, brown and dry at this late season, with nothing to catch the eye but an occasional clump of bare cottonwoods in creek or river bottom. One long weary day was much like any other—except that each grew colder.

Nor did they dare keep campfires burning at night, for the Indians worried them by following their wagon constantly. Every day Indian horsemen could be seen on distant ridges riding a parallel course. Now and again the painted braves would come charging toward the wagon to beg trinkets, coffee, tobacco, sugar, and firewater. Though Larimer's patience was sorely tried, he never quite had the courage to deny his friendly but unwelcome outriders. Late every afternoon the Indians rode off, not to be seen again until the party was breaking camp next morning. The

Indians rode away a safe distance because they had good reason to distrust the whites. But the General was not one to appreciate this and lived in constant dread of a night attack. No matter how bitterly cold the weather, all fires were regularly stamped out before sunset.

Along the way the Larimers were joined by a small party of gold-hunters from Oskaloosa, Kansas. Some days later the combined party was surprised to spy three horsemen riding toward them down the trail, obviously on their way back to the States. The riders stopped to talk, and one identified himself as Green Russell, to the surprise and concern of General Larimer.

What did this mean? Was he abandoning the country?

Green Russell explained that he was returning to Georgia to bring out a large party in the spring. More reassuring, he showed them several small bottles of "dust." But he frankly told them how matters stood at the diggings.

"If I'd met you at Leavenworth," he concluded, "I would have advised you to stay where you were. But as you've started, I would say, go on and see for yourself."

Even so little encouragement renewed enthusiasm, and the party pressed on toward the Picketwire (Purgatoire) River, passing Colonel William Bent's great stone fort at Big Timbers.[1] Mounting four cannon on its walls, the fort covered more than an acre of ground and housed a number of hunters, trappers, traders, teamsters, and general hands—the nucleus of Bent's private army, small but formidable. Bent was known to the Indians as Wa-Si-Cha-Chis-Chil-La, or Little White Man, for he had been only fifteen years old when he first came into the territory some thirty-five years before as an agent of John Jacob Astor's American Fur Company. Always on the best of terms with the Indians, he had married among them—first, Owl Woman, daughter of a Cheyenne medicine man, and subsequently her sister, Yellow Woman, after the death of his first wife. The Colonel was induced to sell the Larimers a dozen apples for $1, their first fresh food in a month, and his fort somewhat quieted their fears as they passed up the Arkansas into wilder country beyond.

Nearing the mountains, they noted signs of travelers ahead and came up to find campfires burning in the river bottom near Pueblo, a cluster of adobe huts occupied largely by Spanish-Americans and Mexicans, all that remained of Jim Beckwourth's old trading post. A few years previously, on a riotous and drunken Christmas Day, it had been sacked and burned by a band of Ute braves, who killed and scalped more than a dozen men, only a Mexican girl and two children escaping alive.[2]

Somewhat apprehensive, Larimer sent his party off across country to the north before advancing to the campfires by the river, where he found eleven men from Lecompton, Kansas, under the command of "Colonel" Ed Wynkoop. The latter announced their intention of wintering where they were, and Larimer was not displeased until he learned that they had been authorized to organize the gold fields as Arapahoe County, Kansas, and had arranged to have themselves appointed as its chief officers.

This entirely changed the complexion of the matter in Larimer's eyes. These men were obviously needed as allies, and he now began pointedly to argue the necessity of proceeding immediately to Cherry Creek before everything of value had been pre-empted. But the Lecomptonites were hesitant and held back. It was too late in the season, they feared, to cross the high divide that lay between the Arkansas and the South Platte. They were aware that a large military command had been almost overwhelmed here by disaster not five months previously, late in May, when a severe blizzard had suddenly swooped down upon them from the mountains. The soldiers had suffered cruelly. Two had perished, and all had been badly frost-bitten. Many ponies and mules, not to be replaced within a radius of many hundred miles, had been lost, to the great peril of all survivors.

But General Larimer finally prevailed, and the combined Leavenworth-Oskaloosa-Lecompton party, praying for good weather, hitched up and hurried north past Jimmie's Last Camp and Fagan's Grave, ominous names. On the crest of the divide, some 7,500 feet above sea level, the wind suddenly rose with a roar in the pines, heavy clouds came scudding over the mountains, flurries of snow swept round the wagons, and before camp could be made, the storm burst in full fury upon them. Huddled together in the icy wagons, with the gale threatening at any moment to carry away the booming canvas tops, the shivering and frightened Argonauts scarcely dared think of what might happen as the oxen, maddened by the driving sleet, plunged and kicked and finally broke from harness. All night the blizzard raged, with the wind and cold increasing.

The morning, fortunately, broke clear, though it was bitterly cold. The oxen were found to have taken shelter under a rock ledge near by. By noon the wagons were again moving forward and on November 16th, almost fifty days out from Leavenworth, the Larimer party and its allies came rolling down Cherry Creek and pulled up in the cottonwood grove where Auraria was rising to busy sounds of axe and saw and hammer.[3]

Camp was no sooner made than Larimer went on a round of inspection. Decisive measures taken that very night reflect his disappointment and alarm at the progress made. An Auraria Town Company had already been formed, and some thirty log houses were built or building to either side of the Jack Jones-John Smith double cabin. Not a moment was to be lost, obviously, and the General called a council. Whitsitt and a partner were sent up the Platte to have a look at the town of Montana. Two others were dispatched downstream to survey the situation there. Larimer and his son sat quietly in camp until nightfall when the General, shaking off the fatigue of his long journey, slipped from camp, stealthily waded across Cherry Creek, and spent a chill fireless night on the far bank where he proposed to stake out a rival townsite.

His son Will joined him at daybreak, and together they hastily began building a cabin, for by the unwritten law of the Frontier no claim to property was recognized unless it had some pretence of a structure upon it. Land could not simply be engrossed and held out of use by a paper claim. The Larimers were only well started on their task, however, when a horseman came galloping up and ordered them off the ground. Several of John Easter's party, it seems, had made precisely the General's estimate of the situation and had already staked out the sand flats as the town-site of St. Charles. In organizing their town company they had invited the squawmen, John Smith and Jack Jones, to be members for the curious but adequate reason, as one of the St. Charles promoters later explained, "that we thought they might help protect our interests to a certain extent, for the land belonged to the Arapaho Indians."

The Larimers, having "jumped" the sand flats like any squatters, defied the horseman and stubbornly refused to move, quickly organizing a town company of their own. Then followed long and earnest debate on the question of the best name for the still nebulous settlement. Golden City ruled as a general favorite until some shrewder person, perhaps Larimer, suggested the desirability of honoring James W. Denver, governor of Kansas Territory.

Denver City they named it—only to have all hopes of special favor from that quarter suddenly dashed when word came at length that Governor Denver had resigned his post some weeks before.

The St. Charles promoters now pressed the Kansas legislature to pass a bill incorporating their company and granting it title to the disputed land. This the legislature was expressly forbidden to do, for in creating Kansas Territory the United States Congress had specifically denied it the right to alienate any lands owned by the Indians through treaty with the Federal government. Nevertheless, the Kansas legislature passed the St. Charles bill.

Hearing of this, General Larimer hurriedly dispatched one of his men in a frantic attempt to persuade Governor Denver's successor to veto the St. Charles bill. The agent did his persuasive best but failed in his mission, for reasons perhaps not then known to him:

"On the last night of the session, at 11:30 P.M., I went to the Governor's office and stated briefly that if anyone had any rights, we had priority," wrote a leader of the St. Charles group. "Knowing the Governor had a son, I said to him, 'If you will sign this bill, I will give your son one hundred lots.'—He signed the bill."

General Larimer, still refusing to admit defeat, now desperately proposed that the two companies compromise and unite to promote a larger and finer Denver City. After much negotiation, it was so arranged. The St. Charles Company accepted $250 in cash for its rights, and each member received a share in the reorganized town company.

The Arapaho were given a barbecue of three tough oxen.

By spring the two rival camps on Cherry Creek contained perhaps one hundred small cabins, all similar in style and construction, like the cabins of every early mining camp.[4] Logs, round or hewed, laid up to a height of seven or eight feet, supported a flat roof frame of split timbers, covered first with dry grass and then with six inches of dirt. Doors were made of canvas stripped from the hood of prairie schooners. Oiled cloth stretched over window openings kept out the cold and admitted some light. Such cabins were very dark, very warm, and also very wet, "the rain usually continuing three days indoors after the weather has cleared up outside." But they were not too uncomfortable, and life in them offered a number of simple pleasures.

"You have no idea how nice Will and I are fixed up," Larimer wrote his family. "We have plenty of everything to eat. Today we had nice cakes, venison, beans, and molasses for dinner. We have a nice door with an old-fashioned wooden latch, with the string on the outside of course. The fireplace, as is the custom in this country, is made of sods. In the southeast corner is the bunk; in the northwest corner the window, four panes of glass with sash. On the north side, between the end of the bed and the fireplace, we have two shelves and a bench, all made with a nice slab. We cut the meat on the bench and set water buckets on the other two shelves. . . . I have the remaining hams hung up; also, the saw, auger, and hatchet, also the two bed cords, and two pairs of boots and sundry little matters. On the northeast side and corner we hang our coats, guns, and things. I have a nail box, shovels, and old boots and buffalo overshoes under the bunk. . . . I am writing on a nice pine table under the window, covered with the gray horse blanket as nice as the day we started. On this table I have my books and papers, ink stand, and all the other nice things, together with a candlestick and candle, with some matches ready to light. Will scoured up the candlestick today; it looks clean and nice.

"We have also another pine table to eat on. Will has on it a nice table cloth of muslin. We have four nice stools with my trunk and waterbag to sit upon. I have the comb and hair brush on the window sill. Will made a nice willow broom. I have David Copperfield, my Bible, and your Prayer Book, together with some old newspapers and a lot of Mr. Collier's books on this table.

"We have three sacks of flour and some crackers, with plenty of candles, soap, dried apples, rice, onions, about three gallons of molasses, 100 pounds of bacon, 50 to 60 pounds of sugar, 30 or 40 of coffee, 1/3 of a bag of salt, and nearly a bushel of beans. . . . You have no idea how comfortable we all live. We sleep warm and nice."

The General indeed was prepared to speak well of almost everything but the lack of news from home, a want soon filled by Saunders' Express, one of the most important institutions of the day. Late in November, Jim Saunders and his squaw departed in an open wagon for Fort Laramie. Upon their return two months later the entire camp crowded about their wagon. As names were called, men fought their way forward to pay twenty-five cents for each newspaper and fifty cents for each letter. Larimer stood confidently to the last and could scarcely credit his ears.

"Our mail is in," he wrote his oldest son in great anguish, "and only think, John, we did not get either letters or newspapers from you or any other. . . . Oh! the sad disappointment when the next thirty days will have to pass without another mail. I never felt such a sore disappointment. I have no heart to write more today."

"Congregate one hundred Americans anywhere beyond the settlements," remarked one with an eye to the local scene, "and they immediately lay out a city, form a State constitution, and apply for admission to the Union, while twenty-five of them become candidates for the United States Senate."

Little more than a month after Larimer's arrival, at a time when the entire region did not contain more than two hundred persons, an ambitious attempt was made to cut the gold fields from Kansas and organize them as the Territory of Colona. A delegate to Washington was chosen at an election marked by considerable irregularity. In general, Denver City was aligned against Auraria, but liquor was also an issue. Party lines were rather confused, however, with abstemious General Larimer campaigning for "wet" William Clancy. But as Clancy also represented the General's town company, Larimer could forgive him his morals.

On election day a great blizzard was howling so that few in Denver City came to the polls, a deficiency which Clancy decided to remedy himself. With a few supporters he slipped away to a secluded cabin. There the younger Larimer, according to his own story, read a long list of names from a Kansas directory as the candidate and his friends cast their votes. But if congratulations were exchanged, they were rather premature, for with the approach of evening Aurarians came valiantly to the support of their candidate.

"After supper," so one of them related the story, "I told the boys I was going to fix up a ballot box, and, taking a cigar box, I soon had a good one. Then arose the question as to who would administer the oath of office to the election board. Some contended it would make no difference in this far-off country whether they were sworn in or not. Others made it plain that everything should be regular. They finally put it to a vote that I should administer the oath. After supper, in the midst of the blizzard, we wrapped up our books and ballot box, and started out to the different cabins for more votes from those who had failed to brave the storm, and by nine o'clock we had enough votes to beat Mr. Clancy—I think it was about a seven majority—and thus we prevented the sending of a drinking man to Congress."

Delegate Graham inspired only smiles at Washington, but the Cherry Creek camps did not lose hope. Within a few months a number of self-appointed delegates assembled, with General Larimer in the chair, to proclaim "many strong reasons why a State government should be adopted." They resolved that the "name of the proposed new State shall be Jefferson." This movement failed when the working portion of the population—the miners—refused "to take the slightest interest in these political maneuvers."

But aspiring politicians are never easily gainsaid. They called another convention of self-appointed delegates who proceeded to establish a provisional government for the Territory of Jefferson. As the proceedings had no constitutional warrant whatever, this extra-legal provisional government was recognized neither at Washington nor by Kansas, which continued to administer the region as the County of Arapahoe. The gold fields remained subject to two rival sets of authorities till '61, when Congress organized them as the Territory of Colorado, rejecting the name Jefferson as smacking too much of Democracy, then fatally identified with the slave-holding South.

No mining at all was done along Cherry Creek during the winter, and gold-hunters dared not venture into the mountains before spring. Although they did not quite believe, miners were not yet prepared to deny trappers' tales of winter there—of fabulous blizzards sweeping down without warning from the high white ranges to bury the pines under forty or fifty feet of snow. All had lost faith in the local diggings. During the long winter the only mining in the entire region was done at the mouth of Dry Creek by one Andrew Jackson of the Oskaloosa party, who worked every pleasant day with an occasional profit of a few dollars. In fact, as the younger Larimer once declared without great exaggeration, "there were only a few prospect holes on Cherry Creek, and in all the region around there was never found (as long as I was in the country) enough gold to fill a goose quill."

Restlessly awaiting spring to be off into the mountains, miners turned to the few simple pleasures at hand. Drinking and gambling were the most congenial. For months there had been little whisky in camp. No doubt many a demijohn started from the Missouri River, but few survived the arid prairie and thirsty Indian. On Christmas Eve, one that was long remembered, a wagon loaded with all kinds of merchandise was driven in by Richens Lacy ("Uncle Dick") Wootton, old trader and trapper, friend of Colonel Bent, Kit Carson, and Jim Bridger, and once as renowned as any of these. Wootton had come north from Taos to trade with the Arapaho and Cheyenne, who knew him both affectionately and fearfully as "Cut Hand." The miners crowded round his wagon, eager to buy flour, sugar, and all that he carried. Greater profit was to be had from trade with the Indians, but the miners were so clamorously insistent that Uncle Dick at last agreed to sell and in the end remained several years to become a leader in camp.

Auraria, he found, had "no such thing as a store or anything like one." Moving into a log cabin, Wootton started business "without waiting for any such things as shelves or counters to be put in." But there was no need of counters, for the miners' eyes were fixed on three large barrels in his cargo, all filled with "Taos Lightning," a staple of the early days—a raw rank Mexican distillation of which it was said that none indulging in it ever lived long enough to become an addict. Wootton rolled the barrels inside his cabin, ranged them on end as a bar, tapped one, filled a number of tin pans from the gurgling bung and with a friendly open-handed gesture endearing him to all but a few, invited the miners to drink their fill. The "Lightning" struck fast, hard, and often that first Christmas Eve, but with no fatalities.

"You have no idea of the gambling carried on here in Auraria," Larimer wrote his wife. "They go it day and night, Sundays and all, and Oh, how they drink! You cannot conceive of anything as bad as they carry on here. . . . Neither Will nor I go out at night."

Nor do the Larimers appear to have dissipated their quiet evenings at home with *David Copperfield* or Mr. Collier. Practical matters fully occupied their minds. With four shares and twenty choicest lots in Denver City, they now seized two large tracts abandoned by the town company. They also envisaged the necessity of still another townsite. One cold morning at dawn they hastened to the Platte, forded its icy waters, clambered up the bluffs on the far side, and there staked out the City of Highlands. A few cabins were erected, but development was slow and Larimer turned to other things. The diggings needed a hotel. At first sight it seemed certain to pay handsomely. On second consideration, the General decided not: a floating population of miners and squatters was not apt to pay its bills.

Late in January, to the amazement of all, six men from Michigan came stumbling into camp "with their hand-carts, . . . a most destitute lot." They had almost miraculously fought their way to safety up treacherous Smoky Hill, pushing their heavy handcarts more than seven hundred miles through deep sand and snow. The first of thousands of even more reckless gold-hunters, they came bringing news of a virulent gold fever sweeping the States. Men were everywhere talking of the new Eldorado and preparing to rush to the Cherry Creek diggings.

Larimer hastily wrote his son John at Leavenworth, exhorting him to expand his land and banking business to include a wholesale and retail grocery, "with iron and nails on the side." For, as the General declared with less exaggeration than he can ever have dreamed possible, "All the world and the rest of mankind will be fitting out there by early Spring." [5]

his gains fell into the hands of Kansas editors who by familiar devices easily swelled his profits from $2.50 to $25.00 a day. It was these same editors who gave the gold rush its name, for their confident knowledge of the richness of the diggings was not matched by their knowledge of where they lay. They placed them vaguely at the foot of Pike's Peak, almost a hundred miles south of the already abandoned diggings along the South Platte.

"Now there is *Shenanigan* going on," a Denver City miner indignantly protested upon hearing that enterprising promoters at St. Louis were publicly exhibiting three-ounce nuggets allegedly from Cherry Creek. "This thing is being done by speculators in town property out here and on the Border, and should be denied by all the papers; it was never found in such lumps, within a thousand miles of Pike's Peak, and the originators of such stories, to advance their own interests, *should be lynched,* and the emigrants who come out here next spring will, if they find out the originators of these stories, do this thing. Now, tell any of my friends who may think of coming out here next season, that they will curse the day they started; tell them to *stay at home* and not listen to all the stories they hear. There is a bare possibility that enough gold may be discovered here next season to pay for the emigration. If so, it will be a wonder."

From end to end the country was swept by the gold fever. During '59 more than a hundred thousand people, all conservative estimates agree, abandoned their homes in the Middle West, East, and South to join the rush to the new Eldorado. In a mounting flood they converged upon the Missouri River towns—by train, by river steamboat, by stagecoach, by covered wagon, on horseback, and on foot. Early in the spring, before the snows had melted, long lines of prairie schooners came wallowing axle-deep in mud across Iowa and Missouri, with *Pike's Peak or Bust!'* blazoned on every canvas top.

Gold-hunters from every walk of life crowded the wagons. Hal

Sayre and a friend, two young engineers from the East, arrived at the Mississippi by train and lay stranded there for days, unable to obtain passage in any of the prairie schooners passing by. They were finally picked up by two farmers in an old battered wagon drawn by a single yoke of feeble oxen. As the price of their passage, they had to buy a year's provisions for the party.

Finding times dull on the lower Mississippi, Captain Peleg Bassett persuaded three friends, all steamboat pilots like himself, to resign their commands and ship with him on a prairie schooner. Far away in Georgia, the Reverend Hezekiah Porter recruited sixteen hardy souls among his Methodist congregation and led them forth toward New Canaan.

By Horace Greeley's *Tribune* the excitement was carried to a quiet Connecticut village where an unemployed youth of nineteen decided to join the rush. Young Ryan worked his way west to St. Louis, hoping to find a job there and earn enough to carry him on to the diggings. But times were bad, and jobs not to be had. One day, while idling away an afternoon along the levee, he spied the *S. S. New Monongahela* loading for a trip up the Missouri. From stem to stern ran a large white streamer, reading: *Ho! for the Gold Fields of Kansas!* From another youth, a chance acquaintance, Ryan borrowed money, and both took passage. The steamer, large as it was, was densely crowded, with "seven hundred people aboard," the majority bound for the gold fields. As there were not berths for so many, almost all had to sleep on deck. Five days later Ryan and his new friend Rice disembarked at Leavenworth, dropping from sight for a time in the seething confusion that reigned in every Border town.[1]

In how many thousands of farmhouses in the East and the Middle West occurred scenes like this on the homestead of Robert Teats, in Michigan, when the Detroit *Free Press* and New York *Ledger* first brought news of Pike's Peak gold—scenes that profoundly affected not only individual lives but the fate of families for generations to come.

"How vividly I recall the interest of the family in the news," wrote Eugene Teats of these exciting days of his boyhood. "Father, after a hard day's work in the fields, going out to the gate to get the mail from the hired man whose duty it was to go for it every Saturday afternoon—and how we children would be allowed to sit up later than usual to hear him read of the great unknown country beyond the Missouri. Each week, through the winter, the news became more interesting and finally by Spring, after most of the hard work on the new and only partly-developed farm had been performed, Dad decided to go to Detroit (some 20 miles away) and make a more careful study of the conditions reported in the papers. In a few days he returned, fuller than ever of enthusiasm. That evening he and Mother sat up later than usual talking the subject over. We children, of course, were sent to bed early, but my own enthusiasm would not allow me to sleep. So, waiting until my elder brother who slept with me had dropped off into a sound slumber, I carefully slid out of bed and tiptoed across the floor to the stove-pipe thimble and putting my ear to the holes, found I could hear perfectly all that was being said in the room below. The upshot of their talk was that Mother thought she could handle the farm that year with the help of two trusted hired men and us boys, if Father wanted to go, which was surely his desire."

The question of finance bothered, as did the problem of caring for the family in case the crops failed, which was all too likely. But these matters were finally arranged, and Uncle Phillip, the father's only unmarried brother, was summoned to a general family conference.

"As I knew what was going on, my interest in the conference can easily be imagined," said Eugene, "for absurd as it may seem, I had hopes that I might soon be drawn into the adventure although at the time I was just past eight years old. No such luck, however, for Uncle Phillip took up the scheme with the greatest enthusiasm. Then all fell to studying such maps of the West as were available in those days, discussing routes and deciding upon necessary equipment, for the journey would have to start at our own front door, and with our own animals, and it was one of considerably more than a thousand miles."

A bright new "dead-axle" wagon was bought and, when wheeled under the carriage shed to be remodeled, centered the eyes and energies of all. The farm itself furnished tough young hickories to be dressed down and bent into the great bows which, when spread with canvas, transformed a plain farm wagon into as romantic a schooner as ever sailed the seas. Eugene had his part in the glamorous adventure; he helped bend the bows.

"This was accomplished by selecting a level area in the yard where stakes were firmly driven in in the shape of a great letter 'U,' around and between which the tough pliant slats were slowly bent by means of hot water, which it was my duty to heat and pour over them.

"Next, on each side of the top of the wagon box, shelves were extended out over the wheels to serve as beds for the travelers. At the ends, cupboards were built for clothing and other uses. So, gradually, after the long hickory bows were set in place and covered with stout canvas, the little home on wheels began to look so inviting that I could not resist frequent pleading to go. But I was always reminded that Mother depended more upon me than some other members of the family. And at last, early in the summer, with Nell the pet mare of the family in harness with her mate, Father started off one bright morning for the long drive to the Rocky Mountains. Little conception had any of us of the magnitude and perils of the undertaking. It was fully six months before we heard of his safe arrival in Auraria, the little settlement on the left bank of Cherry Creek."

But fevered gold-hunters, ignorant of even the rudiments of pioneer travel, began to rush blindly forward as early as February. A large number traced the steps of the Lawrence and Leavenworth parties up the Santa Fe Trail. A larger number followed the Oregon-California Trail as far as the South Platte, up which they turned to toil through long stretches of deep sand to the diggings. Many parties along this route were snowed in for weeks at a time.

Up this road, soon popularly known as the Overland Trail, raced William N. Byers "with his shirt-tail full of type," frantically eager and quite determined to establish the first newspaper in the gold fields, though none too familiar with the workings of the press, having been a surveyor at Omaha. One day Byers spied a strange white object astern. A wagon with two great sails bellied out by the wind rapidly overtook his ponderous prairie schooner, flashed by, and disappeared in the sunset. Next morning it was seen again—a total wreck in a deep ravine.

Two other routes were soon opened to the gold fields. One ascended the Republican Fork, the other the treacherous Smoky Hill Fork of the Kansas River. Both were shorter than the main routes, but many times more dangerous.

As the rush increased, it was not long before all trails from the Missouri to Cherry Creek were lined "with cooking stoves, clothing, and mining tools thrown away to lighten loads"—with the rotting carcasses of oxen, mules, and horses that had perished along the way—and with "many fresh graves." Upon a secluded island in the Platte the "bloody remains of a little girl with a broken skull" were discovered by a Boston journalist who found it "difficult to surmise the motive of the murder of the poor child."

Up the Republican River trail came Horace Austin Warner Tabor, with his wife and year-old baby, both weak and ailing. Although wholly undistinguished at the moment and destined to remain so till late in life, Tabor is a man to mark—with his large head and great black handle-bar moustache, his thick heavy body and curious loping gait, his slow fumbling habits of thought and speech. After long bitter years of failure and defeat in the mountains, he will awaken one morning to discover himself, thanks to a pilfered jug of whisky, Colorado's first great Bonanza King, a man of vast influence and power. He will become a banker, a patron of the arts, and go on to grace the United States Senate, trailing involved matrimonial troubles that boiled up into a national scandal—altogether, a fantastic career that, with its high tragedy and low comedy, has become legend in the West, an epitome of frontier society at its gaudiest and most ironic.

A poor stonecutter from Holland, Vermont, where he had been born in 1830 to Sarah (Ternin) and Cornelius Tabor, a small farmer and country schoolmaster, Horace early left home because of difficulties with a stepmother. Making his way to Quincy, Massachusetts, he there joined an older brother who taught him his trade. Tabor later drifted to Portland, Maine, where in the panic year of '57 he married his employer's daughter, Augusta Pierce. A frail and delicate girl, she was rather angular perhaps both in figure and manner, as New England girls are apt to be. But whatever Augusta may have wanted in physical strength, comeliness, and charm, none ever denied her remarkable moral stamina, her steadfast loyalty, and great unpretentious courage.

As times were bad, Augusta immediately acquiesced in Tabor's desire to seek his fortune in the West. They journeyed by rail to St. Louis and thence by five-day boat to Westport (Kansas City). There, said Augusta, "we purchased a yoke of oxen, a wagon, a few farming tools, some seed, took my trunks, and started westward. The trip was not very pleasant, for the wind blew disagreeably, as it always does in Kansas."

At Zeandale, near Manhattan, the Tabors claimed an abandoned homestead and started housekeeping in a deserted cabin standing quite alone upon the open rolling pairie.

"To add to the desolation of the place, the wind took a new

start. Our only furniture was a No. 7 cook stove, a dilapidated
trunk, and a rough bedstead made of poles, on which was an old
tick filled with prairie grass. I sat down upon the trunk and
cried," declared Augusta later, vividly remembering the anguish
of those days. "I had not been deceived in coming to this place.
I knew perfectly well that the country was new, that there were
no saw mills near and no money in the territory. But I was homesick, and could not conceal it from the others."

Here Tabor broke ground and put in seed, exchanging day
labor with neighbors to save hiring help. Augusta worked in the
fields as well, until brought to bed with her first and only child,
Nathaniel Maxcy. During that first summer no rain at all fell.
When harvest came, there was nothing to gather. That winter
Tabor went to Fort Riley near by to work at his stonecutting
trade. Augusta remained at home to mind her baby and raise
chickens. Indians and snakes infested the neighborhood, and Augusta lived in constant dread of both, especially of the rattle-
snakes which she occasionally found coiled in her cabin.

The next summer brought much rain and an abundant crop.
But the Tabors were little better off than before, as they could
find no market for their produce. What little money the family
had was earned by the tireless efforts of Augusta, who "kept
boarders and made some butter to sell."

Certainly, Kansas seemed to offer little hope of fortune.

"In February, 1859, Mr. Tabor heard of Pike's Peak through
someone of Green Russell's party who was returning, and at once
decided to try his luck in the new Eldorado. He told me I might
go home to Maine, but I refused to leave him, and upon reflection
he thought it would be more profitable to take me, as in that case
the two men would go along and board with us, and the money
they paid would keep us all. . . . Mr. Tabor worked at the Fort
through March and April, earning money for the outfit. The fifth
day of May we gathered together our scanty means, bought supplies for a few months, yoked our oxen and cows, mounted to our

seats in the wagon, and left the town of Zeandale with the determination of returning in the Fall, or as soon as we made enough money to pay for the one hundred and sixty acres of Government land and buy a little stock."

Unsuspecting their destiny—their separate tragic destinies—the Tabors drove off never to return. Soon they were plodding up the Republican River through lush green prairies starred with crimson anemones and blue larkspur, shadowed with dark belts of purple bunch grass. Timber along creek and river bottoms gradually thinned out and finally disappeared. Now they were among the buffalo, antelope, and Indians on the high brown Plains. The Tabors passed Hurricane Creek just a few weeks after it had been named for a tornado that "overturned heavy freight wagons, blew a light buggy into fragments, tore open boxes and scattered dry goods for several miles, and rolled cooking stoves forty to fifty yards."

The Tabors encountered no hurricanes or cloudbursts such as endangered the lives of thousands traveling the prairies before them and since. But every afternoon they anxiously watched towering white thunderheads pile up in the west to cast an indigo shadow over the sultry, suddenly hushed afternoon. Great shafts of rose-colored lightning flashed across the heavens. With a deafening report the thunder crashed and rolled heavily off into the distance. Then, with a sudden cyclonic blast, the storm burst upon them with blinding torrents of water. Not even the terrifying white squalls on tropical seas, according to a world traveler who followed this road a few years later, equaled the sudden violence of these prairie thunderstorms which often shot down hailstones as large as pigeon eggs to whiten the earth for miles around.

Day after day the Tabors followed the strenuous and almost invariable routine imposed upon all gold-hunters. By seven each morning they had breakfasted, struck their tent, repacked the wagon, captured the grazing cattle, and yoked them, driving a full five hours before dinner at midday. They then usually rested an hour or two while the sun was hot overhead, sometimes amusing themselves with a game of cards, more often creeping under the wagon to nap in the shade. After three or four hours of driving in the afternoon one of the men rode ahead to scout for a campsite.

Again, while supper was preparing and the tent being raised, the cattle were turned out to pasture. More often than not, there was no wood, and buffalo dung had to serve as fuel. Even this was not always easy to find. It sometimes required an hour or two to gather sufficient to cook beans, bacon, and coffee. The weary work of gathering buffalo chips—*bois des vaches*—fell to Augusta's lot, for the men had all they could do in caring for the teams and in making and breaking camp. Supper was finished before dusk. The oxen were herded back once more to be tied securely to the wagon wheels. The wagon itself was frequently staked down against the wind. Smudges were built to drive off the clouds of insects that constantly harassed them. White stars were always out before Augusta and the men were ready for bed. The watchman for the night took his post. Rifles and revolvers were looked to and placed within easy reach. At last, all lay down to rest as best they could—to be up again next morning at daybreak.

"Indians followed us all the time," declared Augusta, "and though friendly, were continually begging and stealing. Every Sunday we rested, if rest it could be called. The men went hunting, while I stayed to guard the camp, wash the soiled linen, and cook for the following week." But Augusta often accomplished nothing at all on Sundays, for the departure of the men emboldened the Indians in their worst practices. When not begging and stealing, they wallowed in the water courses from which the party drew its supplies and were generally pretty filthy, said Augusta.

"My babe was teething and suffering from fever and ague, and required constant attention day and night. I was weak and feeble, having suffered all the time I lived in Kansas with the ague. My weight was only ninety pounds.

"What I endured on that journey only the women who crossed the plains in '59 can realize."

Altogether, it was a searing experience, but years later Augusta looked back upon it without regret.

"I can almost see the approach of each night's camping ground. I can tell how, when, where, and how many buffalo my husband killed. I can see just how the Indians looked as they came on begging expeditions to our wagon. The antelope, the great herds of buffalo, the wild flowers I gathered, the prairie chickens, the bright mornings, the fragrant atmosphere. . . . I was a girl then, filled with enthusiasm. I feared nothing."

Of Augusta it should be said here rather than later that she, almost alone among her contemporaries, looked upon the antelope, the buffalo, and the prairie chicken as something more than meat for the pot. She was one of the very few who saw more in the lush green prairies than potential real estate. No one else in later years recalled gathering wild flowers on fresh spring mornings under a bright yellow sun. And never did she come to look upon the mountains merely as heaps of rock perversely piled up by the gods to hide gold and silver treasure.

Now came another with eyes to see and ears to hear. On the far bank of the Missouri suddenly appeared Eugene Teats, all of nine years old, in "red-topped boots (long hoped for), a suit of blue overalls, one just a little better, and a little carpetbag well loaded not only with a change of underwear but good home-cooked food." Eugene had left home alone for St. Joseph, Missouri, where he was to meet his father's partner, Colonel John Wanless, who was to take him on to the diggings. Eugene had just arrived by train.

"What a crazy old road it was in those days, that Burlington and St. Joe. First ride aways, then walk aways, and those able to do so were expected to be prepared to help put the cars back on the track everytime they slipped off, which was often. We were all day, all night, and until four P.M. of the second day in reach-

ing St. Joe. The slow run was very tiresome, and I will admit that
I was ready to turn my back on Pike's Peak after listening to the
talk of the passengers, many of them bound for the P.P. country.
When I heard of the discomforts and dangers they were looking
forward to, more than ever did I long for home and Mother, and
consider going back while I still had money enough in my little
belt so securely fastened around my waist. So, when we landed
and I strutted about the rickety old platform, expecting someone
to grab me, and no one even inquired who I was or where I was
going, my feelings do not have to be explained. So I went to the
agent and told him my troubles, asking for a ticket and the time
the train went back."

The kindly station agent smiled and took the boy home with
him for the night. Next day Eugene got trace of the Colonel by
making inquiries among the horse dealers. Learning the name of
the hotel at which the Colonel's family was stopping, he knocked
on the door and was "at once invited by Mrs. Wanless to come
right in." The Colonel was off in the country buying stock, but
several days later returned with horses and two farm hands, who
in their desire to reach the gold fields had signed on as teamsters
without pay.

Within the week the party set out in two heavy wagons, each
drawn by two teams of horses, followed by the Colonel's "ambulance," a light strong vehicle favored by army officers crossing the
Plains. Eugene was given an honored place on the box beside the
driver of the leading wagon. With the Colonel's ambulance bringing up the rear, the party was ferried across the Missouri and
drove off into Kansas. Passing through a thick forest, with cultivated clearings here and there, they emerged in open grass land.
That first night camp was made near a deserted cabin offering
wood and water and shelter for the stock. After supper the Colonel ordered nine-year-old Eugene to stand watch till midnight,
under strict orders to call the next watch at that time. Although

he did not pretend to know what was to be done, or why, Eugene obeyed without asking questions.

"Being very proud of the confidence placed in me, I had no difficulty in keeping awake. The night was fine, the camp fire was alive, and the fragrance of fried ham and pancakes still lingered around. It was not at all unpleasant; besides, I had a double-barreled shotgun and was already feeling myself a man among men, as a boy will under such circumstances. But about ten o'clock I was startled to attention by a long-drawn-out howl that seemed far away, followed almost immediately by another coming apparently from exactly the opposite direction, then by a succession of howls, each seemingly nearer than the one before. To say that I was alarmed would be to put the matter mildly. None of the sleepers seemed to hear the sounds that were so terrifying me, or if they did, did not take any notice of them. Nor were the stock in the least disturbed. So I managed, though badly scared, to stand my ground and refrain from calling for help. After a while, as usual, the chorus died out or came from such a distance that my courage revived.

"But the experience drove all thought of time out of my mind. Midnight came and went, and left me still tensely listening for repetitions of what I still fancied to be a threatened attack by a group of pernicious wild brutes. At last, close to four A.M., the horses, being more or less strange to one another, began to quarrel and move about uneasily. This finally resulted in a kicking bee which culminated when one big animal broke the rail to which he was tied in his stall, which, of course, made such a racket that the whole camp came awake. Three of us at once saddled and started in pursuit."

Several hours later Eugene found the runaway horse. But he was lying prostrate, with his back broken. In attempting to jump a small stream, he had been thrown and killed when trees along the bank caught and held the dragging rail. The Colonel gave the boy a "well-deserved lecture" before turning back to St. Joseph to procure another animal, leaving the party in camp at the deserted farm. Eugene improved the interim with sly questions to establish the cause of his alarm and was somewhat chagrined to see his "troup of pernicious wild brutes" turn into a band of sneaking coyotes.

"But those who know what kind of a noise one coyote can make when on his mettle will understand the impression made on a youth (under ten)," he said, "on hearing hundreds of them at night for the first time."

After more than a week of monotonous travel the driver of the leading wagon, a powerful young Scot, Eugene's favorite in the party, asked permission to quit his job, saying he wanted "to strike out with some others on foot and get to the mountains and mines sooner." The Colonel was greatly upset and pointed out the difficulty.

"No trouble about that," said Scotty, "for that boy can beat me to death driving and caring for the teams. Let him try for a day or so, and I'll stay along until you satisfy yourself that with help in greasing the wagon and in handling the feed, he can take my job to your advantage."

Scotty departed, and Eugene now reigned alone upon the wagon box though the Colonel ordered him to drop back to second place in line. As they were plodding forward four days later, they came upon a fresh grave by the roadside. Eugene was overcome when he discovered it to be Scotty's.

"But whether he was killed by whites or Indians we never learned, but we inferred the former, because the grave was evidently not the kind of one a savage would have given him. We knew that he had a good-sized wad of money when he left us, and as he was gifted with a love of whisky, like many of his countrymen, and a rather loose tongue, we reached the conclusion that his new companions were in some way responsible for his death. But in those days when laws had not yet crossed the Missouri and a man was supposed to take care of himself or suffer the consequences, no one had the time or inclination to follow up a matter of that kind."

Colonel Wanless had chosen to proceed by the dangerous route up Smoky Hill, and the party was soon struggling through the Ridge Country, barren and stony. Grass was thin and water scarce, most of it alkaline. The grain supply, even at half rations, was rapidly disappearing. All that cheered them was sight at last of the snow-capped mountains far on the horizon. Eugene was in raptures, but more than a hundred difficult miles yet separated the party from Cherry Creek and safety.

The horses were now too hungry, weak, and footsore to go on. The Colonel decided to lighten the ambulance and push on for help, leaving Eugene and the driver of the other wagon to make what progress they could after allowing the horses a full day's rest. When the teams were harnessed up again, one of Eugene's leaders collapsed, and they had to remain in camp on the hot dry Plains another day. Eugene was "pretty blue."

Next morning they learned of a stage station some miles in advance. But they had no money and Eugene said nothing of the gold in his belt, having long ago resolved not to be parted from it. He was persuaded, however, to ride forward to use his wiles upon the station agent. He returned soon with corn and hay received on credit. Good feed so quickly restored the horses that they were hitched up for a drive during the cool of the evening. Progress was so rapid that it was decided to keep moving all night. Guiding themselves by the white stars, they rolled slowly forward through the dark with nothing to be seen and nothing to be heard but the heavy breathing of the horses and the creaking of the wagons. But about midnight they heard a distant tramp of horses, apparently in the rear. Eugene was frightened, thinking the station agent was pursuing them to demand his pay. Then the sounds shifted and appeared to come from in front. And now someone was riding up close by in the dark, and a voice rang out.

"Is there a Eugene Teats in your party?"

The boy was too overcome by mixed emotions of fear and joy to reply. The driver of the other wagon answered for him, and Eugene was soon in his father's arms, sobbing loudly.

"You can imagine the reunion there in the middle of the night on the barren plains. Father was riding a beautiful little Indian pony that he had bought for me, and on another horse had a sack of grain for the animals and some lunch for us. We proceeded at once to feed ourselves and the animals, while McKnight rode back to pay for what we had procured from the agent. Well, to make a long story short, we started off in good shape the following morning, I on my new mount, Father driving my team, and with old Long's Peak rising up majestically higher with every mile we made, until, late in the afternoon several days later, we drove down Cherry Creek and into the little town of Auraria. What a relief it was to have someone of my own blood to talk to about home and family, and for a few days every leisure moment was put in in that way. We all lived at the Elephant Corral. My bed was on the ground, made of a few soft pine boughs known as 'Irish feathers,' then some hay with a blanket over it, with my clothes for a pillow or sometimes my saddle.

"What more could a boy desire?"

Whatever their hardships and dangers, the Teatses and the Tabors experienced the gold rush at its best. At its worst, it was one long delirium and hideous nightmare. Poorer gold-hunters by the thousands, unable to buy wagons or even adequate supplies, resorted to the most desperate measures to reach the diggings where they had been led to believe that nuggets might be gathered as readily as pebbles on a beach. If it was madness to attempt to cross the Plains before May in wagons carrying food and clothing and affording some little shelter, it was little short of suicide to attempt it, as thousands did, early in the spring—hitched to handcarts, pushing wheelbarrows, or trudging along on foot with only a few day's provisions on their backs.

"One came almost hourly upon hand-carters and footmen slowly journeying over the sandy undulations of the plains," wrote Henry Villard, later a railroad king of the Northwest, who first crossed the Plains at the height of the rush.[2] "Not a few started with such clothing only as they wore on their backs and small bags containing a few pounds of corn-meal and meat. We met two individuals, one fifty, the other sixty-two years old, who had left Leavenworth with just twenty pounds of corn and $1.68 in money. Nor was this reckless infatuation confined to representatives of the less well-informed classes." Young lawyers and doctors, dapper clerks in remnants of broadcloth and patent leather, could be seen toiling with farm hands and laborers across the apparently endless prairies.

These poor handcarters and footmen, wantonly deceived by guidebooks and editors, were soon "hungry, in rags, shoeless, with sore and swollen feet, and without shelter from the rains, snows, and chilling winds. Not a few had to meet death in its most awful form, starvation, and, what was worse still, were driven by the maddening pangs of hunger to acts of cannibalism, such as living on human flesh, and alas! as in the case of the wretch Blue, even on brothers' bodies. . . . It is doubtful whether such scenes of human misery as were enacted on the Plains last Spring were witnessed even at the height of the California excitement."

Young Ryan and Rice were among those who attempted the journey with handcarts. After disembarking from the S. S. New Monongahela, they sought work in vain at Leavenworth. Finally, in despair, they bought a handcart, having heard that the Mormons in '47 "had used such go-carts, one to two men, with one pushing and one pulling." Ryan and Rice set out in high spirits but soon found "that it was hard work pushing the cart and progress was slow." Rice lost heart in a week or two and turned back.

Disgruntled gold-hunters were soon denouncing "all the Kansas gold excitement as the most stupendous humbug ever perpetrated upon the American people." One experienced miner indignantly exclaimed that he had "visited all the claims and diggings and saw no man who made more than twenty cents a day, or found dirt yielding more than one per cent per pan."

Suddenly panic seized the destitute Pilgrims along Cherry Creek. A stampede back to the States developed, as wild and reckless as the rush itself, and in its day as famous. Every morning Villard was awakened by the clamor of auctioneers in "all the principal streets of Denver and Auraria, offering rifles, pistols, clothing, boots, picks, shovels, etc., etc., at prices that did not in most instances cover one tenth of the original cost. And then the last spare shirt, the reserved new boots being sold and the proceeds pocketed, off they went afoot, their packs on their shoulders, on horseback, and in wagons."

A large boat yard sprang up along the Platte, and departures from the Port of Denver were so numerous for some time that the *Rocky Mountain News* devoted a special column to local shipping news. Accidents on the swift shallow river were many. The correspondent of the *Missouri Daily Democrat* barely escaped drowning, and young Ryan reported five men lost when their crude leaky boat struck a snag, overturned and sank, pinning all beneath it.

For weeks the Stampede carried all before it, hurling back even the more determined and adventuresome. Every trail was crowded with long wagon trains carrying home thousands of hungry ragged men, "all swearing mad."

On every canvas top could still be read the words that so recently had been painted there with such resolve and hope, *Pike's Peak or Bust!* But a line had been drawn through them with obvious disgust, and below had been added *Busted, by God!* —often with some such sentiment as *Bound for America!*

Along the way, angry Pilgrims talked earnestly of lynching all editors in the Border towns. Every westbound traveler was stopped and told the most harrowing tales—the Cherry Creek camps had been sacked and burned—thousands were dying of starvation there—all town promoters had been shot or hanged.

One sullen band of Pilgrims chanced to meet a traveler westbound with sawmill machinery. They stopped him, as they did all, to relate their grievances and persuade him to turn back. The stranger's face seemed somehow vaguely familiar, and at last one Pilgrim recognized it. This was unfortunate, for D. C. Oakes of Denver City was well known—at least by name—as author of a popular Pike's Peak guidebook. At the moment, he was returning from a hurried trip to the Missouri to obtain means of exploiting the excitement.

The Pilgrims with a common impulse seized Oakes and prepared to lynch him. In the end he got off with nothing more serious than a rough handling and was allowed to proceed. Several days later he came upon what seemed to be a fresh grave by the roadside. Above it stood a "headboard made of a polished shoulder of a buffalo—in those days a favorite bulletin board of the Overlanders."

Oakes stopped and was somewhat surprised—and curiously relieved as well—to be able to read his own epitaph:

> *Here lies the body of D. C. Oakes,*
> *Killed for aiding the Pike's Peak Hoax.*

IV

GULCH GOLD AND BLOSSOM ROCK

"Hell! I expected to see them backing up carts and shoveling it in."

IN THE black days of the Stampede a single hope shone bright—gold might be found in the mountains.

As a matter of fact, it had been—months before.

But as yet only two men knew the secret.

Ten miles west of Denver rise two high table mountains. Between them comes tumbling down the waters of Clear Creek, once sweet and sparkling, but long since discolored and polluted by tailings from mine and mill. Here, where plain meets mountain, there once stood the City of Arapahoe. It never comprised more than a score of cabins strung irregularly along the creek bottom. But in its day it appears to have sheltered a hardier lot of Argonauts than any of its rivals. While Denver City and Auraria were idling away the winter of '58 with whisky, cards, and dreams of fortunes in real estate, Arapahoe sent forth into the cold forbidding mountains two bold prospectors who were to find real treasure at last.

One white morning in the dead of winter George Jackson, Indian trader and miner, cousin of Kit Carson, set out up the creek with his friend Tom Golden and a character known only as Black Hawk. They had with them Jackson's two dogs, Kit and Drum. It was bitterly cold, but the men were warm in heavy windbreakers, fur caps, high leather boots, and buckskin gloves. Under packs heavy with provisions, blankets, gold pans and skillets, with rifles slung over their shoulders, they stumbled up the creek between the table mountains and on into the foothills. After hunting deer a few days Golden and Black Hawk turned back. Jackson went on alone. Striking north to Ralston Creek, he trudged up it through deep snow to its source, stopping occasionally to dig down through the heavy drifts to try his luck. Raising no color, he crossed south and came back down the North Fork of Clear Creek. Nor did he raise color here, and his provisions were running low.

"Mountain lion stole all my meat today in camp; no supper tonight—damn him!" wrote Jackson in his diary early in January, adding next day, "Killed a fat mountain sheep and wounded a mountain lion before sun-rise; ate ribs for breakfast; drank last of my coffee."

Realizing that he had to hasten home, Jackson nevertheless decided to try his luck on the other fork of Clear Creek. Scaling the high intervening divide, he hurriedly worked his way down a small tributary. Just above its junction with the South Fork, his practised eye fell on a long low sand bar which seemed worth the risk of stopping to prospect thoroughly. He built a great fire on the sand bar and kept it blazing all night to thaw the frozen sand and gravel.

"Clear day," reads Jackson's diary for January 7, '59. "Removed fire embers, and dug into rim on bed rock; panned out eight 'treaty cups' of dirt, and found nothing but fine colors; with cup, I got one nugget of gold. Dug and panned today until my belt-knife was worn out, so I will have to quit or use my skinning-knife. I have about a half ounce of gold, so will quit and try to get back in the Spring. Feel good tonight, dogs don't." The dogs were ill and hungry.

Jackson filled up the hole with charcoal and then built another large fire over it. With belt-axe and knife he marked a large fir tree near by and cut the "top off a small lodge-pole pine on a

line from the fir tree to the hole, 76 steps in a westerly direction
. . . all fixed now; will be off down the creek tomorrow."

Next morning he started for the Plains, only to be caught in a
heavy blizzard.

"Storming like Hell!" he recorded three days later with increasing concern. "High wind and cold; in camp all day."

Once again in Arapahoe, Jackson quietly slipped into the routine of camp, with not a word or gesture to betray him: "Spent
the night playing poker for buckskins; won 20 green hides and 7
dressed ones." Next day he grained the best of these and fashioned them into coat and trousers, cutting up old flour sacks and
sewing them in as lining.. "The pants," he remarked, "fit like a
dish rag on pot hooks."

Then Jackson calmly drove off to Fort Laramie [1] to bring back
the mail, taking with him a rather sinister figure, Big Phil the
Cannibal, whose shadow occasionally falls across the records of
the day. Jackson remained away several months without the least
apparent concern: "Tom Golden is the only man who knows I
found gold on the head of the creek, and as his mouth is as tight
as a No. 4 Beaver trap, I am not uneasy."

A richer strike, unknown to Jackson, had been made on the
North Fork of Clear Creek—just a few days, in fact, after Jackson himself had passed down the stream prospecting it in vain.
Here rich beds of spangle gold were discovered in a narrow side
gulch by John H. Gregory, another miner from the Georgia fields.

By all accounts Gregory was a lazy good-for-nothing fellow—
an "ignorant corncracker," according to several, who objected
that he was "very profane, talked loud, and a very great deal."
But he showed no want of energy and acumen in the winter of '58
when he found himself stranded at Fort Laramie on his way to a
gold excitement in British Columbia.

Coming south along the mountains, Gregory panned every
stream between Cache la Poudre Creek and Pike's Peak, tracing

many to their source. Apparently he found something to interest him in Clear Creek, for he quickly returned from Pike's Peak, stopping for a time at Arapahoe before he plunged into the mountains. Three days after Jackson's strike was made, Gregory made his and hurried back to the Plains to await spring and obtain supplies.

At the height of the Stampede early in May, Gregory fell in with an Indiana party led by Wilkes Defrees. He told them his story, and they offered him a grubstake—provisions and a little working capital, in return for equal shares in his discovery. Gregory accepted and with his new partners floundered up Clear Creek through deep snow. At the mouth of the gulch soon to take his name, Gregory stopped to dig for "float" gold—small nuggets and "dust" washed down from outcropping veins on the mountains above. Raising color here, as he had in January, he decided to prospect further.

"Bring your shovel and come with me," said Gregory, summoning Defrees and leading the way up the narrow timbered gulch.

"Stick your shovel in there," he suggested.

With considerable difficulty Defrees turned over a few shovelfuls of gravel.

"Here, give me some in this pan."

Kneeling at the small cold stream that came leaping down the gulch from the snow and the ice fields above, Gregory washed the dirt and became more and more excited as he washed other panfuls. Defrees was commanded to dig here—and here—and there! Each panful showed more color than the last.

"The ice and snow prevented us from prospecting far below the surface," Gregory informed Horace Greeley several weeks later, "but the first pan of surface dirt on the original Gregory claim yielded $4. Encouraged by this success, we all staked out claims, found the 'lead' consisting of burnt quartz, resembling the Georgia mines in which I had previously worked. Snow and ice prevented regular working of the 'lead' till May 16th—From then on until the 23rd, I worked it five days with 2 hands, result, $972."

Within a week Gregory panned more gold than Green Russell's party in an entire summer.

And now Green Russell, just returned from Georgia, made a third rich strike. Gregory's discovery had confirmed his own theories about gold in the mountains. He hastened up Clear Creek to strike it rich in a side gulch three miles below the Gregory diggings. Within a month nine hundred miners were working in Russell Gulch, panning more than $35,000 of "dust" a week—a better initial average than the best of the California and Australia fields.

George Jackson had meantime returned, distributed the mail, and paid off his friend the Cannibal, who lost "his $50 the first night, Big Wallace getting it all at Twenty-one." Jackson walked to Arapahoe to find Tom Golden had kept faith. Meeting several Chicago men with money, he sought to interest them in his prospect. An incorrigible optimist, Jackson later enjoyed a reputation as the "damndest liar in the mountains," leading friends into one fiasco after another. But whatever he said in this instance, he can scarcely have exaggerated. The Chicago Mining Company was formed and on May 6, '59, began the first profitable gold mining in the Pike's Peak country.

Denver City and Auraria learned of Jackson's operations within a few days. Shortly came word of Gregory's strike, and then Green Russell's. So thoroughly discredited a few weeks before, the Pike's Peak country suddenly became "richer than California in its palmiest days," according to Larimer's report in a triumphant and somewhat exuberant letter home. "From $4 to $16 a day is now taken out from a single pan of dirt about thirty-five miles from here. One party took out $1,950 in three days last week. Plenty of men are making from $50 to $100 a day."

With one accord, destitute Pilgrims loitering along Cherry

Creek hurled themselves into a second mad rush. Even those stampeding home across the prairies faced about and raced again toward the mountains. By the thousands, gold-hunters poured into narrow Clear Creek canyon. Dangerously overcrowded but the day before, Denver City and Auraria were almost deserted overnight. Merchants locked up their stores, saloonkeepers packed up their bottles, gamblers pocketed their cards, the few carpenters busy building cabins threw down saws and hammers as one and all, including the "county judge and sheriff, lawyers and doctors, even the editor of the *Rocky Mountain News*," joined the general rush.

Even the Larimers were swept along into the mountains. Happy enough to be relieved of the menace of so many desperately hungry men, they were nevertheless uneasy. What if Denver City became merely a way-station on the road to the mines?—another La Platte City early falling to ruin as the Frontier swept on? In his perplexity the General made his first and last trial of mining. His small party struggled up Clear Creek and did a little prospecting. But as none of them was "much inclined to undergo the hardships and labor of digging and washing gold," according to the younger Larimer, all returned within the week to more leisurely and genteel pursuits.

At the height of the Clear Creek excitement the parties of Hal Sayre and Horace Tabor arrived, passed directly through Denver and on toward the mountains. Both pitched camp above Arapahoe. Sayre and his friends, thinking gold was likely to be found almost anywhere, paired off to prospect all the surrounding country. This way and that they ran "over the ground, like fox hounds seeking a trail and almost as rapidly, stopping to stick a pick in here and there, but without any knowledge of indications as to where to go to work." Everywhere they met green prospectors making search much as they were doing. Always they stopped to talk but learned nothing.

At last, Sayre's party reached Chicago Creek to interview

George Jackson. In battered old hat, red flannel shirt, and high boots, Jackson impressed the tenderfeet and showed himself kindly and affable. His easy lush profanity was particularly impressive, but the diggings themselves proved to be a sore disappointment.

"Hell!" remarked one, echoing the feelings of all, "I expected to see them backing up carts and shoveling it in."

Before long Sayre and his friends returned, one by one, to their respective trades and professions, early learning that prospecting as such is the least profitable of callings.

It took Tabor many years to learn this truth. Certainly, at the moment, his hopes were high. Inquiring the way from a miner down from the diggings, Tabor set out with Augusta's two boarders to dig his fortune.

"Leaving me and my sick child in a seven-by-nine tent that my own hands had made," said Augusta, "the men took a supply of provisions on their backs, a few blankets, and bidding me be good to myself, left on the morning of the glorious Fourth [of July]. How sadly I felt, none but God in whom I then firmly trusted, knew. Twelve miles from a human soul save my babe! The only sound I heard was the lowing of the cattle, and they, poor things, seemed to feel the loneliness of our situation and kept unusually quiet. . . . Three long weary weeks I held the fort. At the expiration of that time they returned.

"On the twenty-sixth of July we again loaded the wagon and started into the mountains. The road was a mere trail; every few rods we were obliged to stop and widen it. Many times we unloaded the wagon and by pushing it, helped the cattle up the hills. Often night overtook us where it was impossible to find a level place to spread a blanket. Under such circumstances we drove stakes into the ground, rolled a log against them, and lay with our feet against the log. Sometimes the hill was so steep that we slept almost upright. We were nearly three weeks cutting our way through Russell's Gulch into Payne's Bar, now called Idaho

Springs. Ours was the first wagon through, and I was the first white woman there, if white I could be called after camping out three months.

"The men cut logs and laid them up four feet high, then put the seven-by-nine tent on for a roof. Mr. Tabor went prospecting. I opened a 'bakery,' made bread and pies to sell, and sold milk from the cows we had brought. Here one of our party, Mr. Maxcy, had an attack of mountain fever, and for four weeks he lay, very ill, at the door of our tent, in a wagon bed, I acting as physician and nurse. A miner with a gunshot wound through his hand was also brought to my door for attention."

Here Augusta first tasted the isolated life of toil and care she was to lead in the mountains almost without respite for twenty years. Here she mastered the arts which enabled her to support her family and keep it together through the long period of discouragement and defeat that followed. Tabor staked a claim along the creek near the Jackson diggings and worked hard. But his prospect here, like many another later, came to nothing, and the Jackson diggings themselves began to decline rapidly as the summer advanced. Soon Chicago Creek had an air of dilapidation and premature decay as miners deserted it for the richer diggings in Russell and Gregory gulches.

One morning early in June when thousands of miners were feverishly at work along Gregory Gulch, all hands dropped pans, picks, and shovels at the approach of a curious figure mounted precariously upon a mule. His face was almost concealed under a "variety of extemporized plasters." A battered old white hat was pulled tightly down about his ears. As he bounced forward from group to group, he announced that he was Horace Greeley, come in person to inspect the diggings.

Greeley's plasters and bandages covered painful bruises received in an accident on the Plains a few days previously. Eager to visit the gold fields on a tour across the continent, Greeley had

secured passage (at $125) on one of the first of the Leavenworth
City and Pike's Peak stages which, within a short time, were ply-
ing tri-weekly up and down the Republican River. Attracted by
the new coach, bright red with gleaming canvas top, friendly Indians came charging up with a whoop, frightening the horses
which sheared off the road down the side of a gully. The coach
toppled over to give Greeley a "pretty smart concussion generally."

With Greeley were two other journalists—Henry Villard of the
Cincinnati *Commercial Enquirer,* and A. D. Richardson of the
Boston *Journal.* The party rode slowly forward through a hopeless confusion of tents, cabins, wagons, oxen, horses, mules, and
excited bustling men, all literally breathless in the high thin mountain air as they raced about stripping sand bars, shoveling pay-
dirt, building dams, digging ditches, felling trees, sawing riffle
boards and sluices. Some had mounted their pans on barrel staves,
or rockers, to form a "cradle." Others were using the "Long Tom"
—a large log hollowed into a trough and rolled from side to side
with a long stick as a handle, a variation of the cradle. More were
using sluices—long wooden troughs, usually three or four in series, each with a riffle board along the bottom. Behind the wooden
cross bars of the riffle frame lay pools of quicksilver. These caught
and held the heavy gold sinking to the bottom as pay-dirt was
shoveled in to be washed down the sluices by a steady stream of
water from ditch and dam.

Through their sluices Greeley found the miners running not
only bedrock gravels but broken "blossom rock." This blossom
rock—white quartz streaked and seamed a rich orange-brown—
was found up the mountain sides in surface veins so soft and de-
composed that to a depth of several feet they could be mined with
nothing more than pick and shovel. Gulch gold lost its allure as
all turned to search frantically for this rich "burnt" quartz. Soon
it was coming down the slopes by the ton, usually in rawhide sacks
on the backs of miners themselves. Only the richest could afford

to keep a horse, mule, or even a small mountain burro with hay, when obtainable, selling at $100 a ton.

Greeley was frankly impressed with what he saw. But the miners had no great faith in tenderfoot journalists and decided to take no chances.

"The boys," so the story goes, "took an old shotgun and fired dust into a partly worked mine until it had all the richness of a Golconda." Greeley, carefully directed, filled a pan and went to the creek to wash it. He was amazed, as it was intended he should be. He washed a second panful, and a third, and was even more astonished.

"Gentlemen," he exclaimed, "I have washed with my own hands and seen with my own eyes, and the news of your rich discovery shall go forth over all the world as far as my newspaper can carry it."

As good as his word, Greeley sat down with Villard and Richardson that very afternoon to start writing his famous report on the Gregory diggings.[2] First published in a special edition of the *Rocky Mountain News* early in June, the report was featured in Greeley's New York *Tribune* and reprinted throughout the country. Although it ultimately became a "source of slander and abuse to its authors," as Villard complained, it immediately brought the Pike's Peak rush to its greatest excitement.

The journalists, having first specifically denied any personal interest in local mines or real estate, went on to list what actual profits they had been able, more or less, to verify—among others, these:

> *Defrees & Co., (from South Bend, Ind.) have run a small sluice eight days, with the following results: first day, $66; second day, $80; third day, $95; fourth day, $305. . . . Have just sold their claim for $2,500.*
>
> *Zeigler, Spain & Co., (from South Bend, Ind.) have run a sluice, with some interruption, for the last three weeks; they are four in the company, with one hired man. They have*

*taken out a little over three thousand pennyweights of gold,
estimated by them as worth at least $3,000; Their first day's
work produced $21; their highest was $495.*

*S. J. Jones & Co., from Kansas, have run own sluice two
days, with three men; yield, $225 per day. Think the
quartz generally in this vicinity is gold-bearing. Have not
seen a piece crushed that did not yield gold. . . .*

*John H. Gregory, from Gordon Co., Georgia. . . . "Ar-
rived in this vicinity, May 6, . . . found the 'lead' consisting
of burnt quartz, . . . worked it five days with 2 hands; result, $972. Soon after, I sold my two claims for $21,000, the
parties buying, to pay me after deducting their expenses, all
they take from claims to the amount of $500 per week until
the whole is paid. Since that time, I have been prospecting
for other parties, at about $200 per day. Have struck another
'lead' on the opposite side of the valley, from which I washed
$14 out of a single pan."*

Conscious of having dealt rather handsomely with the diggings,
Greeley and his colleagues felt free to assert their humanity and
good sense by protesting most earnestly against a renewal of the
gold rush.

"There are said to be five thousand people already in this ravine, and hundreds more are pouring into it daily. Tens of thousands more have been passed by us on our rapid journey to this
place. For all these, nearly every pound of provisions and supplies
of every kind must be hauled by teams from the Missouri River,
some seven hundred miles distant, over roads which are mere
trails, crossing countless unbridged water courses, always steep-
banked and often miry, and at times so swollen by rains as to be
utterly impassable by wagons. Part of this distance is desert. . . .
To attempt to cross it on foot is madness—suicide—murder. To
cross it with teams in midsummer, when the water-courses are
dry and the grass is eaten up, is possible only for those who know

where to look for wood and water. . . . A few months hence—
probably by the middle of October—this whole Alpine region will
be snowed under and frozen up. . . . There then, for a period of
six months, will be neither employment, food, nor shelter within
five hundred miles for the thousands pressing hither under the de-
lusion that gold may be picked up like pebbles on the seashore.

"We charge those who manage the telegraph not to diffuse a
part of our statement without giving substantially the whole; and
we beg the press generally to unite with us in warning the whole
people against another rush to these gold mines as ill-advised as
that of last Spring."

Tired as he was from several weeks of hard travel, Greeley
could not resist an opportunity to address the miners the evening
of his arrival. Several thousand assembled—many out of curiosity, some to participate in the disturbance expected. The many
Southerners in the gulch knew and hated Greeley for his anti-
slavery views. But the slavery question was not mentioned—apparently one of the few subjects neglected.

Greeley first advanced a theory of his own about the formation
of the quartz beds, then mounted his "usual cold-water hobby,"
gave the gambling fraternity a scorching, recommended industry
and thrift, expounded the blessings of an agricultural community,
and concluded with a "description of the present condition of the
political world of America and Europe."

Rather more interesting than all this, according to Villard, was
the scene itself: "The illumination of the place of meeting by dint
of pine torches, the unique and picturesque costumes of the audience, the vigorous vibrations of the voices of the speakers and the
cheers of the crowds from the surrounding mountains, the frequent discharge of firearms and the distant songs of those encamped in the upper part of the valley—all united to heighten the
grandeur of the spectacle."

After several other long speeches the miners got down to the

and cursing stubborn burros. Somewhere in the throng wandered
W. A. Clark, later an Anaconda copper king, and W. H. Stanley,
adventurer and explorer, one day to go searching Africa for Dr.
Livingstone.

Necessity soon forced thousands of disappointed prospectors to
abandon all hopes of sudden wealth and hire themselves out to
the more fortunate. From twelve to fourteen hours a day they
labored in the gulches for an average wage of $1.50—or $1 a day
with board, which was chosen by the wiser as the better real wage.

Every night brought the serious problem of where to sleep.
Every small cabin sheltered an astonishing number of miners,
packed tightly away in short hard bunks ranged in tiers along
the walls. In these cabins, according to local tradition, the idea of
the Pullman sleeping car was born.[3] However that may be,
George Pullman here laid the foundation of his fortune. Coming
early in the rush, he bought and sold gold dust, speculated in
mines, and loaned money at the prevailing interest rates—which
ranged from twenty to twenty-five per cent a month—thus acquir-
ing the $150,000 stake that enabled him to perfect his million-
making marvel.

But cabins, however crowded, were too few to house so many.
Thousands had to seek any roof and floor available. Eugene Teats
came to visit the diggings and was forced to sleep in the general
store at Central City, kept by Charles Post, his father's new partner. Post's general store, like all of its kind, was also a gambling
saloon, open day and night. Eugene found it crowded with boisterous men and nauseating with stale fumes of tobacco and whisky,
but he gratefully stretched himself out on the rough dirty floor.

"I recall how Judge Post pleaded with the men to give me a
place near the big wood stove, and how I begged food for my
pony. Crackers were about all that could be had, so the Judge
bought a lot, which I shared liberally with the pony. Some men
in the place, more kind-hearted than the rest, saw me doing this
and rustled some grain from somewhere, and some bacon and

flapjacks for me, until we were both contented and a little more comfortable. Several nuggets were given me by miners that I talked to, who were pleased to see a boy so young in camp, for the place was practically bare of women and children."

But most gold-hunters had to live and sleep in tents and wagons, or in the open by blazing campfires. Even in mid-summer nights were chilly, especially to tired sweaty men after a long hot day in the gulches. Rolled up in a blanket or two on hard stony ground, they found it "utterly impossible to keep warm," as many complained, and got up at daybreak, almost benumbed with the cold, to build a fire and try to thaw out before breakfast."

Breakfast—in fact, every meal—consisted of bacon ("Billy Russell") or sowbelly (salt pork), flapjacks, and coffee, with the occasional luxury of dried fruit. Few could afford fresh vegetables which were worth almost their weight in gold. Scurvy and dysentery appeared, and other disorders, mountain fever particularly, a baffling disorder of typhoid character induced by bad whisky and worse water. Loud but vain complaints arose that all streams were contaminated by piles of filth and ordure accumulating about tents and cabins, and crawling with ants, bugs, and flies. Gold-hunters themselves, for the most part, were dirty and louse-ridden—"to be expected," said one, "when men pay so little attention to personal cleanliness, going from week to week without ablutions or changing their clothes, which they wear continually, both day and night, sometimes until they drop off."

Hazards to health, life, and limb were many—pneumonia from exposure to all kinds of weather and extreme fluctuations of temperature—falling rock in mine shafts—falling timber, and forest fires.

"We have tidings," wrote Greeley, "of one young gold-seeker committing suicide, in a fit of insanity, at the foot of the mountains; two more were found in a ravine, long dead and partially devoured by wolves; while five others with their horse and dog before the initial boom collapsed. Individual properties, some valuable and more not, were snatched up by speculators and combined in large corporations which were almost solely interested in selling stock, gulling the public with fantastic claims about the prospects of the "golden Kingdom of Gilpin, the richest square mile on earth." With the bursting of this bubble in '64, mines and mills closed down, one after another, and for years the Clear Creek camps lay paralyzed and "in cap."

A brief period or two of renaissance came to enliven these tortuous gulch towns high in Gilpin County. The difficult smelting problem was solved in time by Nathaniel P. Hill, a professor at Brown University, who quickly made a fortune and had himself elected to the United States Senate, the goal of every bonanza king. Shafts were reopened, and mills began to clang again. But the return of prosperity found the Clear Creek camps staid and respectable, having much the character and color of a coal camp, "with shapeless houses dumped here and there among the excavations." Absentee ownership flourished, and the wild exuberant individualism of earlier days had given way to organized strikes and lockouts. With every foot of ground staked and claimed, old prospectors were relentlessly driven into the wage system "to toil day and night, weekdays and Sundays, in darkness, begrimed with dirt, amidst the clatter of machinery, under the drippings of shaft and tunnel."

In these days there came, as local watchdogs of the corporations, a number of able engineers and lawyers—among the latter, Jerome N. Chaffee, Edward Wolcott, and Henry Teller. All were to become United States Senators, and Teller was also to be Secretary of the Interior in President Arthur's cabinet, a fact of influence upon Tabor's political and social career in later years.

In 1872, with the building of the Teller House on steep-pitched Eureka Street, Central City could boast—and did—of the largest and most civilized hostelry in the Pike's Peak country.[4] Six years later, in 1878, largely inspired by the presence in the district of a considerable number of Cornish and Welsh miners who had brought with them across the water their native gift of song, the citizens of the town erected by popular subscription a small but quite beautiful opera house, both then and now the finest in the mountains.

Within five years, however, the opera house was in difficulties and had to close its doors. From time to time they were reopened, only to be closed again as the tides of prosperity ebbed, one by one, and left the Clear Creek camps stranded. Today, all are ghost towns smelling of the long slow processes of ruin and decay, though in recent years Central City has enjoyed a spasm of vicarious life—a heady compound of art and alcohol—for a few brief weeks each summer.[5]

The early difficulties which beset Gregory Gulch first appeared not three months after Greeley's report had spread its fame throughout the country. By the end of the summer, gold from gulch sands and blossom rock totaled less than a tenth of the production of May and June. As owners even of rich claims became increasingly discouraged, utter despair seized luckless thousands whose long desperate search for treasure had not paid them for having their picks sharpened. Not one in twenty had made expenses. Not one in many hundreds had acquired even the most modest fortune. Gold-hunters in great crowds were soon deserting the gulches.

"The gambling, which for a while prevailed in this place, has almost ceased," wrote a miner from Nevadaville. "The gamblers could not live as we have to—on hope—and so have cleared out to a man."

A second stampede back to the States developed. The Plains were again white with prairie schooners carrying home thousands of ragged and dispirited men. The more sanguine joined the rush to South Park where the camps of Tarryall and Hamilton boomed

V

THE ELEPHANT CORRAL

"Cool in summer, cozy in winter . . . the center of civilization in Denver."

BY EVERY conservative estimate, the Pike's Peak Gold Rush of '59 swept more than a hundred thousand fortune-hunters from the security of home toward the distant Shining Mountains. Not more than forty thousand of these ever reached Cherry Creek, for many turned back or stopped to settle along the way. Perhaps twenty-five thousand penetrated into the mountains that first summer. But never were there more than fifteen thousand in the gold fields at any one time, according to Villard, who was in an excellent position to judge.

The second Stampede carried off many of these. The approach of winter frightened away many more. By the time the prairies were again snowbound, there remained behind in the Pike's Peak country perhaps five thousand adventurers who had either actively resisted or been left stranded by the ebb tide of the gold rush as it passed into history.

What little life remained on plain and mountain during the winter of '59 was centered in Denver City and Auraria. Here some seven or eight hundred men settled down in scattered cabins along the creek, or in tents and wagons among the cottonwoods where large campfires blazed on frosty nights. Times had been very bad along Cherry Creek since the first days of the rush to Gregory Gulch. Business was so dull that it could not "get any worse unless sales stop entirely," reported one offering such indispensables as smoking and chewing tobacco, pipes, and snuff for sale. But even at the worst of the depression, "signs of Progress—Improvement—Manifest Destiny" were not wanting.

"There was a man about town yesterday who had lettuce to sell," wrote Greeley, "and I am credibly assured that there will be green peas next month—actually peas!—providing it should rain soakingly meantime. . . . To the bread, bacon, and beans, which formed the staple of every meal a short time ago, there have been several recent additions: milk, which was last week twenty-five cents a quart, is now down to ten cents, and I hear a rumor that eggs, owing to a recent increase in the number of hens within five hundred miles, . . . are about to fall from $1 to fifty cents."

Game began to come in, too—deer, and especially antelope, at four cents a pound. And the fact was long remembered that a load of watermelons arrived late in the season to sell at $3 each.

As miners fled the mountains in fear of winter there, Denver City and Auraria began to fill up again. Larimer and his colleagues took heart once more, and in the name of "improvement" impressed the conventional gridiron pattern upon the straggling settlements.

Indian Row in Auraria was extended and dignified as Ferry Street. Along it stood the town's original building, the double cabin of Jack Jones and John Smith, both of whom had grown rich during the Gregory rush from their rope ferry across the Platte. Down the street Uncle Dick Wootton erected a large two-story log building, with a general store and barroom on the ground floor. Here Uncle Dick dispensed Taos Lightning day and night to crowds of noisy men whose uproar frequently disturbed the local court in solemn session on the floor above.[1] Around the corner was the blacksmith shop of "Noisy Tom" Pollock, first City Marshall and official executioner, soon to be busy indeed.

Auraria could boast of three other main streets—Front, Cherry, and St. Louis. Front was graced with the Temperance Hotel, within a short time better and more favorably known as the Tremont House. Cherry had a temple devoted to Masonic mysteries. From a tall pine flagpole along St. Louis Street floated a white silk flag to guide the hungry and thirsty to the Eldorado Hotel, kept by Smoke and "Count" Murat, who claimed to be a nephew of Joachim Murat, Napoleon's King of Naples. Close by, Uncle Dick Wootton built a second large cabin and opened it as a hotel. It was well patronized, for the camp was filled with hungry and homeless men. But the hotel failed financially, for neither he nor his manager, according to Wootton, "could ever understand that only men with money have a right to eat."

Although Cherry Creek was generally regarded as the boundary between the rival camps, both town companies laid claim to its treacherous sandy bed. Indeed, many buildings were erected there by businessmen who hesitated to identify themselves too closely with either community. On a sand flat in the middle of the creek, reached by a wooden foot-bridge from either bank, stood the office of the *Rocky Mountain News,* founded by William N. Byers, who had arrived with "his shirt-tail full of type," only to find a rival project well under way. The *Cherry Creek Pioneer* already had its presses in place. Byers quietly rented space in Wootton's building and quickly went to work.

"Before midnight the Washington hand press was up, the cases were in place and type was being set. The men worked all the first night, all the next day and at ten o'clock on the night of April 22 —twenty-eight hours after the outfit had reached its destination —the first copies were run off in the presence of a large number of citizens."

Next morning the *Pioneer,* taken completely by surprise, published its first and last issue. Byers bought it and merged it with the *News,* which continued as a weekly for several years and was "welcomed almost as a god-send by the community," even at twenty-five cents a copy.[2]

The bitterest jealousy marked the relations of the camps, but

Larimer now staged a coup to end the rivalry. Ten shares in the Denver Town Company and twenty of its best lots were judiciously distributed among influential members of the Auraria Company. The latter reciprocated and summoned the citizens of Auraria to a mass meeting, which was finally persuaded to take the desired action:

> WHEREAS, *the towns at or near the mouth of Cherry Creek, are, and ought to be one; therefor, be it* Resolved, *That from this time forward, Auraria proper, shall be known as Denver City, West Division, and we hereby authorize the board of directors to change the name on the plat accordingly.*

The directors of the two companies thereupon invited prominent citizens of both communities to a meeting of ratification, "held on the Larimer Street bridge by moonlight." The union was effected, and upon the motion of General Larimer the meeting adjourned, "with three hearty cheers for Denver."

Improvements were likewise going forward on the far bank of Cherry Creek. Larimer had laid out Blake, McGaa, Larimer, Lawrence, and Arapahoe streets. The few cross streets were lettered from E to H. Even more bleak and wind-swept than Auraria, wanting even the cottonwoods that somewhat softened the latter's profile, Denver City was a "forlorn and desolate-looking metropolis." But it quickly outstripped its rival, centering within itself every frontier activity, throwing together and mixing indiscriminately men of all kinds from all parts of the world.

Blake was the principal street, important alike for its business and sporting houses. None of the latter was better known than the Denver House, later notorious as the Elephant Corral. Across the street, Gasnier, a Parisian, had his blacksmith shop. Next door a Jewish merchant had hung out a sign advertising "White, Red, and Orange Flannels." Down the street were warehouses, groceries and Vienna bakeries, a drugstore, the office of the Pike's Peak stage line, primitive cabins with dirt roofs, and a chair factory.

McGaa Street had "many tenements occupied as dwellings," the Exchange Coffee House, the "place of Episcopal worship in the Library Reading Room," many livery stables and corrals, and at the far end of the street a large block of stores, with the corner "occupied as a drinking and billiard saloon by American citizens of African descent."

On Larimer Street was the General's cabin, a theater, Simm's Eating House and Billiard Saloon where the territorial legislature first met, and the Broadwell House—"the first thoroughly finished frame building in the city, it being plastered, painted, and grained throughout."

Lawrence Street had a few scattered buildings—a powder magazine, several stores of Indian traders, a large white house first turned into a brothel and then into a Methodist church, and the "neat Gothic cottage" where law was practiced and the affairs of the town company were managed by Secretary Dick Whitsitt.

Even fewer buildings graced Arapahoe. "A half dozen cabins and two or three frame dwellings comprise their number," wrote the town's first historian, "and with them is finished a full account of Denver as it stood in the month of March, 1860." [3]

The historian fails to summarize. Every fifth building is a saloon, every tenth a gambling hell. There are few brothels as yet. The twin camps together, in fact, contain scarcely a half dozen white women. In want of more the men take freely to the charms of Negresses and squaws. Altogether, it is a male society, seeking its diversions in gambling, drinking, fighting, racing, and shooting.

In the groups of weather-beaten men who wander up and down

the dusty streets, all are young and vigorous. There are no older people, and few in middle life. Most are wearing moccasins and dressed in buckskin trousers, woolen shirts, tattered coats, and black slouch hats. Some have fashioned themselves pantaloons from sugar sacks. Even those well dressed on arrival are now out at elbow and knee. Store clothes are to be had, but they are expensive. No one shaves—"some of us bathe, and some do not." All openly carry at least one revolver and often a knife fastened to the belt. The men, for the most part, idly saunter along, having nothing to do, for jobs are scarce.

In the drifting crowd appear a number of familiar faces—Uncle Dick Wootton, with his powerful figure and stiff black hair; John Smith; Jack Jones, with watery blue eyes and red nose; prim Larimer and his son Will. With his braided whiskers, one cannot mistake Green Russell, down from the mountains for the winter. Somewhere lost in the throng is H. A. W. Tabor. But if any notice him here, all signally fail to record the fact.

Suddenly the crowd parts to stand clear of George Jackson's curious friend, Old Phil the Cannibal, a filthy monster, as he comes staggering from saloon to saloon, trailed by a large mangy dog almost as dangerous as his master. A fugitive from justice, wanted in Philadelphia for several brutal murders, Big Phil openly boasts of having in emergency turned cannibal, according to Byers of the *News*. "Said he had killed and eaten two Indians and one white man (a Frenchman). Upon being asked about the taste of human flesh, he answered that the head, hands, and feet, when thoroughly cooked, tasted good—not unlike pork. But the other portions of the body he did not like; they were too grisly and tough."

Down the street, with black cassock flying, harbinger of a different order, hurries good Father Machebeuf, later a bishop, who has just come north from the episcopal seat at Santa Fe to build a chapel and in time establish St. Mary's Academy.[4]

Of a somewhat different stripe is "Professor" O. J. Goldrick, who never appears but in silk hat, frock coat with large shining buttons, white cravat, and lemon-colored gloves. His coat buttons are "not of brass, but of gold—solid gold—Colorado gold, fresh from the mines." On his starched shirt front blazes a "solitaire diamond as big as the end of your thumb." Although he creates the impression of a lackey, Goldrick is, as his epitaph declares, the "Founder of the First Sunday School and the First Public School in Colorado." He has established himself in a primitive log cabin in Auraria and, at the entirely reasonable fee of $3 a month, for the Professor claims to have taken honors at Trinity College, Dublin, undertakes to teach more than a dozen restless pupils, including several Mexican and half-breed children. From time to time he contributes to the *News*. His flowery effusions, masterpieces of their kind, one of which will be noticed later, finally gain him appointment as city editor of the newspaper and the Professor promptly gives up schoolmastering.

And here comes one of the first to rebel against Goldrick's instruction as both dull and irrelevant. Happy at last in buckskins, "just about the proudest boy in the settlement in a new suit made by the Indians, complete with all the fringes and brass buttons, etc., etc.," Eugene Teats gallops by on a wall-eyed pony given him by his friend Left Hand, Chief of the Arapaho. Eugene never considers himself dressed now, he declares, without belt, revolver, and knife. The boy soon knows everyone in camp, from Father Machebeuf to the Cannibal. He is especially fond of Chief Left Hand. He helps the Chief and his braves scour the gutters of the town for the dead dogs to be found there every day, shot because there are so many of them and food for them is scarce. The Chief invites him to the camp of the Arapaho down the Platte where Eugene marvels to see them "cut off the legs of the dogs at the second joint, stand them on their stubs, roast them intact, and have a regular feast, eating hide, hair, tail, and all."

Chief Left Hand proudly shows him still bleeding scalps taken in the mountains from the tribe's traditional enemies, the Ute.[5]

Eugene watches as the scalps are mounted on poles used only for the ritual. As soon as it is dark, the boy rides back with the Indians to town where they collect boxes and barrels, pile them high at some crowded street corner, and light a huge bonfire. With weird song and dance, the painted warriors, carrying the scalps high, circle round the fire faster and faster as the wives of lost braves moan loudly and slit their breasts with knives until the blood runs.

To Eugene it is "not a very inviting spectacle to see them dance and yell, with their knives flashing in the firelight." But, he reflects philosophically, it is "only their way of mourning the dead."

The Elephant Corral where Eugene lives for several years is the old Denver House, the "Astor House of the Gold Fields," where Horace Greeley was entertained and lodged while on his way to the diggings. At that time it was a crude log building with neither floors nor ceiling. Flimsy canvas covered windows, and the roof as well. Still flimsier cotton sheathing served as partitions between rooms. In front was a large gambling saloon. Behind it were ranged six bedrooms, mere canvas cubicles, each containing a rough bed frame with grass mattress, a sawed-off barrel or stump as a chair, and a tin wash basin. Guests were invited to fill the basin for themselves from a barrel in the corridor and to empty it of dirty water by sprinkling it over the earth floor to settle the dust.

Here, so Greeley found, "every guest is allowed as good a bed as his own blankets will make him. The charges are no higher than at the Astor or other first-class hotels, except for liquor, twenty-five cents a drink for dubious whiskey, colored and nicknamed to suit the taste of customers. . . . I had the honor to be shaved by the nephew (so he assured me) of Murat, Napoleon's King of Naples—the honor and the shave together costing me but a paltry dollar. Still, a few days of such luxury surfeited me, mainly because the drinking room was also occupied by several blacklegs as a gambling hall, and their incessant clamor, persisted in at all hours up to midnight, became at length a nuisance. Then, the visitors of that drinking and gambling room had a careless way, when drunk, of firing revolvers, sometimes at each other, at other times quite miscellaneously, which struck me as inconvenient for a quiet guest."

The Denver House soon passes into the hands of Robert Teats, who improves and enlarges it, and renames it the Elephant Corral. By him it is transformed into a complete caravanserai. One unhitches in the corral proper and leaves one's wagon there to be guarded from thieves. Horses are stabled in a large barn to one side. Opposite is the House which offers food, drink, shelter, and the usual amusements of the Frontier. Hal Sayre steps in to find its public room crowded with several hundred men, all "engaged in drinking and bucking the tiger vigorously, and in a variety of ways."

An unusual arrangement exists at the Corral between the house and the professional gamblers who run the games there. Teats, contrary to custom, has no personal interest in the games, merely renting tables and other accessories by the day, week, month, or year. This leads to much scandal, for "transient" gamblers bring in a tenderfoot, fleece him at three-card monte or another confidence game, and then quickly vanish. When the dupe complains, the house refuses to accept any responsibility. In one of the first petitions submitted to the Denver People's Government, "One Hundred American Citizens" unite to demand immediate action "to abate the nuisances existing in this city under the guise of games of chance, to wit: *Three Card Monte,* the *Strap Game,* the *Thimble Game* and other confidence games of a similar character." The City Fathers pass such ordinances but to no avail.

"Here you are, gentlemen," cries a three-card monte expert at the Elephant Corral. "This ace of hearts is the winning card. Watch it closely! Follow it with your eyes as I shuffle. Here it is, and now here, now here, and now—where? If you point it out the first time, you win; but if you miss, you lose. Here it is, you see. Now watch it again. This ace of hearts, gentlemen, is the winning card. . . . I take no money from paupers, cripples, or orphan children. The ace of hearts! It is my regular trade, gentlemen, to move my hands quicker than the eye. The ace of hearts! Who will go me twenty?" [6]

He seldom asks in vain.

Play goes on at the Corral day and night to a repetitious series of tunes offered by a screechy orchestra sitting within a small enclosure at the far end of the hall. Every better gambling hell has its orchestra, which usually consists of four pieces—fiddle, cornet, piccolo, and asthmatic piano, with occasionally a banjo for any of these. Mingled with the clink of glasses at the bar, and the monotonous call-song of the gamblers at the tables, rise the strains of "Lily Dale," "Twenty Years Ago," "Yellow Rose of Texas," and "Sweet Betsy from Pike."

One evening, when conviviality is at its height and the music at its loudest, a miner enters, approaches a faro table, takes a large pouch of gold dust from his pocket, and places it on the five-spot.

"Does it all go?" asks the dealer.

The miner grunts assent, and the dealer begins slowly turning over the cards. Not a half dozen are played before the pouch is lost. The miner desperately grabs for his gold. The gambler whips out his gun and shoots. The musicians, with a single practiced motion, drop both their instruments and themselves behind the low enclosure, which they have thoughtfully lined with sheet-iron. For a few moments the air is blue with smoke and bullets as three hundred men frantically dive for cover or dash madly toward the street. The instant the shooting stops, the orchestra is on its feet again, with Jones, the leader, singing,

Ha, boys, ho!
Ain't you glad you're out of the wilderness—
Ain't you glad you're out of the wilderness?
Ha, boys, ho!

When a guest is killed, as many are, his body is dragged to the rear to be buried at the expense of the house by one McGovern—undertaker, cabinetmaker, gravedigger, and sexton. McGovern is a lean lank man, given to melancholy when business is slow. "But a full-priced customer would always set him whistling and jigging." McGovern owns a cemetery up the Platte where he buries, so it is said, many a corpse but never a coffin. His apprentice, a "camel-backed youth with a taste for the grave business," later hanged as a horse thief, once declared that the same box was used "thirty times for customers and that the Old Man himself was finally buried in it."

The Elephant Corral had a single serious rival as a gambling hell, the famous Progressive, built by Ed Chase close by. With a stake of $1,500 won at poker while working as a railroad brakeman in and out of Saratoga Springs, New York, Chase came west in the rush to spend a fruitless summer prospecting Clear Creek. Recognizing the liabilities of ignorance, as few did, he quickly abandoned mining for more familiar pursuits.

With two Ford brothers, Chase first established a small gambling saloon on Blake Street. An impressive ceremony marked its opening. William Chivington, presiding elder of the Methodist Church and colonel of the Third Colorado Cavalry, attended with his staff in full regimentals. "His benediction was reverently received by the Fords' guests. All bowed their heads, and silence reigned as prayer went forth from our soldier-preacher."

Showered with blessings, Chase soon set up shop for himself across the street. "Furniture was scarce, and the boys considered themselves lucky to have benches to sit on, while the card tables were covered only with woolen blankets." But profits were large, and with them Chase built the Progressive.

"There were seats for all comers. The tables were the best that had been known in Denver up to that time," said Chase. "The entire lower floor, twenty-five feet by one hundred, was devoted to gambling, with the exception of bar space. The second floor was also used by the sporting fraternity, but in a more quiet way. There were private rooms there which were rented to those who could afford to pay for them. The tables were run practically without limit. When one of these big games was on, I generally sat at the head of the table, so arranging it that a customer could place as high as $200 on double cards and $100 on singles. But they never broke any bank of mine. My profits were big at times."

But the police soon began to annoy Chase, demanding an increasingly larger share of the spoils. "I generally found it cheaper in the end to meet the demands of the officials than to try to evade them. I was often 'held up,' but I never found it profitable to kick about it. I would simply give them the money and forget about it."

When their demands became preposterous, Chase closed up the Progressive and departed to try his fortune in Montana. The Vigilantes there proved even more troublesome. Chase finally returned to Denver to amass a fortune, first at the Cricket, and then at the Palace, a celebrated gambling saloon and variety theater where in later years he entertained many notables—Eugene Field, Oscar Wilde, Horace Tabor, and almost all of the mining, smelter, and cattle kings of the day.

The Elephant Corral with its many sources of revenue paid Father Teats and Uncle Phillip rather well. Now they decided their livery business might be improved with a light wagon service. Two small brightly-painted drays were placed on the streets, drawn by fine large horses in shining harness. In an unexpected manner they proved to be an immediate success—"especially with lucky men down from the mines for a good time, with their buckskin pouches filled with dust. When they wanted to show off a bit, they would make up a little party, hire both drays, decorate the harness with bottles and cans, and then drive from saloon to saloon until they were all sufficiently soaked to be ready to turn in and sleep it off. As we charged them a dollar an hour for each dray, and as hardly a day passed without a gang of them coming to town, the drays proved fair money-makers."

Eugene's education at the Corral continued apace, for he was "like all boys with ordinary ambition in wanting to become as proficient as the other fellow in most things." He first set himself to master the Western style of riding, finding it "easy after a while to pick up things from the ground while loping along at a rapid rate, which is done by catching a spur in the hair cinch and locking it in with the rowel." He then learned to throw the lariat and manage the "half-wild stock" brought to the Corral to be cared for. Every morning at seven he drove a large herd of horses to one of three outside ranges where they were pastured for the day. Late in the afternoon he herded them back again so that those wishing to ride or drive in the evening could have their ponies.

Eugene next applied himself to the bullwhip—"built very much like a rattlesnake, about twelve feet long, although many used them longer, with a short handle, a swivel, and a long loop on the lash end." Finally possessed of one "with up-to-date qualifications, having a buck-popper fully two inches wide," the boy began to scourge the barn men. When he could find no fly or insect on which to practice, he pinned a "piece of paper to the pants' seat of some of the good-natured ones." At other times he refined his technique on lazy mules and ponies until at last he could do "almost as good a job as some of the professional bullwhackers, many having eight, ten, or sometimes sixteen bullocks to chastize, each with the name of a famous man, their song beginning this way—Up ahha there, Brigham, and you too, Old Abe, and what's the matter with you there, Franklin, that you're not doing your share to help Old Daniel Boone! And you, Washington, and you, Adams, get into the yoke there!

"During the days when Porter, Raymond and Company had their mule and bull teams moving in and out of Auraria, they used to have about fifty bull teams to a wagon train, with five or six yoke to each wagon and trailer. I used to go out to meet them at the place where they camped until they were ordered in. The drivers would prepare for the occasion by trimming up their bull-whips or 'persuaders' with new poppers—the wider, the louder the noise. Well, when orders came and they harnessed up, it was like the firing of guns all the way in. How I did enjoy snapping flies off the left hip of good Old Brigham!

"Great days and good ones, I tell you, with gambling and booze shops running wide open, day and night. Everybody had mostly gold dust as money. A pinch between the first finger and thumb was twenty-five cents, and you weren't supposed to have long nails either or dig down too deep in the buckskin pouch. Occasionally some fellow would try the big-pinch act, only to find himself looking down the muzzle of a cannon and hear someone say, 'Now, partner, just drop that pinch back and play the game square, and don't try that again in this joint, see!' "

Into the Corral one day rode two strangers astride a large bay gelding, gaunt and footsore, caked with sweat and dust. They had manifestly ridden far and fast on this one horse. Eugene eyed them with some misgiving as he lead their hungry mount off to the stables. As the strangers continued to live for a time at the Corral, Eugene soon knew them well and learned their story long before they—and their horse as well—became the talk of the town.

One was Tom Hunt, his partner being the gambler-desperado, Charley Harrison, in his day the most accomplished gunman in the West. They had just come from Salt Lake City, they explained, "because of a little trouble with the Mormons."

Hunt, as a matter of fact, had been almost on the gallows when daringly rescued by Harrison. Stealing Border Ruffian, a champion racer, and leading Hunt's big sorrel, Harrison rode down upon the lynching party, freed his partner, and away they

Harrison's guns were the old Colt cap-and-ball revolvers, the original type of the formidable six-shooters so renowned in song and story, for the metal-cartridge revolver did not come West until the 1870's. The cap-and-ball was not such a clumsy weapon as would at first appear. It was necessary, of course, to load separately each chamber of the revolving cylinder with percussion cap, powder, and ball. By means of the small lever-ramrod hinged under the barrel, the lead ball was "seated" against the powder. This operation obviously took time and was never attempted when shots were flying. Hence the necessity of a second gun. Many gunmen also carried in their pockets extra cylinders previously loaded and dipped in beeswax to keep the powder dry. As it took but a few seconds to insert a loaded cylinder, a man with two guns could fire twenty-four shots in one almost continuous fusillade.[7]

The speed of the old-time gunman was the more remarkable because these first Colts did not have double action. They had to be cocked with the thumb for each shot. But this was considered a great advantage, according to Masterson, who declared that all of the better gun-fighters of the West always scorned the double-acting revolver, complaining that the trigger pull was too hard for accurate shooting. And the cap-and-ball could be fired almost as rapidly, particularly when the trigger notch had been filed away so that the hammer dropped the instant the thumb released it. This allows the more accomplished to "fan" their guns—i.e., by moving the hammer with their free hand which, palm down, flashed rapidly back and forth above it. Good shots invariably filed away the sights on their weapons. Not only were these apt to catch in holster or pocket when life depended upon a quick draw, but they were considered useless, for a Western gunman's weapon was as much a part of his hand as his index finger, and he pointed it as readily. He cocked his revolver in the single flashing motion with which he drew it, and, as Masterson declares, delivered "his first shot in a half second, six shots in less than two seconds"—and another six shots in even less time from his second gun, which he had meantime drawn.

Colts of this day ranged in size and caliber from the heavy "Dragoon" to the "Suicide Gun." The Dragoon was none other than the well-known Forty-four, the favorite of cowboys and plainsmen because it shot the same cartridge as their .44-.40 Winchester rifles. With its long barrel and weight of four pounds, it required a holster and was rather too cumbersome for any but horseback use.

In mining camps the .41 was generally preferred to the .44, for it was quite as powerful and with less weight had less recoil— "hence faster action at close quarters." Harrison's guns were of this caliber. Although properly a holster revolver, gamblers usually carried the .41 concealed under their vests or in pockets sewn inside the waistbands of their trousers.

But the early boom towns and mining camps generally preferred the Colt "Navy" (.36), so named for a naval scene engraved round its barrel. This and the .38 Smith and Wesson were pocket revolvers, and were variously and ingeniously concealed.

Likely at any time to be challenged, confidence men and the worst class of gamblers adopted a weapon peculiarly their own, the derringer, a light gun of large caliber, so small that it could easily be concealed in a vest pocket, or even in the palm of a large hand. As it had the shortest of barrels, its accurate range did not exceed five or six feet. But it was deadly within that range, which was ample to embrace all at even the largest gambling table. As derringers fired but a single shot, they were always carried in pairs. Although it bestowed an obvious initial advantage, the derringer was nevertheless a dangerous gun to use. For if its one shot went wild, the man using it was left at the mercy of the slower but more accurate and powerful six-shooter.

Lastly, there was the "Suicide Gun," the Colt .32, which was thought to lack power. "When two men got into a smoking argument, the one with the .44 always killed his man, while the one with the .32 gave his foe merely a skin complaint, as the grimly humorous saying went."

Eugene learned all this and more from Harrison, and under his instruction was soon a remarkably fine shot.

And now, Eugene became a jockey.

One day not long after Harrison's arrival, three Greer brothers from Iowa drove into the Corral with four large horses tied to the tail of their wagon. "I paid little more than the usual attention to the bunch," said Eugene, "but when Bill Greer called Father into the room called our office, and I overheard him say that he wanted three of the best stalls we had, and for a long time, and would we fix it so that they could be together, and if possible boxed-in, so that one of the brothers could sleep in the stall— well, so unusual a thing created new interest in the horses to be so carefully guarded."

Eugene soon learned that one of them was a champion half-miler, Bay Chief. When asked by the Greers to exercise the racer, the boy accepted delightedly and every day went speeding through the streets and along the outlying roads. It was not long before a race against Border Ruffian began to be talked of. Hunt still had his half share in Ruffian. But Harrison, not interested in horses, had sold his share to a certain Colonel Miller, "a Southerner of rank ideas called a Secessionist, who was near being invited at times to stop talking or get out of the country." Finally, a race was arranged. "For a couple of months nothing else was talked about, and it seemed that about every week a goodly sum would be added to the first amount of $40,000, all in gold, which was taken down to the old Clark and Gruber mint and lumped together in one retort."

To his great surprise and delight, the Greers chose Eugene to ride Bay Chief, now renamed Rocky Mountain Chief. Colonel Miller had already announced his intention of bringing a professional jockey from Kentucky for the race. Every day Eugene rode down the Platte to the racetrack at the old McNassar Ranch where Chief Left Hand's Arapaho were encamped at the moment. As Eugene put Chief through his paces, the Indians "would come running out with blankets, shaking them and yelling to scare my horse and see him run away." Hunt and Miller went earnestly to work as well, training Ruffian secretly at a private track on the far side of town. But they spent quite as much time in "thinking up every little underhand trick which might advance their chances of making a big winning," according to Eugene.

"Two weeks before the race, Hunt appeared at the Corral and very secretly gave out that he had quarreled with Miller and had given him until the next day to retract his words or he would leave him, or challenge him to fight, or possibly stop the race altogether. Our trainer, McKnight, never thought of Hunt's possible treachery and told him to come back and tell us how his troubles panned out. Poor fellow, he had it in his mind to gain some valuable pointers and have a good two-hundred pound man to help him hold Chief down, for he was becoming very hard to handle when excited. True to his dishonest principles, Hunt showed up on the third day, full of abuse of Miller, who had threatened to have Hunt arrested or possibly shoot him on sight. So it is easy to imagine how Chief's true and honest supporters, in their eagerness to gain every possible advantage, saw the good to come from having Hunt's assistance. He was hired as an assistant starter and immediately began his work. He secretly reported to Miller our speed, endurance, and every move in our training. I must not forget to mention the handicaps our horse was supposed to be working under. Never had Bay Chief graduated above the half-mile class. This race was mile heats, the best two out of three, and our hope was to make a haul on the first heat. Right here was where Hunt knew he could and did do his mischief.

"Well, the final day was on, and if there ever gathered a mixed crowd, it was right there. It was said that seventy per cent of the people of the Pike's Peak country were on the track, all with bags of real gold dust. No small currency was needed. The sun never shone upon a scene more wildly animated than that Frontier race course. There were no high enclosures, no morose ticket sellers, no insolent gatekeepers, no protecting policemen. All was go as you please, where you please, an unending confusion of men and women, encircling the track in a weltering chain—the roughest, the kindest, the poorest, the most vile of the border element mingling without distinction. A temporary judges' stand was up, and the big retort was hung where everybody could see it.

"Just in front of the starting post, a hole in the track had been filled in with dirt from the side of the course, leaving quite a deep ditch, very uneven, from which it was very difficult to get back up on the track without going the whole length of it, about two hundred feet. This Hunt and Miller had decided to use as their safe and certain means of winning the first heat. The rest would be easy. Betting was wild, as high as ten to one on Chief to win the first heat."

When the horses were called up at last, Eugene was amazed to behold on Border Ruffian his friend and playmate, young Jim McNassar, for never did he "suspicion that he was to be my opponent." Eugene tried to talk with him, but Jim remained glum and answered no questions.

"Both horses were behaving very badly, seeming to catch the spirit of evil which pervaded the place. For fully an hour the turning and jockeying went on, and much praise did Hunt receive for his masterful way of heading off any unfair start. He certainly did his work well. Father was one of the judges and on several occasions called Hunt to account. But always Hunt's response was that he was on to the tricks of the Miller gang and intended to give Chief a fair start.

"Finally the limit of patience was reached, and the judges said they would send the horses off on the first reasonably good score, and they did. But big Tom Hunt failed to hear the word *go*, at least so he said, and hung on. His two hundred pounds were too much for poor Chief to overcome, with the result that we found ourselves floundering around in the ditch while Ruffian started off under the whip. When I regained the track; Ruffian had the inside track and a start of a good two hundred feet. Fortunately for me, I did not lose my head and abuse Chief, but just let him have his head. Gradually he closed the gap, and I believe I could have regained all the ground lost by the treachery, had I urged him. But for some unknown reason I did not once use the whip, and Ruffian won the heat by several feet."

The track was a bedlam. Through the surging crowd came Charley Harrison to Chief's paddock, for he had dismissed whatever sentimental debt he may have owed Border Ruffian and transferred his allegiance to Rocky Mountain Chief for the good reason that the Greers contributed heavily to the profits of his Criterion Saloon. Harrison plied Eugene with questions, confirmed his own suspicions, and with drawn revolver marched back to the track to denounce Hunt publicly for his treachery.

"Colonel McNassar, father of Ruffian's rider and a bad man in those days, very ready with the gun, took the lead in championing Hunt's side. This at once brought into action the two most noted gunmen of the day. In the meantime, a crowd had gathered about Hunt and gave him thirty minutes in which to gather himself and his possessions and 'git,' not only from the track, but from the town. He went, mostly because of the antagonism of his old pard Harrison. He knew his man too well to risk a later meeting. Well, one can imagine the turmoil."

Back to the paddock came Harrison to talk again with Eugene about their prospects. The boy was confident, pointing out how well Chief had performed after so poor a start.

"All right, young man. But if necessary, you whip that horse this time and at least try to win," said Harrison, as he departed with the Greers for the betting field in the hope of recouping their heavy losses.

"It was then I saw Bill Greer's woman, known as Moll, go down

fluence of drink, they would try to force me to drink with them, and on several occasions they held me down and tried to force liquor into my mouth. But someone always came to my rescue and saved me. I have always thought that it was Charley Harrison, who, having witnessed the frequent dinners of my chums, decided best that my father should know of the temptation. When he called me to task, the matter was easily settled by sending me off to his partner in the mountains, where I was allowed to run about the hills looking for gold and getting experience which later served me well.

"I have on many occasions in later life wondered how I kept from becoming the real thing, but always when temptation was strongest, my mind would go back to my mother's parting words when leaving the farm in Michigan, 'Leave liquor, cards, and gambling alone, and you will come out all right.' "

VI

BUMMERS AND STRANGLERS

"The town, such as it was, was full of gamblers, thieves, and cutthroats, and by the summer of 1860, soon after our arrival, this element seemed to be running the place."

B L O O D had begun to flow along Cherry Creek before the Larimers' arrival. A gambler named Vincent drifted in from Salt Lake City and a few days later murdered the squaw man Atwell in a quarrel over a game of three-card monte. Vincent fled, but was captured and brought back by Arapaho induced to go in pursuit. Tried before the first People's Court assembled in the territory, he was speedily found guilty. Given a horse, rifle, ammunition, and provisions for a few days, he was commanded to leave the country instantly. If ever found within a mile of camp, so his sentence ran, he would be shot at sight.

Crime and violence increased with the gold rush, which had attracted large numbers of irresponsible, vicious, and lawless men. Murders became "almost every day occurrences," according to Uncle Dick Wootton, "and stealing was the only occupation of a considerable portion of the population, who would take anything from a pet calf or counterfeit gold dollar up to a sawmill." Indeed, the first steam sawmill in the gold fields, he declared, was stolen from a flatboat on the Missouri. But Uncle Dick condoned thievery on the ground that disappointed gold-hunters left stranded on Cherry Creek had all suffered cruelly. Many were starving, for "they had little or no money and there was little or nothing for them to do."

Denver City and Auraria contained a "great deal of low scuff from California," and much of the lawlessness was attributed to them by the gambler Ed Chase. The Californians, said he, "considered themselves a superior class of beings, but the other fellows would not stand for their airs." The former were locally known as "the Self-risers." The Californians in turn dubbed their enemies "the Pike's Peak Skunks." Clashes between them were frequent and often fatal. Chase identified another particularly lawless group as the stragglers and deserters from the armies which had put down the Mormon Rebellion of '57.

Although many men were murdered during the year of the rush, "only fifteen men and women were given notice to leave the country, and only two were hanged." While acting as Larimer's personal bodyguard, Captain Peleg Bassett was shot and killed by one Scudder and a desperado named Carrol Wood. Both escaped from custody and fled the country. But so little respect had Wood for the authorities that he returned shortly to defy them with impunity. A Negro prizefighter killed a rival and in turn was murdered by the old trader Jim Beckwourth, who objected to his attentions to the comely young Negress known as "Lady" Beckwourth. The prizefighter in the first instance and Beckwourth in the second were acquitted on the grounds of self-defense.

A young German named Stoefel, who had assassinated his brother-in-law to rob him of a few dollars in his pocket, was the first to pay the extreme penalty for murder. He was brought to trial before a People's Court assembled among the cottonwoods in Auraria. Three judges were selected from among the crowd and mounted to the bench—a carpenter's bench commandeered for the occasion. A rope stretched from tree to tree kept the audience from crowding the court too closely. Attorneys for the prosecution and the defense were appointed. A jury was selected and seated on a log to one side. The prisoner sat alone on a stump to the other. Quickly found guilty, he was sentenced to be hanged that very afternoon. Anticipating the verdict, Noisy Tom Pollock, the blacksmith, had a stout rope at hand and so loudly clamored for the job of executioner that he finally prevailed.

When Stoefel requested a stay of fifteen minutes to "arrange his spiritual welfare," General Larimer and the Reverend Fisher, blacksmith-preacher, led him away to the hall above Wootton's saloon. The crowd followed and was soon demanding its victim. Larimer's head appeared at an upper window, and after much acrimonious debate another fifteen minutes' grace was granted the prisoner. At last Stoefel appeared and the crowd marched him off to the gallows, a large cottonwood tree in St. Louis Street. The prisoner was commanded to step up and stand in the wagon always used on such occasions. As Pollock was clumsily fitting the noose, the condemned man began to speak, for a final address was customary.

Stoefel talked of his sins and prayed forgiveness in broken English, which moved his audience to roars of laughter. He was obliged to stop again and again "to ask the crowd not to make sport of his faulty language." His self-appointed executioner also interfered, commanding him to hold his head higher. Stoefel obeyed, stretching out his neck, but continued talking as fast as he could. Now ready, Noisy Tom Pollock jumped down, gave the signal for the wagon to be driven from under the condemned man, and stood by with a critical eye as Stoefel, still talking, swung out high in the air, choking and shaken with convulsions.

This first public execution affected the community variously. Some remarked an improved moral tone. Others remained somewhat skeptical. The hanging not only pleased the Larimers but inspired them to new enterprise. The camp, they decided, needed another cemetery.

Father and son quickly laid claim to a high sandy hill up Cherry Creek and seized the bodies of Stoefel and his victim, to bury the two together in one grave. The General then invited a prosperous undertaker to become a partner, but this was a mistake. While Larimer was absent for a brief time, the new partner

was intimidated by the "ominous clicking of the hammers of a dozen revolvers." Complaints multiplied that peaceful citizens were being stopped in the streets by armed ruffians and subjected to indignities and violence. The Jefferson Rangers, a company of recently organized volunteers, were hurriedly called out to patrol the town all night.

Next morning, good citizens met again to proclaim that "Todd, Harvey, and Karl must leave the city within five hours under penalty of being hanged if found within the city limits at the expiration of that time, or ever afterwards." The desperados, supported by a ruffian crew from Charley Harrison's Criterion Saloon, took their time in obeying the command. Todd and Harvey leisurely departed the following morning. That evening Karl was found hiding in an Indian lodge. When granted another five hours' grace, he decided not to try the community's patience further, and after a week of day and night patrol the Rangers were withdrawn from the streets.

The Bummers next fell upon the Indians when Cheyenne and Arapaho came in to trade a few months later, leaving their squaws and papooses encamped a few miles down the Platte. At midnight, drunken scoundrels descended upon the lodges to rape even small children, taking horses and mules as they fled. Left Hand and other chiefs threatened war and massacre. An attack was averted only through the mediation of Jim Beckwourth, old Indian trader, once a famous war chief of the Crow. He persuaded Left Hand to accept the community's apologies and promises of retribution. But the perpetrators of this outrage were never punished.

Matters went steadily from bad to worse. A prominent rancher had been gambling and drinking all day in Charley Harrison's Criterion Saloon. Finally broke, the rancher commanded the bartender to give him a drink on the house. When refused, he began to curse loudly. Harrison was standing well to the front of the saloon, apparently unheeding the row. Suddenly he spun on his heel, walked up to the intoxicated ranchman, and without a word emptied his six-shooter into him.

The murder created great excitement because of the prominence of the victim. A motley crowd collected down the street and after a harangue by a friend of the murdered man, moved, some two hundred strong, upon the saloon to lynch Harrison. Advised of events, Sheriff Middaugh drove up to check the mob.

"Give me a few minutes and I will arrest Harrison," pleaded the Sheriff, and finally gained his point. But the mob insisted upon accompanying him.

"No, I don't want any of you to go with me. All the assistance I need can be supplied by this boy here," he declared, indicating his son Asa, a youth of twenty. Together, they drove up to the Criterion to find it locked and barred. They knocked. Harrison opened the door, shook hands with the Sheriff and his son, and invited them in. There were "fully seventy-five, if not a hundred, cutthroats stationed in the saloon, all armed to the teeth."

"Charley, I have a warrant for you, and I want you to submit to arrest and save your own life as well as that of others."

"Will you protect me?" asked Harrison.

"With my life!"

The desperado drew his two revolvers and handed them to the Sheriff. His gang rushed forward, ready for any command.

"Boys, put up your guns," Harrison drawled, and all obeyed. Harrison stepped into the buggy and was driven away to jail.

Harrison's trial proved to be a farce. A woman of the town, "Ad" Lamont, distributed $5,000 "so discreetly as to bring about a disagreement of the jury after a two days' hearing." This was regarded as an acquittal by the judge, who dismissed the jury and released the prisoner.

Harrison was no sooner free than he himself sat as Judge Lynch. For a purse of $9, a tramp robbed and murdered one of the gambler's friends, a rancher named Freeman. The offense was aggravated by the fact that the murdered rancher was Harrison's brother in Masonry, while the murderer was a Catholic. Harrison organized the gamblers as a Vigilante Committee to wreak vengeance.

Captured as he fled on a stolen horse, the tramp Pat Waters was brought back to the scene of the murder, forced to confess and indicate where he had buried his victim. The body was dug up, and the two men, the live and the dead, were placed in a wagon and driven to town. Here the gamblers took entire charge of the proceedings, "with a gambler as judge, and a jury composed of gentlemen of the cloth." Found guilty, Waters was sentenced to be hanged that afternoon, but a priest procured a twenty-four hours' stay of execution. Next day a long procession wound its way down the Platte to the McNassar racetrack, where a gallows had been erected. Harrison, determined to avoid any mishap, had arranged for a drop of nine feet, "almost sufficient to separate the man's head from his body, but instead of the head coming off, the neck stretched until it was fully eighteen inches long"—the most gruesome sight he ever beheld, according to the young Middaugh, who had a taste for such things.

The authorities seldom interfered with proceedings of this kind. In the disorganized community a mob was generally accepted as the final authority. Also, as the Sheriff confessed, considerable danger attended an attempt to stop a hundred or more determined men, inflamed with passion and rum. Furthermore, there was little or no money to defray the expenses of more formal trials. Lastly, it was expensive to feed and practically impossible to hold prisoners in the makeshift jail. They had either to be summarily dealt with or allowed to roam at large.

Matters reached a crisis in July, '60, with another murder by Harrison. One day Eugene Teats and his schoolmates were eating lunch at a restaurant-saloon on Larimer Street. At the next table a game of poker was proceeding, "with a big black bullwhacker as its chief victim." Harrison walked out from a back room where he had been lunching.

"Charley," shouted the Negro, rising, "I would like to play you a game of poker, for I know you're honest! These fellows are rascals."

"Who are you to address me as Charley and these gentlemen as rascals?" asked Harrison, coldly eyeing the Negro, his Southern sensibilities offended.

"I'll show you who I am. I'll wipe the floor with your carcass," shouted the Negro, one Stark, as he lunged at Harrison.

"Are you heeled?" snapped the gambler as he shook himself loose and backed off. The Negro inadvisedly reached for his gun and in a second lay dead on the floor—"a damn fool and nothing more," according to Eugene, who witnessed the scene. Spying the boy in the crowd, Harrison called him.

"Get Brigham for me, quick!" he said in his quiet way, and Eugene ran to the Corral for his pony. Harrison mounted and rode "out to Bishop Machebeuf's ranch for a few days' outing." Upon his return nothing was said except by his enemy, Colonel Miller, the owner of Border Ruffian, and the Colonel quickly fell silent when Harrison threatened "to riddle his old Secession carcass."

Events moved rapidly toward a crisis and open civil war, precipitated by one Jim Gordon, a well educated and widely read man, a civil engineer by profession, who lived on a ranch down the Platte with his mother and sisters. Though ordinarily kindly and gentle, a man of wit and cultivation, he was a maniac when in his cups.

Just after Harrison's murder of Stark, the Negro, Gordon entered a brothel and in cold blood shot down the bartender, wounding him seriously. Next day he wandered drunkenly about town shooting at random. He was still at large the next night when he staggered into the Elephant Corral, fired point-blank at Big Phil the Cannibal, missing him twice at close range, and staggered out again, "evidently in an ugly mood." In the street he met a man with a dog and without remark shot the animal—a most heinous offense in the early West when a dog was more than wife or child. Making his way to the Louisiana Saloon, in the bed of Cherry Creek, Gordon amused himself smashing glasses and destroying furniture until, tiring of the bartender's complaints, he knocked him down with the butt of his gun, pulled him to his feet by the hair, held his limp figure against the bar, and at last succeeded "in shooting him through the head, after ineffectually snapping his pistol four times." [1]

As no one interfered during all this pistol-snapping or afterwards, Gordon reeled out into the street again and home. Next day, with Sheriff Middaugh in pursuit, he fled the country on a horse stolen for him by Harrison's gang in the Criterion Saloon.

The *Rocky Mountain News,* feeling that matters had gone far enough, uttered a mild protest against this outrage and the Stark murder. Next forenoon, three desperados—Carrol Wood, implicated in the murder of Peleg Bassett; John Rooker, murderer of Jack O'Neil; and George Steele, who had defied two official commands to leave the country—raided the office of the *News,* seized Editor Byers, and carried him off to the Criterion, proclaiming their purpose of "stopping his attacks by stopping his breath." Harrison happened to enter in an amiable mood and went to Byers' defense, stamping out a threatened rebellion among his followers by sheer audacity. He then smuggled Byers out the back door, personally escorting him back to his office.

Angry and resentful, the desperados sent a party to reconnoiter the *News* office. For a time they lay in hiding in a cabin about ten rods distant, hoping to get a shot at Byers through the windows. George Steele finally became impatient, returned to the Criterion, mounted his pony, and walked it past the *News* building. Suddenly wheeling, he came galloping back, firing volley after volley into the office as he sped by. Byers dropped his pencil and seized the revolvers "always within easy reach of the editorial desk."

Printers jumped for the rifles and shotguns always kept stacked beside their cases, and replied with a fusillade from the upper windows. Steele was shot in the back, but not unhorsed.

"At 11 A.M. George S. came down in front of the bank corner on horseback, with a revolver in his hand," reads a diary of this day, as tense as any in Denver's history, "two men on horses after him and hundreds of men on foot."

One of the horsemen was Noisy Tom Pollock, armed with a double-barreled shotgun. He pushed his horse up close to the desperado's and with the two racing along together, leveled his gun against Steele's head and pulled both triggers. Steele dropped into the street, fatally wounded, although he lingered on till nightfall with an "entire side of his head blown away and his brain freely exposed." But he deserved his fate, remarked Sheriff Middaugh, for he was "one of the most desperate men I have ever known."

"Intense excitement," the diary continues. "Orders for all citizens to arm. Several went in pursuit of C. W. [Carrol Wood], R. [Rooker], and others. Wood taken about 1 P.M. Crowd rushed to hang him, but concluded to give him a trial which is to be held tomorrow. W. and R. are guarded by fifty men tonight to prevent a rescue by the gamblers. . . . A large meeting was held tonight to take active measures in regard to the desperados around Denver."

Out of this ominous challenge by the Bummers came the first organized Vigilante Committee in the gold fields. At first it consisted "of one hundred leading citizens." But among them there appears to have been several desperados in disguise, for "proper secrecy" was not maintained. The Vigilantes' decisions had a mysterious way of leaking out to warn intended victims. Within the committee there gradually coalesced a still more secret group of just ten men, arbiters of life and death in the community.

"It is an interesting fact that the names of these less than a

dozen men who cleaned up Denver and put it on a plane of respectability are entirely unknown," the younger Middaugh once
naïvely remarked at a time when he was the only man alive who
knew their identity. But he steadfastly refused to name them on
the ground that "many have descendants still living, and the
revelation might be unpleasant to them."

This is significant. Though the early West showed considerable
indifference to the killing of man by man, it was always somewhat
ashamed of its mob murders, no matter what the provocation.
These violated its sense of fair play, which was the very foundation of communal living at a time when all constitutional authority
was notoriously weak and ineffective.

The "Stranglers," as the Vigilantes were known to the Bummers and also to many good citizens who objected to their arbitrary violence, proceeded at once to make Denver "as quiet as
any Eastern village."

A party was sent with Sheriff Middaugh in pursuit of Gordon.
Along the way the Vigilantes seized three men suspected as horse
thieves. One escaped, the second was drowned while attempting
to swim the Platte under a hail of bullets, while the third was
captured, tried, publicly lashed, and ordered to leave the country
within twenty-four hours. Gordon led the Vigilantes a long chase,
but was at last captured among the Osage Indians in Kansas.
After a second and then a third escape, he was finally returned to
Denver. Tried and sentenced to be hanged, Gordon fastidiously
objected to having Noisy Tom Pollock as his executioner because
of the latter's brutal killing of Steele.

"If I am to be hanged, I want a decent man to drop the trap.
I don't want it done by a murderer."

Sheriff Middaugh was persuaded to accept the responsibility,
and in the traditional address from the gallows Gordon asked that
the Sheriff be forgiven.

"He is only doing his duty," he said, "and is the best friend I ever had." But the Sheriff was shot down in cold blood a year later by one of Gordon's friends.

The Vigilantes now laid hands upon the mysterious Black Hawk, the second of George Jackson's curious friends, who confessed himself a horse thief and implicated John Shear, of the Denver City Council, and J. C. Ford, a prominent lawyer and member of the territorial legislature. Black Hawk and Shear were lynched two days later. Ford clambered on board a stage coach to escape. The Vigilantes rode after him and overtook the coach at the head of Cherry Creek. Ford was "taken from the stage, marched across the prairie to a secluded spot, and his body riddled with buckshot." But at the moment all that anyone knew was the fact that a valuable gold watch, engraved with his name, was recovered in Denver a few days later and "sent to Ford's widow in Iowa." The Vigilantes soon claimed six other victims, the sight of those dangling bodies seared itself indelibly upon the brain of the boy who discovered them.

"At the Elephant Corral we had built up quite a lucrative business," so Eugene told the story, "and had no opposition in our line, which was mostly that of renting saddle ponies for short mountain trips, and of caring for those coming in from the prospecting camps. But soon there appeared on the scene one Jim Latty, who, after carefully surveying the half block just below ours, started to build a barn very much on the order of ours, and announced his purpose of competing with us. Latty was fully six feet tall, with a most beautiful red beard, fine and silky, which reached to his knees when he was sitting. Very often he would take me to the store of Cook and Sears and buy me a new pair of spurs, a lariat, or even a revolver or bowie knife—anything I wanted. Then he would catch me up and swing me over his shoulders where I could gather his beard in two lots, like reins, and drive him down McGaa Street. Oh, how I did like that man!

"But Jim was a gambling fiend, kept a lot of rough-looking fellows about his barn, and often I heard Father, Uncle Phillip, and others talking over Jim's doings and his lack of patronage and wondering how he managed to feed his hangers-on. It wasn't long before we began losing some of our herds, mostly cheap ponies whose owners had received from us receipts of high valuation. This was not a very profitable business."

One day Eugene was ordered to deliver a number of horses to his father's ranch on Plum Creek, some twenty miles to the south. He started early, "knowing the delays likely to beset the long and lonely ride." About halfway he descended into a long hollow and had just reached high ground again when, not twenty feet away, their cold glazed eyes staring at him, he beheld "Jim Latty and five men hanging by their necks in a big cottonwood tree, Jim with his long red beard looking at least twenty feet long."

For a moment Eugene was paralyzed with terror. Then he wheeled his pony and abandoning his herd, raced back to Denver, giving his pony "no let-up until within shouting distance of friends, giving them the alarm, at least two of them telling me to go home and not be so noisy about it, and let the news get out from others."

At last he came galloping into the Corral to report his find. No one seemed much interested. Later he understood upon hearing someone grumbling in the barn, "Why did you let the boy start out before they had been discovered and buried?"

The local Vigilantes soon established espionage relations with those in Montana. The Denver committee sent two men to Helena and received two in return "for the purpose of identifying newcomers in each place as soon as they arrive." This policy bore fruit immediately. Two men, presumably from Helena, were pointed out to the Denver committee, which, without delay or investigation, seized them and dragged them off to the McNassar racetrack "to string them up without ceremony on the starting stand." Who the men were or what their offenses never transpired.

Crime and violence now became complexly involved with questions of patriotism. The outbreak of the Civil War found Denver sharply divided, with Unionists in the majority. But Confederates mustered considerable strength, one third of the population perhaps, and showed themselves more militant under the able leadership of Charley Harrison and a certain Captain McKee.

One morning in April, '61, Denver awakened to see the Rebel flag flying over the warehouse of Wallingford and Murphy on Larimer Street. Knots of armed men gathered to demand its removal, but the warehousemen, supported by Harrison and his gang from the Criterion Saloon next door, refused. Bloodshed was imminent when a compromise was arranged. The Rebel flag was to fly until evening and never to be raised again.

With the arrival of Colonel William Gilpin, first official governor of the Territory, two volunteer military companies were hurriedly recruited—one in Denver, and the other in the Clear Creek camps. The latter was immediately ordered to Denver and quartered opposite the Criterion Saloon, which was publicly regarded as the center of sedition. Several raids were made on it by the military, to little purpose. But sheer weight of numbers drove Confederate activities underground. Captain McKee now proposed an ingenious scheme to render the Unionists' superiority in firearms useless. Confederates quietly began buying up all the percussion caps in the territory.

Now thoroughly alarmed, the authorities ordered the military and police to disarm the whole populace. This led Confederate leaders to quit town in a body. Almost one hundred strong, all heavily armed and well mounted, they moved leisurely up Cherry Creek. In the party went Charley Harrison, Postmaster McClure, Mayor John Moore, and Captain McKee, who was riding Eugene's beloved Rocky Mountain Chief. The party headed for the Santa Fe Trail, hoping to plunder Government wagon trains before going on to Texas. When Colonel Leavenworth mustered a force to pursue and capture the Rebels, he discovered that he first had to send to the Missouri River for percussion caps. By Hinckley's Express, the "Flyer" of the day, the round trip was accomplished in the almost incredible time of six days. Leavenworth now rode rapidly south to overtake the Rebels, who had been loitering along the way, waiting for prey. He managed to capture them and brought them back to Denver, where they were locked up in a stockade as prisoners of war. But all soon escaped with the connivance of their jailer, who fled South with them. With the departure of Harrison and most of his gang, good citizens of Denver felt far more secure.

McKee became a colonel of irregulars in Texas. Mayor Moore joined Price's army in Missouri, became an adjutant general, later campaigned in Mexico with the French Contre-Guérillas, and in time returned to Colorado to edit the Pueblo *Press*. Harrison and McClure likewise joined Price's army, and both appear to have harbored a notion of stealing back to Denver to sack the town and enlist guerrilla recruits.

Early in 1863 a reconnoitering party of sixteen Confederate officers, led by Charley Harrison, now a colonel, slipped out of Missouri for the gold fields. They had penetrated Kansas about sixty miles when they encountered a band of Osage Indians in the pay of the Union. In the running fight that followed, all of the Confederate officers but one were killed and scalped—Captain Park McClure and Colonel Charley Harrison in the first encounter—and the bones of Denver's rather pompous first postmaster and of the engaging gambler-desperado whom Eugene adored lie scattered somewhere along the Verdigris River, near Independence, Kansas.

VII

TOWARD SAND CREEK

"Great God! and are we all gone up . . . But no!"

ALTHOUGH drinking, gambling, and shooting appear to have occupied a large part of the population of early Denver, the straggling settlement on the Plains had its more serious concerns.

A Denver People's Government was formed in October, '60, in a determined effort to suppress lawlessness and improve the condition of camp. A city marshal was appointed, with eight officers as a police force. Contributions were solicited "for the purpose of erecting a jail, or caboose." Houses of ill fame were declared a nuisance within certain districts of the city, and peddling was forbidden on the grounds that it discouraged the construction of substantial buildings and filled the streets with wagons, tents, and other temporary places of business.

The Council appointed a city physician as well as a special committee to consider the "expediency of establishing as soon as possible, one or more free schools in this city." One was established at last in December, '62, but no public school system worthy of the name was organized till '70. Even then, there were constant complaints that school funds were not properly accounted for, or that "my predecessor in office left no records." Meantime, Father Machebeuf had founded St. Mary's Academy. Others organized the Valley Seminary for Young Ladies and Misses, which offered instruction in ancient and modern languages, embroidery, and calisthenics. In '64 the local Methodists incorporated Colorado Seminary, subsequently the University of Denver.

112

Denver soon had several banks, notably the First National and Kountze Brothers'. The Kountzes ultimately ascended to Wall Street to become minor priests there in the financial hierarchy. Tabor was one day to buy a half interest in the powerful First National, which early passed into the hands of David Moffat, later multimillionaire and railroad king. The foundation of his large fortune was laid during these days when Moffat was a purveyor of paper, envelopes, brushes, playing cards, photograph albums, paper hangings, Masonic textbooks, and novels. Another multimillionaire of later years, Walter Cheesman, now opened a drugstore for the sale of pure drugs, chemicals, patent medicines, paints, oils, varnishes, brushes, perfumery, soaps, fancy toilet goods, lamps and chimneys, wines, bitters, fine whiskies, and brandies. Essentially dull and uninteresting men, both were patiently acquisitive and with their great wealth made their influence felt in the later community.

For a time Denver had a private mint—Clark, Gruber, and Company. It struck a number of $10 and $20 gold pieces, with a rude figure of Pike's Peak on one face and the name of the house on the other. For the most part, gold dust continued to be the commonest medium of exchange, though for convenience the merchants and banks issued a large volume of "shinplasters," paper script in denominations of ten, twenty-five, and fifty cents, and $1.

The town early had a theater. At the height of the gold rush, "Colonel" C. R. Thorne had brought a troupe from Leavenworth to perform the *Maid of Croissey* at Gunnell Hall, sometimes known as Apollo Hall. Situated above a saloon on Larimer Street, it had neither ceiling nor plaster, and was lighted dimly by twelve candles. Candles also served as footlights. The theater would seat any three hundred and fifty willing to pay $1 in gold dust to sit huddled upon its rough and splintery wooden benches. Richardson, Greeley's colleague, attended the opening night but could hear nothing above the din of clinking glasses, rattling billiard balls, and uproarious songs rising from the saloon below.

Thorne was shortly a bankrupt and fled his creditors. But "Mademoiselle" Haidee and others of his troupe remained behind to do rather well after discovering a great natural dramatic talent in "inimitable Mike" Dougherty, a miner from Gregory Gulch. Dougherty soon formed a company of his own and was joined by Jack Langrishe, the most famous trouper of his day in the West, who, after long wanderings, will be summoned one day to open the new Tabor Opera House at Leadville. Perhaps Tabor first saw him here to applaud his talent.

Langrishe and Dougherty presented, among other plays, *His Last Legs* and a farce, *Nature and Philosophy,* in which they captivated their audience "not only with their low comedy, but their 'Pat Casey,' 'Night Hands,' and other popular songs." They enjoyed an unprecedentedly long and prosperous season of six months before making a tour of the Clear Creek camps, playing at the Montana Theater in Central City for six weeks.

Upon their return to Denver, Langrishe and Dougherty decided to build a playhouse of their own. Great ceremony marked the opening of their Platte Valley Theater on G Street. "The new and elegant dramatic institution was filled with a very large, intelligent, and respectable audience," the *News* reported next morning. "*The Mistletoe Bough* was placed upon the stage on this occasion in a creditable manner, and the managers and company were welcomed in very flattering style."

Perhaps so, but the theater closed its doors three weeks later when Langrishe and Dougherty departed on a longer tour of the mining camps in the mountains. Next year they returned heavy with dust to remodel their theater and rename it the Denver. Melodrama and farce did not exclusively hold the stage here. "The Great Stereoptican will be exhibited for the first time at the Denver Theater this evening," read one announcement. Another a few weeks later advertised a "Grand Vocal and Instrumental Concert by Alexander Sutherland, assisted by Thirty-one Performers, many of them lately arrived from the East." The program, as announced, was this:

Anvil Chorus (Mr. Meyers having kindly loaned six anvils,
to render the chorus more effective) .... *Full Chorus*
Cornet Solo .... *Mr. Olmstead*
Overture, The Lone Star, or The Opening of the Battle of
Charleston *(the Overture to commence with a Salvo of Ar-*
tillery, Col. Potter and Capt. Hawley having kindly loaned
the use of cannon) .... *Full Chorus*
Cornet Solo .... *Mr. Sutherland*

The St. Louis Serenaders in Quartette
will make their first appearance.
Positively the Last Appearance
of
ALEXANDER SUTHERLAND
before his departure for the States.

"The concert Saturday evening was well attended," read the *News* next day. "We have seldom heard the Anvil Chorus performed with better effect, even by the celebrated bands of Boston and New York. Our music-loving citizens are sorry to lose so finished a musician as Mr. Sutherland."[1]

Mike Dougherty soon died of drink at Central City, and Langrishe now established a dramatic circuit which each year provided Denver with a six months' theatrical season. Central City had one of three, while the remaining three months were variously divided among other mountain camps—Fairplay, Buckskin Joe, and Montgomery in South Park; French Gulch and Delaware Flats on the Blue River; Georgia Gulch and California Gulch on the upper Arkansas. Finally in '71—having meantime visited Montana to gain additional triumphs there at Helena, Virginia City, and Deer Lodge—Langrishe departed for Chicago and there at the Globe Theater staged one of the first performances to be given after the great Chicago fire.

By '61 the Pike's Peak country had a population of perhaps

25,000, and at last the Congress created the Territory of Colorado on a great rectangle of land cut from western Kansas and
eastern Utah. The extra-legal government of the Provisional Territory of Jefferson was dissolved.

Appointed by President Lincoln as Colorado's first official governor, Colonel William Gilpin arrived in May, '61, to establish
himself and staff in the Executive Chambers—a suite of three
rooms above a clothing store on Larimer Street. As the Civil War
had begun, the Colonel hastened to recruit the First Colorado
Cavalry, which with other local units acquitted itself well, first
at the battles of La Glorieta Pass and Pigeon Ranch in New Mexico, then against General Price's army in Missouri. To arm and
equip his "Pet Lambs," as he called the First Colorado, Gilpin
issued $375,000 of sight drafts on the Federal Treasury. Local
merchants and citizens accepted them in good faith, and suffered
great loss and embarrassment when the Federal government refused for years to recognize these drafts, promptly removing Gilpin from office for issuing them without authorization.

The embarrassment caused by the repudiated drafts aggravated
the economic depression from which the town increasingly suffered. The better gulch claims in the mountains had been depleted, and most of the hard-rock mines were "in cap." Quartz
mills were everywhere silent. Not only had the Civil war stopped
immigration, but it now began to carry many away.

Green Russell and a party of Georgians, with $20,000 of dust
in their pockets, attempted to reach the Confederacy by marching
south along the Continental Divide, hoping to slip through New
Mexico into Texas. But they were captured in New Mexico and
held as prisoners of war. Russell and his friends were released in
'63 and returned to Denver. As soon as hostilities ceased, however, they proceeded home to Georgia.

Uncle Dick Wootton found that these were "dull years in the
mountains generally, and particularly dull in Denver." Convinced
that the town would continue to decline, Uncle Dick closed his

store-saloon and in '63 departed for New Mexico to settle down and die there on a large ranch, meantime building a toll road over Raton Pass on the increasingly traveled Mountain Branch of the Santa Fe Trail.

Even the Larimers became discouraged and returned to Leavenworth where the General wished "to spend the remainder of his days in peace and comfort, following farming and mercantile pursuits." He had outdone the squatters at their own game but had not found the pot at the end of the rainbow.

And now Denver was struck by a series of disasters.

Early one morning in April, '63, the fire alarm sounded. A great blaze was crackling in the rear of the Cherokee House on Blake Street. With a strong wind blowing, flames were soon leaping across streets and quickly eating their way through dozens of frame buildings, all dry as tinder. The volunteers of the Hook and Ladder Company and of the two bucket companies did what they could to hold the fire in check, pulling down smaller frame structures in the path of the conflagration, dashing water upon those too large to be quickly removed. At one time the entire town seemed doomed. By dawn the heart of Denver lay in ashes, a mass of smouldering timbers. More than seventy business buildings and great stores of provisions had been consumed. Already high, the price of food mounted higher, to the great distress of many.

But the town was not dismayed. Slowly it built itself up again with new buildings, "of that durable character befitting a city of such importance, and not of that fragile and combustible material distinguishing pioneer buildings."

Then in '64, and again in '65 and '67, came a plague of grasshoppers to devour every green thing above ground. "One morning in 1864, when the corn was in milk and the cabbages well-headed, we drove out to look over our farm and rejoice in the prospect of its yield. While we sat at dinner with the tenant and his wife, the sky grew suddenly black and my husband, thinking a storm imminent, went to bring in the cushions from our buggy. With an exclamation of surprise, he called us to the door. The sun was still shining but was veiled with a myriad of grasshoppers. On our drive home the air for miles was thick with the pests. In a week's time the face of the country was changed from smiling plenty to a desolated waste."

"About the midnight hour of Thursday, the nineteenth instant, when almost all the town were knotted in the peace of sleep, deaf to all noise and blind to all danger, snoring in calm security, and seeing visions of remoteness radiant with the rainbow hues of past associations, or roseate with the gilded hopes of the fanciful future—while the full-faced queen of night shed showers of silver from the starry throne o'er fields of freshness and fertility, garnishing and suffusing sleeping nature with her balmy brightness, fringing the feathery cottonwoods with lustre, enameling the house tops with coats of pearl, bridging the erst placid Platte with beams of radiance, and bathing the arid sands of Cherry Creek with dewy beauty—a frightful phenomenon sounded in the distance, and a shocking calamity presently charged upon us . . . Hark! What and where is this? A torrent or a tornado? These were the questions soliloquized and spoken, one to the other. Has creation's God forsaken us, and has chaos come again? Our eyes might bewilder and our ears deceive, but our hearts, all trembling, and our sacred souls soon whispered what it was. Alas, and wonderful to behold! it was the water engine of death dragging its destroying train of maddened waves, that defied the eye to number them. . . . What does this mean? Have the wild waterspouts from all the clouds at once conspired to drain their upper cisterns, and thus drench us here in death? Have the firm foundations of the Almighty's earth given way, and the fountains of the great deep burst forth on fallen men, regardless of that rainbow covenant which spanned in splendor yon arc of sky last evening?"

This was Professor Goldrick describing the great Cherry Creek flood of May, '64. At two o'clock one morning, as the result of a series of cloudbursts, a great wall of black water twenty feet high came rushing down Cherry Creek, which never before had run more than a yellow trickle. The flood first carried away the Larimer Street Bridge, then the Methodist Church and two adjoining buildings. Here one man was "launched asleep and naked on the watery ocean of eternity, to find his final fatal refuge only in the flood-gate port of death. Precipitately and in paroxysms, the tempestuous torrent swept along, bridging bank to bank with billows high as hills piled on hills—with broken buildings, tables, bedsteads, baggage, boulders, mammoth trees, leviathan logs, and human beings buffeting with the billow crests. Next, reeled the dear old office of the *Rocky Mountain News* as down it sank, with its Union flag staff, into the maelstrom of the surging waters, soon to appear and disappear between the waves as, wild with starts, in mountains high, they rose and rolled, as if endeavoring to form a dread alliance with the clouds, and thus consummate our general wreck."

One of the editors and four employees sleeping in the building narrowly escaped drowning when they plunged from an upper window into the torrent to be rescued at last with the aid of ropes. The *News* lost not only its plant and buildings but even its lot in the treacherous creek bed. Heavy presses were later found two miles down the Platte.[2] The flood next swept away a score of buildings near the Blake Street Bridge, including the City Hall with all of its records and the city jail with its prisoners.

"Great God! and are we all gone up, and is there no power to stem the tide, was asked all round. But no! The inundation of the Nile, the Noachian deluge, and that of Prometheus' son, Deucalien, the Noah of the Greeks, were now in danger of being outdeluged by this phenomenon of '64."

It was not as bad as the Professor made out, but serious enough. Almost a score of persons had been drowned, and thousands of head of livestock. Altogether, Denver estimated its property damage at half a million, a staggering loss for the small and increasingly desperate community.

Almost overwhelmed by flood, Denver now lay paralyzed with fear of an Indian attack and massacre. Before the flood there had circulated vague reports of Indians suddenly descending upon ranch houses in the vicinity when the men were absent and ordering the women to "cook heap." Now, less than a month after the flood, Denver was terrified to learn that a wandering party of Cheyenne, under Chief Roman Nose, had attacked the Hungate ranch some twenty miles distant, and killed and scalped a whole family—man, wife, and small children. The mutilated bodies were brought to town for all to see. A force of volunteers to serve one hundred days was recruited. Governor Evans ordered all stores to close early so that men might be drilled for action. Every evening the streets were filled with marching men. Two nights after the Hungate attack, a rider on a foaming horse raced down Cherry Creek and into town.

"The Indians are coming!" he cried. "The Indians are coming to massacre the town!"

In his wake ran terrified men, women, and children, fleeing in panic from neighboring ranches and the outskirts of the town. The women and children of East Denver sought refuge in the Clark and Gruber Mint; those in West Denver, on the second floor of the brick Commissary Building. Doors were bolted; the iron shutters on both buildings were closed and barred. At the foot of the outside stairs of the Commissary Building stood two men with axes, ready to cut away the stairs at first sight of an Indian.

"In the buildings congregated women in every stage of dress and undress. Some came arrayed in their best, having planned an evening with friends; some came as they sprang from their beds; some carrying clothing in their arms; others carrying valuables. But most had with them whatever was nearest when the alarm was sounded. That night one woman in a nightgown and bare feet carried with her a bandbox with her best bonnet in it. A Titian-haired beauty sought frantically among her neighbors for a handkerchief large enough to conceal her curls, for she had been told that the Indians preferred them of that color."

No Indians appeared, and after midnight scouts were sent out to reconnoiter. They failed to find a single savage. But this was thought to be just another ruse, until it was discovered that the alarm had been caused by the shouting of Mexicans herding cattle in the dark. Most women, however, refused to venture forth before daylight when they returned home to find that in the general panic almost all of their houses "were left with doors and windows open, and lamps burning within, but so general was the belief in a fast-approaching death, or a still worse fate, that no thieving at all was done."

The Indians of the Plains stand convicted of many atrocities, but they had a number of legitimate grievances and in their regard the whites could certainly not boast of clean and bloodless hands. In the beginning the Arapaho had received the Argonauts peaceably enough. Under Chiefs Little Raven, Little Horse, and Eugene's friend Left Hand, who spoke some English, the Arapaho remained very friendly until the night the Bummers attacked and outraged their squaws and children encamped below Denver. Nor were the gold-hunters troubled during the first years by the Cheyenne, a brave and fine-looking tribe, well dressed and mounted, who, for the most part, remained out on the Plains far from the settlements.[3]

By treaty in '51, the Arapaho, Cheyenne, and certain tribes of the Sioux had been granted all the land between the Platte and the Arkansas. In '61 the head chiefs of the Arapaho and Cheyenne were persuaded to cede a large part of these lands to the Federal government in exchange for a meager reservation on Sand Creek, near Bent's old fort on the Arkansas. A majority in the tribes objected to this bargaining by their chiefs and soon began stealing stock and collecting arms. Many stage stations were robbed during the winter of '62. Cheyenne and Kiowa, a treacherous tribe living along the Arkansas, raided ranches and settlements on Cache la Poudre Creek in '63. Early in '64 detachments of the First Colorado Cavalry collided again and again with the Cheyenne in brisk skirmishes. Then the Hungates were murdered. Soon ranch houses were in flames from Mexico to Canada in the country along the mountains. Fifty or more whites were killed and scalped on the Plains east of Denver during the next few months.

As alarm increased, strong defenses were built all around Denver. Every night, picket guards were posted. Governor Evans received authorization to organize the Third Regiment of Volunteer Colorado Cavalry. But in spite of the alarm, enlisting appears to have been rather slow. Evans summoned General Larimer from Leavenworth to stimulate recruiting. But Larimer failed to fill up the regiment, soon resigned, and departed for Kansas, never to return.

Governor Evans now issued an unfortunate proclamation in which he promised recruits that they might keep for themselves everything they captured from the Indians. The proclamation urged all citizens, "whether organized or individually, to go in pursuit of hostiles, and to kill and destroy them wherever found, and to capture and hold to their own private use all the [Indian] territory they can take."

Even more unfortunately, Evans gave the command of the Third Colorado Cavalry to his friend John M. Chivington, presiding elder of the Methodist Church in the Territory. Once a blacksmith-preacher in Kansas during the days of the Border War, a giant of a man some six feet seven inches tall and weighing more than three hundred pounds, Chivington was a "crude but good-natured and well-intentioned Irishman," according to Hal Sayre, who served under him. On the battlefield he was the "very incarnation of war," showing great courage and considerable tactical skill at the battles of La Glorieta Pass and Pigeon Ranch.

Governor Evans now sent scouts among the Indians encamped in the Ridge Country to warn them that the Great White Father was very angry with them, and would certainly hunt down and punish the guilty. But as the Great White Father was a kindly as well as a just deity and wished to spare the innocent, those Arapaho and Cheyenne who were friendly should immediately report to Major Collery, the Federal Indian agent at Fort Lyon, Bent's old fort at Big Timbers.[4] Major Collery, so it was promised, would "give them provisions and show them to a place of safety."

Through George Bent, whose wife belonged to the tribe, the Cheyenne declared their own and the Arapaho's willingness to obey if a similar assurance were given those of the Kiowa, Comanche, Apache, and Sioux who were also on the warpath.

Arapaho and Cheyenne chiefs were now summoned to a conference at Camp Weld, just south of Denver. It was a long powwow, but the Indians were allowed to say very little, being curtly cut off whenever they attempted to state their grievances and complaints against the whites who, in many instances, had been the aggressors. No one at the conference was more antagonistic and openly belligerent toward the Indians than the Reverend John M. Chivington, colonel of the Third Colorado.

The Indians, as was to be expected, quit the conference in a sullen and angry mood. But a large number of Arapaho and Cheyenne nevertheless decided to come in from the High Plains. More than four hundred soon appeared at Fort Lyon and surrendered. A few days later they were ordered off to Sand Creek, some forty miles distant, where they might live and hunt without coming into contact with the whites using the Santa Fe Trail.

Chief Black Kettle of the Cheyenne and Chief Left Hand of the Arapaho led their tribes away, as commanded, and were soon joined by several hundred more of their people until, at length, their Sand Creek encampment contained more than a hundred lodges and some eight hundred people, at least half of whom were squaws and children. All settled down peaceably, thinking that they were securely under the protection of the Federal government. Chief Black Kettle, as head of the encampment, immediately proved his good faith by sending a messenger to warn the authorities that a large war party of Sioux had left the headwaters of the Smoky Hill Fork, evidently with the intention of making a swift raid along the Santa Fe Trail.

Governor Evans had meantime departed for Washington, and in his absence Colonel Chivington planned a coup. With two field pieces and six hundred men, Chivington set out quietly for Fort Lyon. Here he obtained reinforcements and two howitzers, and under cover of night rapidly marched toward the Indian encampment on Sand Creek. The encampment lay in the dry bed of the creek, with steep bluffs to either side. In the center of the village stood Black Kettle's lodge. On one side of it were the tepees of the Cheyenne, while Chiefs Left Hand and Yellow Wolf had established their Arapaho on the other.

Chivington's force arrived just before dawn. Finding the Indians' large herd of ponies grazing on the bluffs, the soldiers stealthily drove them off and then advanced in three bodies. Mounted men circled the encampment to occupy the high bluff to the east. Another cavalry unit occupied the lower bluff to the west. Up the creek bed came a large force of men on foot, led by Colonel Chivington, who had issued sharp orders that no prisoners were to be taken. He had made his dispositions well, for there was no hope of escape for the unarmed Indians except to the north through a narrow opening between the bluffs.

Firing began from the eastern bluff, followed by a fusillade from the south and west. Taken completely by surprise, the Indians ran from their tepees and gathered about the lodge of Black Kettle, unable to understand. Thinking there was some mistake, Black Kettle ran up an American flag. When no respect was paid to that, he hoisted a white flag of surrender. Both were riddled with bullets as the roar of the guns increased. Realizing the truth at last, Eugene's friend, Chief Left Hand, folded his arms and stood before his tepee contemptuously facing the whites until he toppled to the ground without a cry, pierced by scores of bullets. Chief White Antelope, with his hands held high in surrender, was shot down as he advanced toward Chivington singing the Cheyenne death song:

> *Nothing lives long*
> *Except the earth and the mountains . . .*

Old men and women, young girls and small children, all of the sick and disabled, ran madly here and there in hopeless attempts to find shelter behind small ridges of sand, piles of driftwood, and scattered clumps of brush. From one side or another they were maimed or killed. Old John Smith of Denver, who had come to trade with the Indians, ran from his tent toward the advancing soldiers, who recognized him and took deliberate aim at him, cursing him obscenely as a squaw man. He managed to escape, but a soldier who rode out from the ranks to protect him was killed. Meantime, the howitzers had been booming, and squads of cavalry were dashing along the ridges and ravines, cutting down any Indians who had somehow escaped the death-trap.

"It may perhaps be unnecessary to state that I captured no prisoners," wrote Chivington jubilantly in his first report of the massacre, claiming somewhat extravagantly to have killed from five to six hundred Indians and to have seized from four to five hundred ponies. Young Charles Bent, son of Colonel Bent by a Cheyenne mother, was in camp at the time and miraculously escaped alive to estimate the dead more conservatively at two or three hundred, the great majority being women and children.[5]

After the "battle," the soldiers tarried to scalp and mutilate the dead in most horrible fashion. "I saw bodies worse mutilated there than I ever saw before," declared old John Smith, who had lived his life among the Indians. "The women cut all to pieces; scalped; their brains knocked out; children two and three years old; all ages lying there, from suckling infants up to warriors."

Jack Smith, the old trader's grown son by a Cheyenne mother, was also in camp and survived the general slaughter, only to be killed in his father's tent by one of a party of soldiers who had come to search it. The shooting may have been accidental, remarked Hal Sayre, who was present, "but I know there was no mourning in our ranks over it. As a matter of fact, some of the boys dragged the body out onto the prairie and hauled it about for a considerable time." [6] The whites, it is apparent from this and many another incident, hated the squaw men and their offspring quite as much as the Indians. There happened to be in Smith's tent at the time of the shooting another old Indian trader from Denver, the mulatto Jim Beckwourth, who later testified that young Jack Smith had been deliberately murdered.

As the Third Colorado marched off down the Arkansas seeking other triumphs, the corpses of massacred and mutilated Indians were left lying along the creek bed to be devoured by coyotes and vultures, for Colonel Chivington had sworn, according to one of his captains, to hang "any son-of-a-bitch who would bury their bodies or bones."

The territorial legislature formally gave thanks to Colonel Chivington for his success in "maintaining the honor of the National Flag."

Jim Beckwourth, known to the Indians as Medicine Calf, went in pursuit of Chief Black Kettle and some two hundred others who had managed to escape and found them encamped on Box Elder Creek.

"Medicine Calf," they greeted him, "what have you come for? Have you fetched the white man to finish killing our families?" [7]

The Sand Creek Massacre split Colorado into two bitter factions. Governor Evans may not have approved but never publicly raised his voice in protest. He remained silent as the local Republican party vitriolically denounced as traitors and renegades any who found fault with the bloodthirsty and treacherous Chivington. So deeply disgusted and revolted was a large part of the community that the greatest difficulty was encountered in recruiting additional volunteer companies—such difficulty, in fact, that it was necessary to declare martial law and order the suspension of all business before six volunteer cavalry companies could be filled. Colonel Chivington was subsequently court-martialed. Though acquitted by his brother officers, he was quickly removed from his command, dying many years later in Denver as coroner and under-sheriff.

The Sand Creek slaughter incited the Indians to rise in fury and sweep the Plains. They ripped up more than a hundred miles of telegraph. Every road to the east was blocked for months so that Denver's only line of communication with the States was by way of California and Panama. All stage stations along the Platte from Denver to Julesburg were despoiled and burned. The price of flour rose to $50 a barrel, and again many were starving along the mountains. The *News* had to print its editions on brown wrapping paper or any other odd bits found about the town. The roads were not again open until '65, and they were periodically closed after that time. In '67 the Sand Creek Reservation was taken from the Arapaho and Cheyenne, who were assigned lands in Oklahoma. Peace was not fully restored to the Plains till '69, after General Custer at the Washita had defeated a large force of Cheyenne, Arapaho, and Kiowa under Chief Black Kettle.[8]

In time, the Sand Creek affair came under the eye of a Special Joint Committee of the Congress which, after a sharp denunciation of the outrage, recommended the award of a section of land each to Black Kettle and other head chiefs, and a half section to every squaw who had lost husband or parent at Sand Creek. The

Congress adopted this recommendation and undertook to recompense all those who had lost property at Sand Creek by making them annual payments in "goods, provisions, or such other useful articles as may in the discretion of the Secretary of the Interior be deemed best adapted to their respective wants and conditions."

After the Indian uprising Denver entered the most critical period in its history. Mining in the mountains declined year by year. Although farming and ranching had begun in river bottoms and mountain parks, and would one day assume first place in the state's economy, they had not yet made any great forward strides. Even the advance of the rails of the Union Pacific across the Plains affected Denver adversely for a time. As the railroad chose a route through Wyoming, Denver lost the advantage it had enjoyed in the stagecoach era of being on a main road of transcontinental travel. Many moved north to Cheyenne to establish themselves on the railroad there.

During these years one catches a last glimpse of many familiar faces. Green Russell returned again from Georgia to settle on a ranch near the Spanish Peaks, below the Arkansas, but did not long remain. With his wife, he joined the Cherokee in Indian Territory and soon died there among her people. Mourning their son killed at Sand Creek, John Smith and his squaw drifted away to the farther Frontier. Old Jim Beckwourth also disappeared to die soon in the mountains. William McGaa, alias Jack Jones, died of drink "in the caboose of Denver with none to mourn his sad end." His heart had been broken by the fact that as he grew steadily more disreputable, the name of McGaa Street had been changed to Holladay in honor of the stagecoach king of the day. The gambler Ed Chase moved away for a time to Montana. The trouper Jack Langrishe departed for Chicago.

Larimer and his son had retraced their steps to Kansas and never returned. Although they still owned property in Denver, they despaired of the town's future. They had little to show for their enterprise, but before his death some ten years later the General was assured of at least one fortune in the family, for he married a daughter to a Mellon—a Pittsburgh Mellon.[9] It is said, in fact, that of all the founders of the Denver Town Company only Secretary Dick Whitsitt made even a modest fortune from the enterprise.

Robert Teats sold the Elephant Corral before the fire of '63 in which it was destroyed. Taking Eugene with him to Central City, he turned to mining but was not markedly successful in his efforts to solve the problems of smelting the refractory ores of Gregory Gulch. Eugene was soon sent away to the University of Notre Dame. In time, he returned to Colorado to become an operator of mines, moved from camp to camp as one after another they rose and fell, later spent many years in the gold fields of Dutch Guiana, and finally returned to Denver, dying there in 1929.

As the first days of wild excitement and wilder speculation subsided in the Pike's Peak country, an air of premature decay crept over Denver. A traveler passed in '68 to find it already dilapidated:

"The old mining excitement has ceased. The old Overland stage has stopped and its business rushes past on a railroad one hundred miles to the north. Business is dull; the town is quiet, almost as an Eastern village. I see scarcely a new house going up, plenty of places *To Let.*"

VIII

CALIFORNIA GULCH AND
BUCKSKIN JOE

". . . everything in sight filled with the metal, the pure gold—"

STAGNANT and uneventful for the most part, the long years of deflation and depression following the first boom days in the Pike's Peak country were illumined occasionally by bright flashes of gold in the mountains. Strikes were made here and there to set gold-hunters' eyes blazing again with the hope that never quite deserted them. Thousands upon thousands rushed desperately from one short-lived camp to another—none more persistently and few with less immediate success than Horace Austin Warner Tabor.

When last seen in '59, Tabor was idling away the winter in Denver upon finding his Clear Creek claim jumped by a treacherous old miner. Augusta was minding her baby, washing and cooking for her boarders. During that winter many rumors circulated of rich strikes in the mountains—now here, now there, in widely separated districts. Tabor at length decided to investigate and knowing as little of one alleged gold field as another, chose the nearest, having "to sell the cow to buy supplies."

The family's battered old wagon was greased and repaired. The two scrawny oxen which had drawn it so far were yoked up again, and on a cold blustery February morning Augusta was lifted from a sick bed and driven off by her husband and boarders toward Pike's Peak, its white hood gleaming in the distance.

Their slow progress along the base of the mountains was recorded by Augusta in her diary:

> . . . *pitched tent, made a fire. Soon had a dish of hot coffee for supper. . . . Retired for the night at six. The boys made themselves merry singing songs.*
>
> *March 1st. The sun arose bright and beautiful, not a cloud to be seen. . . . Breakfast of venison ham and sasphras tea. this I call a poor appology for coffee—We camped for noon at the mill. The wind blew very high. I had a walk after dinner. At night we camped on plum creek. The wind blew al night.*
>
> *March 2. Morning is very windy. Nat [the baby] has a bad cold and is very cross, breakfast of venison ham and coffee. We stopped under a hill to break the wind of and to have dinner. . . . . 4 o'clock we camped for the night beside a log cabin in which lived a woman and five raged dirty chuldren Here the prairie caught a fire, and the men worked an hour or so in trying to keep the fire from a small hay stack, but in vain. We retired early as usual, and slept sound until the sun was up on the day.*
>
> *March 3rd. Windy and cold, I kept the bed al the morning. At noon we stopped at a ranch and built a fire in a cabin but the smoke was so bad we were oblidge to move it out side. The wind is still blowing hard, have kept the bed al the afternoon. . . .*
>
> *4 Sunday. the wind is still blowing we came near to the mountains and passed some natural monuments, some nearly white as marble and standing thirty or forty feet. We drove into a beautiful valley and halted for noon. There a man overtook us with some cows, and kindly offered us some milk which was thankfully received as we had had no milk for coffee since we had left civilization.*[1]

Next morning they pitched camp at the foot of Pike's Peak. For a few days the men prospected the Fontaine qui Bouille and neighboring creeks. They then hired themselves out as laborers on the toll road building up Ute Pass. When rumors began to fly of discoveries on the upper Arkansas, they gave up their jobs and vanished up the pass, advancing so slowly up the steep grade that at night they often saw the "smoke sent up by the dying fire of the camp of the night before." Why Tabor left burning fires behind him to kindle the forests is another matter. For two weeks the party toiled on over high ridges until one evening they were suddenly looking down into South Park—a great flat grassy basin, veined with many silver streams, cupped round with blue pine-clad mountains rising to sharp glistening points of snow. Augusta at least was impressed, pronouncing it "gorgeously beautiful." That night they camped by a clear stream, had broiled trout for dinner and later a game of whist in the firelight.

Through the Park they attempted to guide themselves by Frémont's published maps and letters. Four days later they encamped by Salt Creek. As its waters were too brackish to be drunk by themselves or cattle, all went thirsty and hungry to bed. All nights were cold, and this one especially—so bitterly cold that a half-wild burro strayed into camp to stand in the fire embers until his fetlocks were burned off. Augusta adopted him, and he proved to be a great comfort. In the morning they moved on to fresh water and stopped. They were uncertain of the way and could find no exit from the Park. Someone recalled that a party had left Denver for this region just before their own departure. Tabor and the men shouldered their rifles to go in search of this party or at least traces of its passing. A rifle shot was to be the signal of discovery. All day Augusta sat alone in camp, listening anxiously. The silence in the lonely valley grew more and more oppressive. Night came, and the men had not returned. When the little burro wandered into the tent, Augusta bowed her head upon him and wept "in loneliness of soul."

Late that night, one by one, the men came in, guided by the fire Augusta had kept blazing, having learned nothing. Next morning they decided to throw a stick into the air and proceed in whatever direction it happened to fall. Providentially, it fell pointing south-west. Two days later they descended into the Arkansas valley and after many mishaps forded the icy roaring torrent. They moved up the river to Cache Creek, where all staked claims. They found much fine gold, but so mixed with a heavy black sand that it could not be extricated with the means at hand.

"For four weeks we worked there," said Augusta later. "Our supplies were almost gone, and we felt discouraged. It had been a long year since we had heard of the loved ones at home."

A rumor comes of another strike higher up the valley. The Tabors pack up and are again on the road. Great shoulders of granite force them to cross and recross the swift river. Augusta and her baby are almost lost during one crossing when the wagon slips from a rock ledge into the deepest part of the channel. The wagon bed floats off and goes whirling downstream, rapidly filling with water. Augusta clutches at some willows under a steep bank and manages to hold on until she and her child are rescued. The wagon is salvaged and at length, three months after leaving Denver, the Tabors enter California Gulch, where they will suffer many bitter defeats before their ultimate triumph twenty years later.

Here in California Gulch, more than ten thousand feet above sea level, just a few hundred feet below timberline, Abe Lee and other Georgians from Russell Gulch have just discovered the richest placer diggings ever found in Colorado. They, too, had stopped to work Cache Creek, with no more success than Tabor. They then joined a passing crowd of Iowans and moved up the Arkansas almost to its source. Here, the Iowans decided to proceed up one gulch, the Georgians another, both struggling forward through heavy snow, stopping now and again to try the frozen sands below. It seemed a hopeless venture, but Abe Lee suggested another trial or two. One panful showed color, and soon they were in rich pay-dirt.

"I found it!" shouted Lee. "I got it—the hull state of Californy in this here goddam pan!"

And so the gulch was named.

When the Tabors arrive, there are perhaps fifty miners working in the snow. Having staked out claims, Tabor and the boarders hasten to erect a cabin of green logs to shelter Augusta and her child. It has no door, window, or floor, and is roofed with bark and earth. The wagon is sawed up to provide furniture—tables, shelves, and three-legged stools. The oxen have to be slaughtered for food. This enables Augusta to take in more boarders though, as she said, she has "nothing to feed them but poor beef and dried apples."

Better luck attends Tabor here than he has known before. By the end of the summer his mine shows a profit of $5,000, but he is not among the richest in camp. Scores of men do far better. Indeed, the claim just below Tabor's yields $80,000 of dust, according to Augusta, who personally weighs it on her scales, the only pair in camp, for she now has to tend not only her boarding house but a general store and post office established by Tabor. This store-post office gradually becomes the center of a scattered settlement of log cabins, pine-bough shelters, and dugouts in the hillsides. It is first known as Boughtown. But as it grows larger, it is more pretentiously named Oro City. Father Machebeuf early arrives to build a log church and almost succumb to mountain fever. Colonel Chivington comes to bless a Methodist chapel. Here gather land and mine speculators, bandits, gamblers, prostitutes, and others of their kind to prey upon the miners. Within a few months California Gulch is swarming with more than ten thousand fortune-hunters.

Saloons, gambling houses, and brothels line the gulch road for miles. The Georgians from the Clear Creek diggings enjoy the reputation of contributing most to their support. But all the miners are "roysterers and spenders, not savers." All pay "their devotions to John Barleycorn, Maude Cyprian, and Pasteboard Greencloth." Few in Oro City are unacquainted with "Red Stocking," who within a year departs "with more than $100,000," announcing her intention to reform.

"Money was of no account here then," said Augusta in later years. "Ordinary workmen were paid $6.00 per day in gold. They received their pay every night, and the majority spent it before morning. The miners would clean up their boxes, get their gold weighed, go to town (where Leadville now stands), spree all night, and return dead broke in the morning to commence again."

Tabor no doubt indulged in his passion for poker, for "no old-timer," as one remarked, "has any trouble in associating the name of Tabor with cards—they were one and inseparable." But his games here were necessarily yet too modest to be talked of.

The bonanza kings of this early camp were Jack Ferguson and Pete Wells, two illiterate old prospectors who owned the richest gold pocket in the gulch. Often they took out a "panful of almost pure gold in a day." Every evening they repaired to the saloons and before morning returned "without a color in their possession." What Ferguson did not spend for drink, Wells lost at the gambling tables. Preparing to make the rounds one evening, Ferguson invited a miner friend to his cabin, which contained nothing but a filthy bunk in one corner and a washstand with a dirty drape in another. But the miner never ceased talking of what else he saw:

"Ferguson went to the stand and pushing the cloth aside, revealed a gold washing pan full of nuggets. I would not undertake to say how much yellow stuff there was, but there could not have been less than $10,000. He then produced a bag five or six inches deep, and taking a small spice scoop, filled up the bag. Again I am unable to name the sum, but the bag could not have held less than $800 or $900. . . . Such a bonanza did these two appear to be possessed of, that their gambler friends built a saloon and gambling house on the very brink of their claim, so as to make sure of having first access to the wealth these two were taking out and squandering daily."

The camp, too, had its full share of gunplay and horseplay, often in combination. A stranger one day came galloping through Oro City, splashing mud widely. A miner drew his revolver, covered the rider, and drawled:

"Hold on thar, Stranger! When you go through this yar town, go slow, so's folk kin take a look at you!" The stranger proceeded circumspectly up the gulch. On his return he was walking his pony meekly through town when a shot rang out and a bullet whistled by.

"Stranger," drawled the now tipsy miner, "when you go through this yar town, go as if you hed business, and meant to get somewhar!"

As winter approached, California Gulch almost emptied. Practically all miners decamped for the Plains to return in the spring. Tabor allowed Augusta to go home to Maine, following her shortly when he found he could not work his frozen claim. They returned in the spring with flour and other merchandise. Again the second summer the Tabors prospered. Their profit from mine and store amounted to $15,000, according to Tabor's always generous estimates. But they were nevertheless worried. Although the diggings had yielded several millions during very few working months, production began to drop off sharply. Recklessly exploited, the diggings were nearing exhaustion. The camp was obviously doomed.

Miners began to desert the gulch hurriedly, some returning to the Clear Creek camps or the towns on the Plains. Others pushed on over the Continental Divide to prospect more distant valleys. A few remained behind to prospect Strayhorse and neighboring gulches. But they found nothing but the same weighty boulders and the same heavy red sand which they had so often cursed for impeding their operations in California Gulch. No one suspected that these were virtually pure lead and silver, in a simple and almost obvious combination. If any could have foreseen the great fortunes built upon them twenty years later, they would have searched no farther. As it was, miners rushed desperately here and there as rumor beckoned. With the gulch slipping rapidly to ruin, the last large gambling saloon was torn down by a few stranded miners who, from the debris, panned $2,000 of dust carelessly spilled by those who had once reveled there.

The Tabors, faced with abandoned claims and cabins, again found the future clouded. Their mine had been washed out rather sooner than most. Tabor, in his ignorance, had deliberately staked his claim on a slope above a waterfall, thinking to exploit it more quickly and economically. As he soon discovered, the harder he worked, the more pay-dirt he washed down on the claim below— the very claim which yielded $80,000 the first summer, as Augusta had good reason to remember. The Tabor mine, it was evident, would produce no more dust. Nor did a store-post office in a ghost camp hold out any great hopes of fortune.

A report came of a strike in South Park by that precious pair, Ferguson and Wells, who had early left camp penniless upon exhausting their claims. By air line the new Eldorado was only a few miles distant. But by the rough treacherous trail over the high Mosquito Range it was many long hazardous miles. Although it was dangerously late in the season, the Tabors took to the road again in the wake of the gamblers and barkeepers gone in pursuit of Ferguson and Wells. These two had made their strike in a bleak rocky gorge above timber line, at the source of the South Platte, where the camp of Montgomery boomed for a day. The camps of Buckskin Joe and Fairplay sprang up down the valley as rich strikes were made there.

Buckskin Joe, named for the old prospector who first discovered gold near by, was to be the Tabor's home for several years.

The camp owed its existence to the Phillips Lode, certainly as curious and for its size as rich as any ever discovered. Neither a placer nor a lode mine, properly speaking, it consisted of a thick iron-gold deposit at the very grass roots. It was opened up and worked like a stone quarry. It had been discovered, according to legend, by a hunter who one day shot at a deer standing so close to him that he could scarcely believe his eyes when it bounded off. Certain of having wounded the animal at least, the hunter went to search for traces of blood. He found these and also the gash ploughed through the grass and sand by the bullet—and forgot the deer instantly in what lay revealed before him.

The hunter, one Harris by name, was soon a rich man. Gold poured from his mine in such profusion that his cabin was filled with it—"everything in sight filled with the metal, the pure gold —pots, pans, baskets, even a pair of old boots stuffed and stowed away under the bed."

Harris took in one Stancill as a partner and upon the munificence of these two the whole town rioted. They provided the camp with three luxurious dance houses and a theater where Stancill at his own expense kept a Negro minstrel company performing almost continuously for his amusement. Soon the town had a newspaper, a bank, and several quartz mills. It had every appearance of permanency, "with streets regularly laid out and cabins fairly well built." As its hopes and ambitions mounted an attempt was made to change its name to Laurette—a Philistine agitation that fortunately failed.

Upon arrival Tabor staked several claims and purchased twenty more. All proved to be worthless. But his general store in Augusta's capable hands kept the family alive. Nothing more is known of their life here. In later years neither Tabor nor Augusta talked of the days in Buckskin Joe. Nor can anything be learned from the records of the day. Tabor's name, in fact, is mentioned but once by a contemporary here. When laid up with frosted feet, the Reverend John L. Dyer "sent to H. A. W. Tabor, our storekeeper—now ex-Senator—and paid him sixteen cents a pound for corn to make hominy, . . . a great luxury."

Of all the men in this or any other early camp in Colorado, none was more remarkable, none had higher courage or greater personal integrity, than this same "Father" Dyer, renowned and beloved as the "Snow-shoe Itinerant." [2] Suddenly appearing in Buckskin Joe at the height of the excitement in '61, a gray-haired man of almost fifty, Dyer built himself a pine-bough shelter within a few hours and set out to talk quietly to all who would listen. Every night he preached on the street corners and not unsuccessfully, he declared, in spite of two balls a week, a dancing school, a one-horse theater, and many murders. Dyer knew the ways and speech of the miners, for he had spent many years in Wisconsin and Minnesota both prospecting and preaching. Then he had gone as a missionary into the country of the Chippewa before coming to the Pike's Peak country.

As Buckskin Joe did not begin to use up all of his abounding energy, Dyer walked several times a week to preach at the neighboring camps of Montgomery and Fairplay, some ten miles distant in opposite directions. Even this did not satisfy his zeal. During the winter he mushed his way on snowshoes over Mosquito Pass to California Gulch, thence over the Continental Divide into the Ute country along the Gunnison, back to California Gulch, down the Arkansas to Cache Creek, again to the Gunnison, and back to Buckskin Joe. Within two months he traveled by snowshoe more than five hundred miles, carrying a heavy pack with all that he owned, preaching to any who would listen, frequently having to stop along the way to find a job so that he might eat, for collections were everywhere poor, amounting to just $43.

Father Dyer was no sooner in Buckskin Joe than he set out on foot to attend the Methodist Conference in Denver. As he did not possess $10, he could not take the weekly stage. The Conference assigned him Breckenridge and the neighboring camps on the Blue River, at a salary of $125 a year. Even Dyer found this a rather difficult assignment, for board alone cost him almost $10 a week in that far-off district. But he was resolved to tend his flock, even though he quarreled with them occasionally because they helped themselves to his small organ to furnish music for their frequent dances. Very few people realize, exclaimed Dyer, "how little regard people have for sacred things, and what a preacher has to contend with."

Nevertheless, he did not despair of Breckenridge and went to almost incredible lengths to bring it spiritual comfort. He established himself again at Buckskin Joe and made this his invariable Sunday schedule, even in the depths of winter: an early morning service at Fairplay; a walk of ten miles and another service a few hours later at Buckskin Joe; another walk of ten miles and a noon service at Montgomery; and finally an evening service at Breckenridge, more than twenty miles distant over the Continental Divide, here some fourteen thousand feet high. Often he was buffeted for hours in terrific storms during which he kept his course only by the wind. On one occasion he returned from Breckenridge in a blizzard to find Montgomery completely buried under ten feet of snow.

Now starvation forced good Father Dyer to accept a job at $18 a week carrying mail from Buckskin Joe to Cache Creek, by way of California Gulch, a journey of more than forty miles. Over snowdrifts from five to twenty feet deep, carrying a twenty-five pound mail sack and usually one or more large express packages, Dyer trudged weekly to Cache Creek, often having to travel at night when the crust on the snow was harder. On his day of rest at Cache Creek, Dyer held services for the miners there. With the approach of Sunday he hastened back under an even heavier load, usually carrying much gold dust from all the camps on the upper Arkansas. It was Father Dyer, in fact, who delivered most of the dust which was lost on the Buckskin coach when it was held up and robbed by the Reynolds Gang, whose sudden appearance in South Park in '64 occasioned the greatest excitement of all these years.

The leaders of the bandits, John and Jim Reynolds, the latter famed as "Jim the Bold," knew the mountain country well. During the boom in California Gulch they had both worked as miners there until arrested for their Southern sympathies. They were later taken to Denver to be imprisoned in the compound along with Charley Harrison, Captain McKee, and others. With these they escaped into Texas. There the Reynoldses joined McKee's force of irregulars. Early in '64 they approached McKee, now a colonel, with a plan to organize a gang of freebooters to overrun Colorado and even sack Denver, as Quantrell's guerrillas had ravaged Kansas and sacked Lawrance.

McKee gave them a pass through the lines, and the Reynoldses with twenty-two men rode rapidly north to the Santa Fe Trail. Here they attacked and plundered a large wagon train, obtaining $40,000 in currency and $6,000 in drafts, according to a reasonably measured account of their exploits by City Marshal David Cook of Denver, later Major-General of Militia.[3] The gang immediately quarreled over the booty. More than half deserted when Captain Jim appropriated all of it on the ground that it was needed to arm and equip the many recruits they hoped to gain among the Southerners at the mines.

The Reynoldses and their gang of eight men cached their plunder on the Spanish Peaks, rode up the Arkansas, crossed into South Park, and proceeded on to California Gulch, traveling in small parties to avoid suspicion. As the gulch was already too decayed to interest them, they quickly returned to South Park and fell upon the Buckskin coach, robbing it of $10,000 in dust, most of it delivered by Father Dyer, a much smaller sum than the coach usually carried. The robbers burned the coach and raided a stage station, where they committed a fatal error in pretending to be the vanguard of a large Confederate force raiding north from Texas. This report spread rapidly to throw the entire territory into a panic, for no aid could be expected from the East with every line of communication blocked by Indian uprisings on the Plains. Everywhere military companies were formed and hastily drilled. Troops from Denver guarded all coaches through the mountains. As nothing was certainly known of the number or movement of the robbers, alarm steadily increased. With every rumor, the danger was magnified.

Wholly unsuspecting the general terror they had inspired, the Reynoldses moved slowly through South Park, waylaying travelers and robbing ranchers, treating all with exceptional consideration. So considerately, in fact, that one robbed rancher warned them of the many large posses converging upon them. The bandits rode up into the heavy timber and left the Park, dropping down the north fork of the South Platte to the mouth of Geneva Creek. Here, in a thick grove of pine trees, the robber gang made camp as the two Reynoldses rode up the creek to bury their loot. That evening all were sitting around the fire as Captain Jim, with a spoon, was distributing shares of gold dust. A shot rang out, and he fell wounded.

A posse of miners from distant Boulder Creek had stumbled on the camp, as much to their own surprise as the bandits'. A terrific fusillade ensued. One bandit was killed. The others broke for the brush, abandoning their horses; all but one escaped. The miners cut off the head of the slain bandit and carried it in triumph to Fairplay, together with their single prisoner. The head was publicly displayed on a pole for several days and then preserved in a jar of alcohol; only in recent years has it disappeared.

After a long chase, all of the bandits were captured except John Reynolds and one Stowe, both to be heard of again. Captain Jim and five others were taken to Denver and given a "sham trial," according to Cook, being sentenced to life imprisonment, for there was no proof that they had ever taken life. As Denver's jail was not thought trustworthy, the prisoners were delivered into the hands of Colonel Chivington, who had just ordered his Third Colorado Cavalry south to Fort Lyon, where Reynolds and his men were to be held for safekeeping. It so happened, rather curiously, that the prisoners were placed in the immediate charge of Sergeant "Ab" Williamson, driver of the Buckskin coach which the Reynoldses had robbed.

On the first days of march, the prisoners were offered every opportunity to attempt an escape. They cautiously resisted temptation, knowing full well that upon the slightest pretext they would be executed. The third evening, a certain Captain Cree was approached and thus questioned by one Sergeant Aston Shaw, according to the latter's daughter.

"How does it happen, Captain, that I have to be with the prisoners all the time?"

"Shaw, I want a man with them that will keep those fellows prisoners and not let them escape."

"Well, I'll tell you this much, Cree, I am not going to herd 'em every night."

"What will you do about it?"

"Go kill the whole bunch."

"That's just what we want done."

In the morning, Sergeants Shaw and Williamson assembled the prisoners, ordered a squad of men to follow, and marched several miles off the road to a deserted cabin. The prisoners were stood up in line and blindfolded. Captain Jim made a last plea for his life and his men's, reminding Williamson that his had been spared when at their mercy. Argument was vain. Placing his soldiers ten paces away, Williamson gave the command to fire.

"The sight of six unarmed, blindfolded, manacled prisoners being stood up in line to be shot down like dogs unnerved the soldiers," according to General Cook, "and at the command to fire, they raised their pieces and fired over the heads of the prisoners, so that but one man was killed, Captain Reynolds, and he was at the head of the line opposite Williamson. Williamson remarked that they were mighty poor shots and ordered them to reload. Several of the men flatly announced that they would not be parties to any such cold-blooded murder and threw down their guns, while two or three fired over their heads again at the second command to fire, but Williamson killed his second man."

Snatching a gun from a soldier, Williamson then shot a third. At this point Shaw offered to help him finish the sickening job. "Suiting action to word, he raised his gun and fired, and the fourth man fell dead. Then he weakened, and Williamson was obliged to finish off the other two with his revolver."

Removing the irons from the prisoners' bodies, which were left unburied on the prairie to be devoured by coyotes, the sergeants hurried their soldiers away to overtake the remainder of Colonel Chivington's command, which was hastening by forced marches to the larger slaughter at Sand Creek.

But one bandit, though seriously wounded, was not killed. He crawled into the deserted cabin and ultimately reached Denver. When recovered from his wounds, he went in search of his two friends who had escaped capture, John Reynolds and Stowe, finding them at Santa Fe. Reynolds led them to the treasure buried on the Spanish Peaks. But in robbing ranches for fresh horses, all were killed but Reynolds, who soon spent the treasure and came north again with a desperado named Brown. After many holdups along the way, Reynolds was shot from his horse. Brown rescued him, however, and escaped to an abandoned ranch in a sheltered valley. As he lay dying, Reynolds revealed the secret that he alone knew—where the loot from the Buckskin Joe coach was buried.

"You go up there a little ways [along Geneva Creek] and find where one of our horses mired down in a swamp. On up at the head of the gulch we turned to the right and followed the mountain around a little farther, and just above the head of Deer Creek we found an old prospect hole at about timberline. There was

$40,000 in greenbacks, wrapped in silk oil cloth, and three cans of gold dust. We filled the mouth of the hole up with stones, and ten steps below we stuck an old butcher knife in a tree about four feet from the ground, broke the handle off, and left it pointing to the mouth of the hole."

With a final effort, so the tale runs, Reynolds sketched a rude map of the area on an envelope and expired. Having buried Reynolds, Brown hastened to Denver and made three unsuccessful hunts for the treasure. Disillusioned, he robbed a stagecoach and fled to Fort Laramie, where he perished a few years later in a drunken brawl.

"There is no question but that the treasure is still hidden in the mountains," wrote General Cook in 1897 after Reynolds' map had come into his possession. "Though the topography of the country has been changed somewhat in the last thirty-three years by forest fires, floods, and snowslides, someone may yet be fortunate enough to find it."

If any have tried, none has succeeded, and the buried treasure is still there.

But guerrilla raiders, however disturbing, worried Buckskin Joe less than the sudden complete collapse of the boom. It had never been more than a one-mine camp, and now the stream of gold from the Phillips Lode abruptly ceased. The granite walls bounding the deposit were struck on all sides at once. Montgomery and Fairplay had already declined. Prospecting in the vicinity failed to unearth more treasure. Prosperity departed from the high lonely mountain valley as quickly as it had come.

Stancill fled from $40,000 of debts to become a spiritualist in Chicago, ultimately dying in Denver a pauper. The lucky hunter Harris drifted away penniless, not to be heard of again. Almost overnight Buckskin Joe was depopulated. Soon it contained less than twenty of the four or five thousand miners who had rioted

there during the boom. Three years later a prospector passed by
and noted that the camp was a tumbled ruin.

"There are perhaps forty or fifty houses and cabins still standing—in various degrees of dilapidation—not counting the piles
of logs which show where houses once stood. Gay signs tell of
former billiard halls, barrooms, saloons, etc.—the more modest
ones enumerate necessary articles kept for sale. The bank is in
ruins, and its books are kept as a curiosity by one of those who
remain."

In this bleak deserted camp the Tabors lingered on. They were
still living here in their small cabin-store when the prospector
passed. Why they chose to linger on is a matter of speculation.

Perhaps Augusta was tired of the hardships of travel. After all,
where had they to go? Back to Kansas and farming? But they
had sold their farm. To Maine and stonecutting? They had no
money. There was prospecting and mining, of course, but where?
All Colorado camps were "in cap," and no new Eldorado had been
discovered to succeed Buckskin Joe, the last boom town in the
mountains for almost fifteen years. Tabor, too, was tired and apparently discouraged at last as a miner. At least, he never again
went prospecting.

In '68 necessity finally drove the Tabors from Buckskin Joe,
now entirely deserted. They climbed back over the high Mosquitos to California Gulch, where Fortune had once smiled on
them, and at Oro City established themselves in an abandoned
cabin.

A slight flurry of excitement unsettled them immediately. Gold
had been discovered on the Printer's Boy lode up the gulch. A
small stamp mill was erected near by. What little there was of
Oro City moved up the gulch. The Tabors followed with their
store and post office. This new Oro City sheltered perhaps fifty
miners along one short street containing "several saloons, eating
houses, and corrals." It never grew larger. Indeed, it soon declined, for neither the mine nor the mill yielded much profit.

In Oro City, isolated high in the mountains, the Tabors built a cabin and settled down, apparently content to live here in poverty and obscurity for the remainder of their lives. Tabor, now forty, was resigned to his lot. He spent his days tending his small store-post office and playing poker. Augusta took in boarders.

IX

THE CARBONATE KINGS OF LEADVILLE

". . . great bodies of carbonates, twenty and thirty and even forty feet deep, milling from one hundred to three hundred ounces of silver a ton, . . . enough to test the credulity of the oldest miner."

THE Tabors at Oro City watch ten long uneventful years pass slowly by. California Gulch, littered with broken sluices and falling cabins, lies almost forgotten in the mountains, another name on the growing list of ghost camps. The gold yield of the gulch, which aggregated millions in '60 and '61, drops steadily until it totals less than $20,000 a year.

During these years the gulch sands are reworked by "Uncle Billy" Stevens, farmhand and iron miner from Minnesota. In '59 he had joined the rush to Gregory Gulch, staking a claim and erecting a quartz mill there. Defeated by refractory ores, he drifted away to South Park, worked at Buckskin Joe during its boom days, and moved on to California Gulch in the hope of finding some neglected gold pocket there. He finds none but discovers that some profit can be made by rewashing the abandoned placer claims so recklessly exploited during the first years. He does rather well in spite of profane complaints about weighty boulders in his way and heavy black sands forever clogging up his sluices.

Stevens, after a time, takes in a partner, A. B. Wood, a trained metallurgist, who is apparently the first with any curiosity to know the exact nature of the impeding sands and boulders. That they contain much lead is generally known. Blowpipes have long been used on them to make bullets.[1]

Collecting specimens here and there, Wood tests them to discover that some run as high as forty ounces of silver per ton. Wood and Stevens begin a quiet search for the source of the silver sands. They prospect slowly up the gulch and at last, in '75, find a surface vein along both sides of the gulch and soon satisfy themselves that they are on the point of making a rich discovery. But they say nothing until they have staked nine claims along the vein—first locating their Rock mine, then the Stone, and in '76 the noted Iron Silver, which in its day yields twenty millions.

Old miners in the gulch, with their hopes centered on another gold strike, pay little or no attention to Stevens and Wood until the latter sells his claims for $40,000 to Levi Leiter of Chicago, partner of Marshall Field and posthumously father-in-law to the great nabob Lord Curzon. California Gulch begins to stir with life again. Old sourdoughs are genuinely excited and begin to examine the mountain sides with a fresh eye. Only now do they suspect that for years they have been living blindly in a treasure house of silver.

Three Gallaghers, poor Irish laborers at the Rock mine, quit their jobs, climb over into Strayhorse Gulch, and there start digging a prospect hole. They are down only a few feet when their provisions run out. Unable to obtain money or a grubstake, the brothers return to the Rock mine to work. As soon as a few dollars are saved, they again depart to dig and dig. Once more their provisions are running low. One brother is sent back to work at the Rock. The manager hesitates to re-employ him, but finally tells him to report in the morning. That night his brothers climb over Iron Hill and stumble breathlessly into the bunkhouse to whisper the news. The three creep silently out to reappear shortly as men of substance and position. The Gallaghers name their mine the Camp Bird and go on to strike the Charlestown and the Pine. From these they are soon hoisting tons of carbonate ore rich in silver. A small furnace to smelt their ore is erected at Malta a few miles down the valley.

Excitement increases though it is still largely local. Two sawmill hands bring in the Carbonate mine on a spur of Iron Hill, selling $87,000 of ore within a few months for a net profit of $70,000. Old Abe Lee returns after wandering far to strike the Dana on Long and Derry Hill. The Shamrock is found and named by old Tom Wells, king of the gulch in earlier days. Bill Yankee stakes and immediately sells the Yankee Doodle for $50,000. Other poor prospectors locate the Morning Star, Evening Star, Catalpa, Crescent, Adelaide, and A.Y.—which, with the Minnie, provides the stake upon which the Guggenheims later build their tremendous family fortune, with mining and smelting interests embracing the entire Western Hemisphere, from Alaska to Chile. And this, in turn, sends another bonanza king to the United States Senate—Simon Guggenheim, sixth of the seven shrewd and ambitious sons of old Meyer Guggenheim of Philadelphia, an importer of Swiss embroideries.[2]

With rich strikes multiplying on Iron and Carbonate hills, prospectors and miners begin to pour in from other camps. An owner of a lunch counter at Fairplay, one George Fryer, abandons his business there, hastens into camp, and from "Chicken Bill" Lovell, a rascally but competent old prospector, buys a prospect hole on a neglected hill for a six weeks' grubstake. Fryer starts earnestly to work, laughed at by practical miners and theoretical experts who pronounce the hill outside the "scientific" limits of the field. For weeks he toils alone sinking a shaft, always a painfully slow and laborious task when performed single-handed—one good reason why prospectors usually travel in pairs. Fryer, with nothing more than pick and hand drills, pries loose the "drift" rock, shovels it into a heavy iron bucket, climbs to the shaft head, strains at the small hand windlass to bring the swinging bucket slowly up, dumps it, lowers it back down the shaft again, and descends after it, repeating this clumsy performance scores of times a day. Fryer's supplies are soon exhausted, and he has to sign away a half interest in his prospect to obtain a grubstake.

Finally, at fifty feet, Fryer strikes white-green porphyry. Excitedly he hammers his way through this to the iron "cap" usually signifying silver treasure below. He smashes this to come upon a rich body of carbonate ore, the first of the thick "blanket" veins of silver to be found on Fryer Hill, one of the famous names in mining annals. With a wry smile at the "experts" who sneered at him, Fryer names his mine the New Discovery.

Now Dennis Carter, John Taylor, Richard and Pat Dillon, four Irish roustabouts given to working occasionally and drinking continuously, strike the Little Chief near by. To Pete Finnerty, a teamster, Carter immediately sells his share in the mine for $2,000, which he spends almost overnight in a drunken carouse. With his dividends, Finnerty buys out Taylor for $30,000. Within the year, already rich from huge dividends declared each month, Finnerty and the Dillons dispose of the Little Chief for $400,000.

Excitement rapidly grows as rich strikes are made from week to week. Smelting companies rush in to erect sampling works and furnaces at the lower end of California Gulch.

Tabor, almost alone among all old miners, does no prospecting. He has apparently put mining behind him. Now almost fifty, having lost all faith in his luck, he aspires to no greater fortune than his store and Augusta's boarders are likely to bring him. When Oro City moves back down the gulch to be near the new mines and smelters, the Tabors follow to establish themselves in New Oro City, familiarly known as Slabtown, forming under the smoke and fumes of the smelters. It consists of several dozen slab huts, two saloons, and Tabor's "hotel," a four-room log cabin, larger and more pretentious than any he has yet known. It contains the customary store-post office, to which is now added a small bar-room and a spare chamber to accommodate transients.

Here Augusta cooks, sews, and washes for her boarders, tending the sick upon occasion—an "angel of mercy," said one, "smoothing the pillow of many an ill, homesick, and destitute man." Tabor, too, is kindly and helpful, and a "much better man than in later years he has credit for being." When a trader drives in at this time with a wagonload of eggs, butter, and fresh vegetables, Tabor sells them at cost to the miners with the remark that they have lived upon nothing but beans and salt pork through the winter. In leaving camp for the mountains, many a prospector entrusts his money and valuables to Tabor, for he is altogether honest according to his lights.

Crude and small as it is, the sprawling new camp with its bustle and vitality seems a very metropolis to old miners in the gulch. It pleases Tabor to see business increase. Customers are now so many that he must assist Augusta in "weighing out sowbelly and flour, selling picks, and shovels, assorting and delivering letters and packages." Tabor is pleased as well to observe gambling increase, poker particularly. The first gamblers to swarm into camp boast confidently of owning Tabor's store before the winter is past. But long dull years in the mountains have not been altogether in vain. Tabor more than holds his own.

In January, '78, eighteen miners assemble in a small blacksmith shop for the purpose of merging Slabtown with another small camp forming about Charles Mater's grocery store about a half mile distant up the sandy flat. They desire to have the two incorporated officially as a city. A name is chosen, Leadville, and a provisional government established, with Tabor as mayor. At the first regular election a few months later Tabor is continued in office for a term of one year. The combined camp at the time contains perhaps three hundred miners.

A month later two of the strangest prospectors Tabor can ever have seen stalk into his store. They come seeking a grubstake.

One of this curious pair is George Hook, and the other August Rische—"the worst played-out man I ever met," according to one who saw him at this time, "his entire wealth consisting of a pick and a spade and a faithful old dog."

Poor German shoemakers, both have been cobbling at Fairplay for some years. Declining business there has at last persuaded them that they can do no worse as prospectors. The two have already asked several in camp for a grubstake. One has been vaguely promised them by Edwin Harrison, president of the St. Louis smelter, but they are tired of waiting. Tabor also puts them off. But they are doggedly persistent and come back—not once, but many times—and finally, to be rid of them, Tabor exclaims:

"All right, come and get what you want—and don't bother me now!"

What Tabor happens to be doing at the moment—serving a customer in the store, sorting mail, or playing poker in the bar —will never be known. In any case, his attention is so engrossed that Hook and Rische, in assembling supplies, help themselves to a jug of whisky—certainly not intended for their grubstake —and hurriedly depart.[3]

They select a hill—most mines are on hills—and start climbing. Soon they are winded and less than a mile from camp sit down to rest in the shade of a pine. Tired and thirsty, they open the jug and soon feel restored and much more confident. As all parts of the mountain look alike to them, they decide they might just as well start digging right here in the shade. Having begun to dig, they go on and on, the next day and the next.

Within a week, at a depth of twenty-five feet, they strike the famous ore body of the Little Pittsburgh mine, so named because Hook had once been an ironworker in the Pittsburgh mills. They strike the vein at the "only point on the whole area of the hill where rock in place comes so near the surface," according to an official report of the United States Geological Survey on the shoemakers' startling discovery. If the prospectors had driven their shaft a few yards forward, or a few yards to either side, so the report reads, they would have struck nothing. If they had started their shaft a few yards back, they would have had to go down several hundred feet to make contact—a task far beyond both the means and the patience of the shoemakers.

As it is, they have come down squarely on the tip of a steeply-tilted vein running deep into the hillside.

"We've struck it! we've struck it!" cries Rische, bursting into the Tabor store, his hands full of ore.

"Mr. Rische," says Augusta coolly, "when you bring me money instead of rocks, then I'll believe you."

For once, however, Augusta is much too skeptical. Rische and Hook run a thirty-foot "drift" off to the side and find solid ore up to the last foot. All Leadville visits the shaft. Every foot of ground round about is quickly staked out. Owning a third share of the mine by reason of his grubstake, Tabor can scarcely contain himself.

To Augusta's relief, he sells the store, for within two months the Little Pittsburgh is producing $20,000 of ore a week, with hoisting capacity its only limit. Tabor and Rische now buy Hook's interest in the mine for $100,000; the latter invests his money in Government bonds and departs to visit Germany—one of the few wise men in camp. Rische disposes of his half interest to bankers for $265,000, having already realized $145,000 in dividends. The latter rapidly mount to $100,000 a month. Within the year, having netted a half million from his $64 grubstake, Tabor is paid $1,000,000 in cash for his interests, selling them to Jerome N. Chaffee and David Moffat, Denver bankers and speculators. The latter combine the property with other neighboring mines under the name of the Little Pittsburgh Consolidated, a stock-selling concern capitalized at $20,000,000. Tabor is granted shares in this enterprise and quickly makes another million when Little Pittsburgh stock soars from $5 to $30 a share on the New York Mining Exchange.

Tabor is now a millionaire twice over, Colorado's first great bonanza king.

That rascally and nimble old prospector, Chicken Bill Lovell, inadvertently helped Tabor to several millions more. Having virtually given away the shaft that George Fryer proved as the New Discovery, Chicken Bill removed his operations to the far side of Fryer Hill, where he laboriously sank a deep shaft without uncovering anything of promise. Finally, at forty feet, he struck water and loudly cursed his luck. His time and labor seemed wholly wasted, but Chicken Bill was never at a loss.

Next morning, bright and early, he was at Tabor's office to tell him a pitiful and most interesting tale. He had just struck the richest kind of ore, said Chicken Bill, when water came pouring into his shaft. He could do nothing about it, unfortunately, as he did not have the capital to drain the bonanza. If he had, of course, he would not sell at any price. As it was, anyone who was interested could buy the prospect cheap.

Tabor decided to investigate and, sure enough, there was much rich ore "in the water at the bottom of the shaft and liberally sprinkled about on the surface," as Hook later told the story. A few miners who were standing about noted its striking resemblance to Little Pittsburgh ore, but offered no comments. Greatly impressed, Tabor sat down, wrote a $40,000 check, and with a flourish handed it to Chicken Bill, who all but flew to town to have it cashed before the banks closed.

Next morning, when Tabor sent up a force of men to drain and work the shaft, all Leadville roared with laughter. Now deep in his cups, Chicken Bill was telling everybody how the mine had been "salted" with Tabor's own ore, stolen from the Little Pittsburgh dump.

In an attempt to brazen his way out of a ridiculous position,

Tabor kept his men at work. Within three days they had sunk the shaft eight more feet, "to encounter the richest body of ore ever found on Fryer Hill." This fabulous mine, the Crysolite, paid cash dividends of $100,000 a month for more than two years. Tabor also profited handsomely from the incorporation of the Crysolite Mining Company, capitalized at $10,000,000, selling his stock at top prices when it bounded from $5 to $45 a share.

Tabor's apologists have tried to discredit this account of the buying of the Crysolite mine, contending that Tabor knew that the mine had been salted and bought it because he felt certain of striking silver treasure below. Such apologists appear to have exercised themselves rather needlessly, for the incident never troubled Tabor. One day Hook asked him if he had suspected Chicken Bill's knavery. Tabor at first pretended that he had. But when Hook remained skeptical, for he had been present at the time, Tabor finally laughed and said,

"Anyway, I was willing to take a chance on the Crysolite, as Lovell owed me a long overdue $600 bill for provisions, and what I paid him, in addition to canceling his bill, wasn't much of a speculation, considering the times." [4]

Tabor never spoke more truly. An orgy of speculation and frenzied finance swept Leadville. Tabor bought a non-productive mine for $117,000, spent $40,000 in liquidating conflicting claims, sank tens of thousands more into it against all competent advice, and finally proved it as the Matchless, famous alike for its richness and the tragic story of the second Mrs. Tabor. At a time when it had yet to produce a ton of ore, Tabor bought a third interest in the Vulture for $11,500. Next day he paid $18,000 for another third and offered $20,000 for the remaining third, refusing to buy when $25,000 was asked. But a few months later he paid $250,000 for it. For a half interest in the Maid of Erin, once offered him at $700, he now paid $43,000. George Fryer accepted

$50,000 for his half share in the New Discovery, which was immediately resold to Tabor and Rische for $162,000.

At wit's end to manage the silver stream flooding in upon him, Tabor poured it in varying amounts and not altogether profitably into the Scooper, Dunkin, Union Emma, Denver City, Tam O'Shanter, Henrietta, Empire, Hibernia, May Queen, Elk, Little Willie, Climax, and Wheel of Fortune—the last controlled by George Robinson, a bankrupt banker from Michigan, who drifted into camp to open a small store and make millions from a grubstake. George Trimble and A. V. Hunter, local bankers, made fortunes from the Winniemuck and speculations in other mines. Almost any hole in the ground could be sold for thousands. So general was the speculative fever, that a "mining company composed wholly of ladies has been organized in this city," announced the Leadville *Democrat*.

To climax all, came the discovery of the Robert E. Lee, to make Leadville in its day the largest producer of bullion in the world. Long an undeveloped claim on the peak of Fryer Hill, the Robert E. Lee was bought for $15,000 by one Jim Dexter, who worked months sinking a shaft. It was far below one hundred feet without a sign of ore. When offered $30,000 for the prospect hole, Dexter snatched the opportunity to recompense himself in part for all of his expense and labor.

"Come up, boys! Come up!" he shouted, running to the shaft. The miners below were filling a drill hole with powder and suggested that they "shoot" once more. •

"No! Come up! I don't want you to work any more. I won't put another damn cent into this hole."

Dexter paid the men off and congratulated himself on his luck. Next morning the new owners "shot" the hole, to lay bare a thick vein of almost pure silver. One subsidiary shaft alone produced a half million within three months. During one twenty-four hour period, ninety-five tons of ore worth $118,500 were mined and hoisted at a total labor cost of $60. Two of the owners offered their partners $200,000 to be allowed to work twenty men in the mine for thirty-six hours. Another offered $10,000 for permission to work one man for an hour on an area four feet square in one of the tunnels.

Both offers were rejected with scorn.

Iron, Carbonate, and Fryer hills were soon a tangled patchwork of claims, overlapping and running across one another from every point of the compass. Confusion and conflict resulted in endless litigation, brutal murder, and private war. So endless and expensive was litigation that Uncle Billy Stevens once declared that lawsuits had consumed seven of the eleven millions taken from the Iron Silver up to that time.

"If I ever locate another mine," he said, echoing the feeling of the day, "I'll stand over it with a shotgun, and shoot every damn man who comes on it. It is cheaper and safer to defend yourself against murder than to defend your property in the courts."

After a prospector had driven his stakes, he had sixty days within which to start a shaft or tunnel. If he failed in this, anyone could take possession of the claim—that is, it could be legally "jumped."

But many men jumped undeveloped claims without distinction, ripping up all stakes in their way. Once in possession, they were seldom dispossessed but by force. For just this emergency, a guide-book of the time advised newcomers "to come provided with a good pair of navy revolvers."

Again, a miner upon striking mineral had to have his claim officially surveyed and recorded. He could run his survey lines in any direction so long as the discovery shaft stood midway between the sides of the claim. This allowed a miner to run his survey squarely over the shafts of neighbors who were near ore but had not yet struck it. These lost all their labor, for title went to him who ran the first survey. The race was not only to the swift but to the rich, for many poor miners with good prospect holes had to work elsewhere for wages three or four days a week to keep themselves alive.

"Men with money and machinery," as one poor miner complained, "have squatted alongside the poor toiler, asserting he has no rights and depending on their cash and power to overreach the start the poor man has made and intends to follow up faithfully. Thus, they often strike mineral ahead of him and secure a legal title to hidden treasures which ought justly to have been his reward. Is it any wonder a man should be exasperated at such legal injustice and strive, on first notice, to hold his own ground by force of arms?"

But many made no parade of legality to justify their depredations. A desperado named Williams attempted to jump the Iron Silver. On the claim above he drove a shaft straight down toward the sloping tunnel Stevens and Leiter had driven along the vein. Deep in the mountain, he cut the Iron Silver tunnel, erected heavy barricades, manned them with blacklegs, and warned Iron Silver workers off. Stevens and Leiter moved quickly and secretly, recruited a larger army, and attacked in force. There was a furious battle hundreds of feet underground. Driven from the barricades, Williams' forces resisted stubbornly, sniping as they retreated along the tunnels. Several were killed and many wounded, but the desperado's army was ultimately routed. Stevens and Leiter then posted a guard of thirty men, each armed with two revolvers and a shotgun, or Winchester repeating rifle. This guard was retained for years. The Carbonate and other mines adopted like precautions.

Poorer miners and prospectors formed two strong organizations to combat claim-jumpers—the Miners' Mutual Protective Association, with branches in all the gulches, and the Miners' Guard, composed, said its founders, of "what is known as low-capital men, or those whose means of defence against mine jumpers lies wholly in bullets."

Ten armed men jumped the O'Donovan Rossa claim, seized

the shaft house, and fortified it. Constable Shires approached and was ordered back. He retreated, ostensibly for reinforcements, but failed to return. The dispossessed owners then called on the Miners' Guard, which sent a large party to attack at night. Firing was so brisk and stray bullets so numerous along California Gulch that travelers turned back to spend the night in town. Spectators and reporters watching the battle from afar were "put to ignominious flight by the whistling of the bullets in the neighborhood." At daybreak, the Miners' Guard deployed as skirmishers and crept closer. Their Indian tactics gave them a great advantage over those caged in the shaft house, who attracted a shower of bullets at the slightest exposure. "The indiscretion of Matt Lynch in peeping over the breastworks, caused him a bullet through the ear, and a moment later a Winchester rifle caught him in the right hip. Another of the party stopped a bullet with his shin. . . ."

Those besieged in the shaft house soon pitched their arms on the dump and crawled out after them to surrender unconditionally. "No arrests have been made," remarked the press, "but another batch of suits is likely to follow."

George Robinson heard that his mine was to be jumped. He closed the tunnel with a heavy door and posted behind it a large armed guard under instructions not to open under any circumstances. As the Carbonate King hastened away, he remembered something left behind—no one knows what. He returned, banged on the door, and was instantly blown to pieces by his own men.

It was not long before great dumps of gravel and "drift" rock, smaller dumps of pay ore, came creeping down the hillsides, felling all timber in their way. As the beauty of the valley declined, mining methods improved. The primitive hand windlass on mine shafts gave way to the "whip," a gallows with pulley arrangement by which a mule, driven straight out and back, hoisted and lowered heavy ore buckets. The whip gave way to the "whim," a large wooden drum pulled round by a mule or horse to wind or unwind the bucket rope. Finally, the steam engine came to be enclosed in a shaft house sturdy enough to withstand the assaults not only of fierce mountain storms but predatory mine-jumpers. Eight hissing engines were soon working full blast over the shaft of the Little Pittsburgh.

From almost inaccessible mines, hundreds of heavy ore wagons came lurching perilously down steep rough roads on their way to the smelters roaring in the valley and belching forth great clouds of yellow noxious fumes. Here teamsters dumped their loads down a large chute into a long dark gallery, where the respective lots of ore were shoveled into separate bins to remain until sampled and paid for. Opposite the bins a series of large iron cylinders stood dimly revealed by a lantern or two. Chains of men with wheelbarrows poured ore down the iron mouths of these cylinders, from which sounded the crunch of the ore-chewers and the fierce hoarse rumblings of white-hot furnaces below. Chewed up in the grinders, the ore reappeared in time as molten slag and bullion on the floor below, where there was nothing but a hot metal mass covered with soot and dust of arsenic and oxides of lead. Here a sweating worker, stripped to the waist, darted a lance at a sizzling furnace to release Hell itself as, with blinding showers of sparks and long tongues of strange blue and green flames, a stream of white molten rock fell hissing into the slagpots. These were wheeled out boiling and bubbling to be dumped on the lava mole burning its way down the slope. In a small well at the base of the furnace, lead and silver came gurgling up and were ladled out into iron molds and allowed to cool into forty-pounds "pigs," with silver seldom exceeding more than one pound of the total. These pigs were shipped to New Jersey to be refined.

Not only ore by the thousands of tons but whole pine forests were consumed by the smelters, which could not afford coal or coke at $55 a ton. Soon the valley and sidehills were stripped of trees and left a waste of stumps. In the process, all brushwood and grass were burned away. Round the smelters spread a desolate black waste, dotted with the white cones of charcoal ovens. Through the desolation wound the main road into camp, picking its way uncertainly among the stumps, ovens, and scattered log houses of the town.

Although Fryer, Carbonate, and Iron hills were now brown, bleak, and scarred, the hills at a greater distance were still blue with pines, set between the white sawtooth range of the Mosquitos and the long high hogsback of Mt. Massive, both shining in the sun. But fortune-hunters had eyes only for black chlorides and "crumbling, ill-smelling brown carbonates" to be found deep in cold dripping shafts. All that mattered was that Leadville was mining more than three hundred tons of silver a year—that no camp in the world was producing more bullion.

As Leadville's fame spread, the state paid honor to the camp through its greatest citizen. Leaders of the controlling Republican machine, eager to turn his wealth to their and the public advantage, waited upon Tabor and offered him a place on the state ticket. Tabor was nominated and in November, '78, became lieutenant-governor of Colorado. Ex-officio, he presided over the State Senate for two years, with no very serious lapses.

As he now had to live for long periods in Denver, Governor Tabor bought a large house there for $40,000 and spent $20,000 more in improving and remodeling it to suit his taste and his requirements as a public figure. When he led Augusta to it, she hesitated to enter. She was still highly skeptical of their sudden riches, perhaps sensing inevitable disaster.

"Tabor," she said, "I will never go up those steps if you think I will ever have to go down them again."

X

MAGIC CITY

"You can't imagine the excitement going on here."

IN JUNE, '77, when Charles Mater drew up a half mile above Slabtown to unload a wagonful of groceries and build a cabin there under Carbonate Hill, his small log store stood quite alone on the sandy pine flat, soon the site of Leadville. The next year came the fabulously rich strikes on Fryer Hill—the New Discovery, Little Chief, Little Pittsburgh, and Crysolite. By '79 the local *Chronicle*, in a series of "Midnight Notes," could grow almost lyrical about the rise of the "Magic City":

> *Leadville never sleeps. The theaters close at three in the morning. The dance houses and liquoring shops are never shut. The highwayman patrols the street in quest of drunken prey. The policeman treads his beat to and fro. The music at the beer halls is grinding low. A party of carousers is reeling through the streets. A mail coach has just arrived. There is a merry party opposite the public school. A sick man is groaning in the agonies of death. Carbonate Hill with her scores of brightly blazing fires is Argus-eyed. Three shots are heard down below the old court house. A woman screams. There is a fight in a State Street casino. The sky is cloudless. A man stands dreaming in front of the Windsor looking at the stars —he is away from home. A barouche holding two men and two women comes rushing up Chestnut Street. Another shot*

is heard down near the city jail. A big forest fire lights up the mountains at the head of Iowa Gulch.

"Give you the price of a bed, did you say?"

"Yes, I've not seen a bed for a week. Believe me, kind sir, I'm sick and in need of a friend. Help me, stranger, and as true as I live I'll repay your kindness."

The clock on the Grand Hotel points to one. Shots are heard from Carbonate Hill. The roar of revelry is on the increase. The streets are full of drunken carousers taking in the town.

Into the camp in a mounting flood poured miners, gamblers, and barkeepers—teamsters, lumberjacks, smelter hands, storekeepers, blacksmiths, and carpenters—engineers, lawyers, doctors, preachers, temperance lecturers, and quacks of all kinds—variety actors and musicians—school teachers, "fancy" women, and plain prostitutes—"pumpkin haulers" from the Middle West, speculators and bankers from the East, cotton planters from the South—pickpockets, footpads, and highwaymen—Americans, for the most part, but with large numbers of Irish, Germans, and Swedes.

There was room for all, the camp decreed—for all, that is, but Indians and Chinese. In spite of public warnings, three Chinese laundrymen crossed from Fairplay and were kidnapped the night of their arrival, shot to pieces, and thrown down an abandoned prospect hole where they were found months later.

Everyone with a store, cabin, or lot was on the road to fortune. Food and other necessities were expensive at best, for all supplies had to be freighted in from the Plains over more than a hundred miles of steep dangerous roads. At worst, with local storekeepers ruthlessly profiteering, flour and other staples sold at three or four times their purchase price in Denver. Two small barrels of whisky returned a profit of $2,700 to one who soon announced his aspirations to be governor.

Every foot of ground on the bleak pine flat was hungrily coveted and savagely fought for. Although encouraged in the beginning, squatters were not long tolerated as the value of land rose to fantastic heights. Lots bought for $10 soon brought $4,000 and $5,000. On the main thoroughfare, Chestnut Street (there were no chestnuts within eight hundred miles), property readily sold at $250 a front foot.

"Rents have reached seemingly outrageous figures. Stores on Chestnut Street and Harrison Avenue rent quickly at $300 to $500 per month," wrote a local speculator, almost overcome by the multiplying signs of great prosperity. "Rents here are higher than in New York City!"

Upon the basis of a placer mining patent, the Starr Company laid claim to almost all of Leadville. As such patents ordinarily granted rights only to minerals in the ground, the company's pretentions to absolute title were dubious indeed, although later upheld by the United States Supreme Court. Dividing its claim into tiny lots, the company offered these at preposterous prices to miners who had already built cabins on the ground, threatening forcible eviction if they did not pay up quickly. The company received a prompt and startling reply:

> *We will notify you to leaf this town in 10 days or less or come to terms if you do not we will hang you in spite of hell we have done the same thing in Montana we hung sons of bitches like you and come out all right now you can do as you pleas come to terms or you will go to hell quicker than lightning you are a dam dirty stink try to monopolize this town but we will wait on you to sure as Christ.*

The Starr agent, somewhat alarmed, called a public meeting to arrange a compromise. The miners came away quieted, but the company evidently failed to keep its promises.

> *You damn dirty thief told us you would do what was right*

at our meeting now you say $50 a front foot you dam son of
a bitch you will and must die for the people will have rest
                                        Vigulance Committee.

Threats of lynching were repeated at mass meetings of protest against the "patent tyranny." But nothing served to check the company which was guilty of a "long series of outrages such as would disgrace the wildest Zulu camp of savages," as even the conservative *Chronicle* protested.

"Today a quiet and inoffensive man, who had settled on a lot long prior to the issuance of the pretended placer claims and built a humble house, for himself and his family, was beset by a band of men armed with deadly weapons, in the pay of the placer patentees or their grantees, had his house torn down over his head, and his household effects thrown into the streets. We simply note the plain facts without any stilted invective."

Tabor organized the Leadville Improvement Company to exploit a large tract bought from the Starr Company. Tabor, as mayor, had no difficulty in evicting squatters and persuading the City Council to drive a wide street through the property—christened Harrison Avenue, which soon rivaled Chestnut Street in importance. With ordinary residence lots along the Avenue selling at $1,000, the Improvement Company proved to be not the least profitable of Tabor's speculations.

Chestnut and lower Harrison were soon solidly built up with log stores and business buildings—with every third or fourth door opening into a saloon. Nothing but saloons, gambling hells, dance houses, and brothels lined State Street, next above Chestnut. Above State was Main, graced with the more fashionable bagnios of Mollie May and Sallie Purple. Behind these ran Carbonate Avenue, the exclusive preserve of the Carbonate Kings, a bleak dusty street with great dumps from the mines at the top of it and a flat sandy waste below.

Round about stood cabins, shanties, pine-bough huts, tents, and wagons, scattered in such confusion that it was impossible to know whether one was walking the public highway or trespassing upon some jealously guarded lot. All trespassing, however innocent, was dangerous, with citizens armed to kill instantly anyone suspected as a lot-jumper.

Desperados jumped part of the lot occupied by the First Avenue Presbyterian Church. For a time the congregation toyed with the idea of routing them in battle. Then it considered taking the matter to court, but finally decided to abandon the church and build again elsewhere. Armed ruffians twice attempted to jump and tear down the only hospital in camp, St. Vincent's, founded by seven Sisters of Mercy sent from Denver by old Father Machebeuf, now a bishop. Getting wind of plans for a third attack, Father Robinson mustered a hundred men to guard it day and night, under instructions "to shoot dead the first man who dares to try to jump the premises."

Against roughs and criminals the police were almost powerless, numbering only four officers for many months. Now one of them committed the first murder. City Marshal O'Connor was shot to death in a drunken brawl by Officer Bloodsworth, who stole a horse and escaped. In O'Connor's stead Mayor Tabor appointed Mart Duggan as city marshal. A powerful man of medium height, a notorious bully and killer, openly boasting of seven notches on his gun, Duggan swaggered about town eager for challenge. Quick with both fist and gun, he terrorized innocent and guilty alike, boldly hunting out the most bloodthirsty desperados to force a duel, just as boldly assaulting innocent citizens on any or no provocation.

One night Rische was drunkenly celebrating his luck when he met the Marshal and invited him to drink. After a time they quarreled and Duggan ordered the Carbonate King to the Pine Street Tombs for the night. When Rische offered some resistance, the Marshal knocked him senseless, dragged him off, and threw him unceremoniously among the felons in the single small crowded cell at the jail. When Tabor attempted to intervene as friend and mayor, Duggan turned sharply on him, "Close your trap, or you'll be run in, too."

But for all his brutality and lawlessness, Duggan retained his position for many years, and it must be said for him that, being absolutely fearless, he was the one man in camp to intimidate roughs and cutthroats.[1]

"Feed the Miners," cried the *Chronicle* as the rush increased from day to day. "All up and down the mountainsides for miles and miles around Leadville are thousands and thousands of diggers after happiness and homes. It is a fact that many of these industrious delvers are destitute of food this afternoon. They have used their last nickel; they know they will have to go down but ten feet more; they do not like to give up or give away their competence for a few mouthfuls of bread and—well, leave your meal boxes open tonight, for but few of these fellows will beg. Neither will they steal anything beyond what is required for the immediate sustenance of life."

Hungry miners walked into restaurants, ate their fill, and suggested that the police be called when asked to pay their bill. Many were so arrested, for the authorities took a very serious view of this practice—a far more serious view than of murder, which was committed with virtual impunity.

A starving prospector entered a store and ran out with a can of peaches. Two clerks pursued, caught, and held him while a third "pounded him over the head with a two-pound weight, inflicting terrible injuries."

The saloons, unfortunately, provided no free lunches. The few making the experiment early abandoned it when mobbed by the hungry. Some, however, offered ten-cent lunches. But as these were few, most men patronized the fifteen-cent eating houses squeezed between the larger buildings along Harrison and Chestnut. Often no more than six feet wide, their walls covered "with muslin calsomined and decorated with cheap prints," these small restaurants contained perhaps a dozen rough pine tables which were always crowded. Miners, teamsters, and blackened smelter workers predominated, but here and there appeared white-collared clerks, variety actors in "flash" jewelry, drunken women of the town, and occasionally a gentleman gambler down on his luck. Everything here smelled and tasted of rancid grease. One had a choice of "Mutton, Lamb, Hog and Steak." Potatoes and bread were included for ten cents, but a cup of weak cold coffee cost five cents more.

It is night—a clear cold night early in the spring of '79. The valley lies deep in snow. Drifts are piled high in the gulches down which icy winds race day and night to howl through spectral pines. In this high valley, more than two miles above the sea, there has been no melting temperature since October. For days at a time the thermometer has hovered about zero, occasionally dropping to thirty or forty below. But as early as February the *Chronicle* finds prospectors swarming "thick as bees" in the gulches.

The five stagecoach lines which are now running have brought in a large number over steep tortuous roads hewn out of the mountain sides, full of boulders and bordering on high precipices. Here a slip by one of the horses, a serious break in the harness, a mistake or even a slight hesitation on the part of the driver, spells disaster.

"May God preserve me from such another stagecoach ride," exclaims a frightened tenderfoot. "I will never go out over the road traversed in coming here, not even if I have to leave in a balloon."

Other men by the thousands, too poor to afford the stages, are walking in over Mosquito Pass, "that highway of frozen death," where many perish during these years—how many will never be known.

In a clearing on the sand flat lies the bursting camp of Leadville, a ragged black splotch against the snow. Along its lower edge, smelters are sizzling and belching forth red flames and greenish smoke. Above them shine two strings of lights joining at a right angle—the lighted windows of stores and saloons along Harrison Avenue and Chestnut Street. Within this angle the larger part of the camp is concentrated. Near its apex is a great blaze of yellow light from hundreds of kerosene flares dancing in the wind before the larger sporting houses on State Street. Behind, and curving round on both sides, looms the sheer black wall of the Continental Divide and the jagged teeth of the Mosquitos, sharply silhouetted against the white frosty stars.

Along Chestnut, Harrison, and State move throngs of rough boisterous men, jostling their way in and out of the bright patches of light cast upon the snow from crowded stores and restaurants and noisy saloons. Many are shouldered from the narrow wooden sidewalks into the streets to stumble along in the deep ruts cut by heavy ore and freight wagons. Although many are drunk, many are not. Most are warmly clad in heavy windbreakers or overcoats. But a number hurry shivering from doorway to doorway, having already pawned or sold their weather coats for a meal ticket or a carouse. For the most part, it is a good-natured crowd, innocent enough in its loud camaraderie. But there are those who snarl and fight.

A freighter sits in a crowded saloon with boots and socks off, warming his frosted feet at the stove. A miner staggers in and shouts an offer to set up the house. All must drink, for it is an insult to refuse. The bare-footed freighter asks the stranger to please hand him down his drink.

"No," bellows the miner, "not by a goddam sight! Any man too lazy to stand up and drink is a sucker, and I can whip him." He flashes out his knife, falls upon the freighter, stabs him repeatedly, and without interference runs out to disappear in the crowds.

Noisy hilarity steadily increases. But as the hour grows late, all have a common care eating at the heart of their abandon. Where are they to sleep out of the wind and cold? Since early evening the more prudent have been searching for a bed. The City Hotel accommodates eight and has already turned away hundreds. The Tappan, Tontine, St. Nicholas, and Windsor are not only expensive but already filled. A few succeed in finding shelter at last in one of the better lodging houses, "happy to pay $1 to share a bed with another in a small room containing eight or ten others." A few have luck at the bunkhouses, or the big tents in the side streets, all dignified as hotels, each with tiers of soiled hard beds occupied continuously day and night. One man crawls out as another crawls in, paying fifty cents for a sleeping turn of eight hours.

Here among the sporting houses on State Street stands a cheaper rooming house, a grimy unpainted frame shanty with a tin sign above the door rattling in the wind, *Lodging—25¢*. A drunken ruffian staggers up and knocks. His clothes are torn, his hair and beard matted with dirt. One eye is closed and black. He fumbles through his pockets and unblushingly displays three skeleton keys, a gnawed plug of tobacco, a muslin tobacco pouch, a string, a pair of brass knuckles, a short length of iron pipe, a pack of cards, a needle and thread, four ten-cent gambling chips, and at last a silver quarter, which he hands to the burly keeper blocking the door. The latter examines the coin, grunts, and steps aside to let the man enter the single large room in the shanty. Its walls of rough pine are covered with cheap muslin, heavy with cobwebs and dust. A smoking lantern hanging from the ceiling reveals the usual tiers of bunks, and in the center of the bare dirty floor a single chair with a broken back.

Now a young man rather too well dressed reels up, knocks, and offers a pearl-handled revolver as security, complaining drunkenly that he has just been thrown from a brothel after having his pockets picked. The keeper admits him, approaches a bunk to push the now snoring ruffian against the wall, and orders the new-comer to get in beside him.

Again there is knocking. The keeper opens and stands leering at a small frail woman before him. He quickly notes she is no longer young.

"Well, old gal, what do you want?"

"I want a bed to sleep in."

"Well, you can't have it here, see! This layout ain't for no women."

"But I have no place to go and no money—except a quarter. Do you want me to sleep in the streets?"

"Aw, get some fella' to take you to his room tonight," he growls, as the door slams to.

Every night thousands of desperate men fail to find beds and are driven back into the saloons to quarrel and fight for places there. It costs anywhere from ten to fifty cents to curl up about the stove on hard draughty unswept floors. The sleepers are annoyed by drunken wags, and overhead the rattle of dice goes on till morning. From the bar comes a hum of voices mingled with the monotonous call-song of the gamblers. At last the sleepers doze off, only to be startled by the angry shouts of brawlers and go scuttling for cover as shots fly wild and fast.

At a time when the camp contained a thousand-odd buildings, a local census revealed "120 saloons, big and little," certainly sufficient for any traditional purpose, but far too few to house all the homeless thousands. Into stable lofts they crept—into "kennels dug in the side hills, and roofed with earth and pine boughs"; into packing boxes littering the streets; into hay piles in the alleys; into open sheds and wagons; even into foul outhouses—into anything, in fact, promising some slight protection from the wind and cold.

The Reverend Doctor Tom Uzzell borrowed $6 from an old

maid and came from Fairplay in pursuit of his parishioners, who had all joined the rush. With him on the Leadville stage came "Billy Owens, now manager of the Denver Dry Goods Company, and a doctor, a tin-horn gambler, and two women of the half-world—that bunch and a preacher, can you beat it?" exclaimed the Doctor rather primly.

But he was pleased enough to accept when the tin-horn gambler made room for him in a large packing case where they lived together for several days.

Striking with great speed and fatality in the high thin mountain air, pneumonia literally swept draughty saloon floors and claimed other victims by the score in hay piles, sheds, wagons, and kennels. The authorities, according to the *Chronicle*, were resorting to midnight burials to keep the death rate from public notice and not impair the boom.

"Died Like a Dog," wrote the *Democrat* in describing the tragic end of a middle-aged man found frozen to death in a shanty behind a popular saloon. "The cabin in which he was found is hardly deserving of the name. It is built of rude slabs through which the snow had drifted and covered the floor. In one corner, where the body was found, was heaped one or two ragged shirts and part of a quilt, which had apparently served as a bed. A paper bag or two, containing a little coffee and sugar, and a fragment of sausage and bread, were strewn about the floor, and on a rude shelf were some matches and tobacco. There was no stove or cooking utensils. When found yesterday morning, he was lying diagonally across the corner, with his head against the side of the cabin, his hands clenched and drawn tightly up against his chin, and his bare feet projecting from the scant covering. Unknown and friendless, he died like a dog, and when the inquest is held, the verdict will be death from pneumonia and exposure."

Tabor was moved by all this to organize the Leadville Life Insurance Company, with his son Maxcy, now a youth of twenty, as president.

It is morning several months later—a chill morning early in June, for only in July and August are frosts unlikely. Even then they are not unknown. A July snowstorm occurs this very year, in fact.

Long before the sun has mounted over the Mosquitos to warm the valley, the camp begins to stir. Special Officer Donnahune awakens early to find a window open, and upon investigation discovers that his coat, with its star, is missing, and the window pane as well. Finding a drunken stranger asleep in his spare room, Officer Kelly is slapping the intruder to his senses. A tenderfoot in a better lodging house is loudly complaining of having lost both watch and bedfellow. In the big tents and bunkhouses, men are being prodded from their beds to make room for others. Thousands are sitting up on saloon floors to stretch stiffly and perhaps discover a corpse in their midst—some poor unfortunate carried off during the night by a powerful combination of cold floors, wet scanty clothing, and too much rotgut whisky. Others, by the hundreds, come tumbling sleepily out of the most unlikely shelters.

Harrison and Chestnut are soon filled with men, animals, and wagons. Prospectors by twos and threes pass by on their way to more distant gulches, belaboring stubborn burros packed high with provisions, blankets, and tools. Laborers in leather boots, patched clothes, and weather-beaten black slouch hats stride powerfully up the streets toward the mines along California and Strayhorse gulches. In the other direction hurry smelter hands and charcoal-burners in grimy "jeans," once brown or blue. Water peddlers are crying their wares at fifty cents a bucket. A wagonload of deer comes down from the mountains, for with the boom hunting has become a business. At headlong speed through the crowds horsemen gallop to and from the mines. More ceremoniously, a mine manager drives by in a bright new gig. Soon heavy ore wagons come bumping down the steep slopes to cross the town to the smelters. Astride the nigh-wheeler rides the driver, shouting and cursing, cracking his long whip, guiding four to six yoke by a single rein to the leaders. A wagon bogs down in Harrison Avenue. The "skinner" lashes his sweating teams unmercifully. A struggling leader gets out of harness. The angry driver rushes forward, seizes the excited horse by the bridle, and "with the loaded end of his whip beats out its brains. . . . He will be arrested."

From a distance comes the scream of sawmills cutting a million feet of the greenest of green lumber a week without appreciably diminishing the booming camp's demands. When lumber doubles and then triples in price, Tabor organizes the Little Pittsburgh Lumber Company as well as Tabor, Pierce and Company. Both yield great profits as Leadville "spreads east, west, and north like a prairie fire." Every street from old Slabtown below, to the new suburb of Poverty Flats above, is lined with foundations and skeleton timber frames. Cabins often go up in a day and sometimes vanish as quickly. Now and again a miner returns from work in the evening to find that marauders have left not a board or nail of his new warm cabin.

Substantial brick buildings begin to appear, occupied chiefly by the banks. The latter are "so overrun with deposits that to find places for their money bags vexes the directors sore." Hunter and Trimble of the Winniemuck, Little Pittsburgh Consolidated, and other rich properties open the Miners' Exchange Bank on Chestnut Street, next door to the Coliseum, a notorious wine theater and dance house. Up the street at the corner of Harrison, in the very center of town, rises Tabor's Bank of Leadville, a "handsome two-story brick with elegantly finished woodwork, and beautifully frescoed and painted ceilings." To top the building with a resplendent symbol that all can see, Tabor orders a huge disc to be made of white sheet metal in the form of a coin. For the purpose, he hires a poor carpenter-prospector who happens to be passing through town, Winfield Scott Stratton, destined one day to be the richest of the bonanza kings. When the disc has been finished and is being placed on the roof, Tabor stands with the crowd in the street admiring it as it flashes in the sun.

"That's just grand!" he exclaims. "Silver Dollar—Silver Dollar Tabor." [2]

One small public school is built at last to the apparent satisfaction of all but a few carping critics who protest that it is "inferior in every way to Madame Purdy's House, and a disgrace to a city of 20,000 people which boasts of its rich mines and growing trade." It is also unfortunate that the school becomes the center of constant political conflict that on several occasions almost results in bloodshed. Almost every day Dr. Stewart, president of the City Board of Education, discharges from his post—or is himself discharged by—one B. F. Jay, "our notorious shilly-shally, wishy-washy, wit-starved expounder of vulgarity, this silly snipe or jay-bird, who calls himself by the name of the County Superintendent of Schools."

In one of their endless quarrels over jurisdiction, prestige, and spoils, Dr. Stewart, once fined $25 for a murderous assault on a county commissioner, meets his rival with leveled pistol and a command not to advance another step toward the school building upon pain of death.

In time, at a salary of $50-60 a month (those "who do janitor work in the rooms are paid $10 extra"), two teachers are hired from a number of applicants eager to reach the new Eldorado—one in Illinois expressing a willingness to teach "in Leadville or anywheres else if wages is good," another in New England frankly confessing that he "can teach anything but would rather get to run a sawmill."

In advertising itself the camp also makes much of its seven churches—Presbyterian, Baptist, Methodist, Congregational, Campbellite, Episcopalian, and Catholic. Tabor donates $105 toward the Episcopalians' log chapel and a handsome set of crystal chandeliers to the Reverend Tom Uzzell for his new Spruce Street Methodist Church. When the Swedenborgians erect a house of

worship, the *Chronicle* is led to comment upon the great variety
of religious beliefs in camp:

"There are here the Materialists, the Positivists, the Buddhists,
the Annihilists, the Infidels, and a few believers in what is termed
Christianity. All these have but one religion and one God in common: it is the Crucified Carbonate."

Leadville could now boast of two large hotels, the Grand and
the Clarendon, both celebrated in the mountains in their day.
The Grand, built over and around the old City Hotel on Chestnut,
attracted the more sober and respectable. It was kept by Thomas
F. Walsh and his wife, a rather refined lady who clapped the name
of St. Keven's upon well-known Sowbelly Gulch when her husband
happened to make a small strike there.[3] Though the Walshes did
well enough from roomers and boarders, they did not rise to fortune during this boom. But Walsh will one day strike it rich, far
to the southwest, at the celebrated Camp Bird, in the towering
San Juans. He will follow Tabor and other bonanza kings to
Washington and there erect a great showplace on Massachusetts
Avenue, to dazzle foreign diplomats and Capital society alike, one
of the most elaborate mansions of its day. He will spurn the offer
of a partnership with King Leopold of Belgium in developing
mines in the Congo, bless the marriage of his daughter to one of
the McLeans, then owners-editors of the Cincinnati *Enquirer* and
influential Washington *Post,* and become the grandfather of the
"world's richest baby." It was here at the Grand Hotel that Walsh
acquired his first stake and polished his wit and manners which
enabled him in later years to consort familiarly with senators,
presidents, and kings.

The Clarendon on Harrison Avenue was likewise respectable,
but with a difference. Less staid and sober, it shone with the well-
dressed and bejeweled respectability of those who could afford
the envious gossip of the vulgar. The Clarendon lobby and bar
were virtually the club of the Carbonate Kings. Here they dis-

cussed their business and personal affairs, conducted their negotiations, and planned their coups. As they moved from bar to
lobby and back again, they were trailed by business satellites,
gentlemen gamblers, brokers and promoters, sharpers of all kinds,
and courtesans almost above reproach. The food at the Clarendon was excellent, prepared as it was by Monsieur A. Lapierce
from Delmonico's, New York. The Clarendon has recently been
razed, but for years it stood, a three-storied frame shell abandoned even as a cheap lodging house, a crumbling monument to
William H. Bush, once almost as well known as Tabor.

Once a teacher of mathematics at Kalamazoo, Bush early left
to seek his fortune in the West, settling at Central City in Gregory
Gulch. There he was "running the Teller House, mining some, and
gambling more when Leadville broke in 1878." Bush arrived in
camp with $10, so it is said, but was soon on the high road to for-
tune. Quick and sharp, the antithesis of Tabor, he quickly made
himself indispensable to the Carbonate King, becoming his chief
lieutenant and then his partner in rapidly expanding operations.
Bosom and almost inseparable friends for a time, one was seldom
seen without the other. Fond of racing and extraordinarily proud
of his blooded stable, Bush named his prize gelding H. A. W.
Tabor, his mate in harness being Lilly Langtry.

Next door to the Clarendon was the new house of the Tabors,
a rather small clapboard cottage, for Augusta remained somewhat
suspicious of Fortune's caprices, refusing to make any great
change in their style of living. The five or six small rooms of the
cottage were rather simply furnished, though there was a large
marble clock and perhaps more gilt than appeared at Oro City.
Augusta was at last free of boarders, and was even persuaded to
take a maid. She and Tabor, it was noted, were seen less and less
frequently together. Tabor was extremely occupied with private
and public affairs, to be sure, but perhaps he was beginning to find
Augusta rather too stiff and uncompromising for the life of opu-

lent splendor he desired. In any case, as Tabor stepped forward to be honored and acclaimed, he was apt to leave Augusta behind. It becomes increasingly difficult to catch even a glimpse of her behind his large resplendent figure.

Augusta was not long settled here in her cottage when Tabor, for business reasons, removed it from Harrison Avenue, wheeled it up the street, and dumped it on Carbonate Avenue, flush with the sidewalk. There was no lawn, no garden, not a flower or bush about it or any of the more pretentious houses along the barren dusty street. It was difficult to grow grass and flowers at such an altitude, but that did not wholly account for their absence. The taste of the Carbonate Kings ran largely to other things—gold watches, diamonds, horses, and champagne.

Tabor spent a small fortune to buy, for himself, a rare diamond said to have been Queen Isabella's of Spain. One of the Gallagher brothers traveled to Denver and as he had never owned a gold watch, bought six of the largest he could find, each with a heavy gold chain. Depositing five with the hotel clerk for safekeeping, he wandered forth "to promote the circulation of currency, good fellowship, and wet goods." Upon his return the hotel clerk pointed out that the chain was dangling and the watch missing. Gallagher asked for another. As he attempted drunkenly to attach it to the chain, it fell with a crash to the floor. After many unsuccessful attempts to recover it, Gallagher demanded another and walked out. The fallen watch disappeared into the pocket of some lounger in the lobby.

But this was the same Gallagher who, upon receiving his share of $225,000, went into the streets of Leadville to buy every poor acquaintance he met a new suit of clothes, "of the best quality and highest price." He then took them to the gay and fashionable Tontine for a great banquet, with oceans of champagne and the prettiest girls for all. At least one old miner looked back upon this day as the grandest of his life, the gayest he had ever known.

Another of the Gallaghers was at the moment building a mansion on Carbonate Avenue, for Mrs. Gallagher was no longer pleased to live up California Gulch, finding the Irish up there not fit to associate with.

"We are goin' to move down to Leadville and have a big brick house in the latest style," she declared. "And be Jasus, it'll have an elbow on it, too!"

Rische had built himself a house on the outskirts of camp, almost a mile from his nearest neighbor—whether to escape the camp's thieves or its tempations is not clear. Like Tabor, he had bought himself a large house in Denver—the mansion of William Byers of the *News*—and began paying court to the Tabors' German maid. When the engagement was broken off, he visited Chicago and fell in with one Clem Pieriolat, dealer in furs, to whom Rische confessed his desire to be married. Pieriolat took him to St. Louis and introduced him to a girl in his store there, Minnie Junghuhn, and the two were married at a fashionable wedding in Chicago. The bride appeared with "solitaire diamond earrings, a breast pin containing a cluster of these, a handsome gold watch and chain, and massive gold bracelets, each set with a large and superb stone." For the occasion Rische was "not arrayed in exactly the conventional costume, though sparkling with gems, but people of immense wealth," as the Chicago press remarked, "can afford to laugh at the conventionalities."

With his bride Rische departed for New York City to take in the sights.[4]

Down Chestnut Street there is a great commotion. A stranger has been stopped and asked to explain where he obtained the horse he is riding—and the silver of the Grand Hotel in his pockets. Hoisted high on a rope, the suspect is seized "with the death throes customary on such occasions before being lowered and given a second opportunity to live by confessing where he got the silver and the horse." His answers are not satisfactory, and up he goes again. A burly miner pushes forward, striking right and left, scattering the self-appointed execution squad. The dying man falls to earth with a thud, "totally unconscious, and rolls over like any fresh corpse." As several men move to lay hands again on the rope, the miner steps back and defies the mob, a revolver in either hand.

"The first one to make a move toward this man will die. He's a stranger to me, but by God! he'll have fair play. No damn man, whether he's a horse thief or not, should be hung like a dog without some chance to prove he's innocent." The suspect and the miner are hauled off to jail.

John Kane, owner of the popular Catalpa Saloon, staggers home to lunch, beats his wife into insensibility, and on his return invades the schoolhouse. He knocks down the clock, kicks it to pieces in sight of the frightened children whose "baby faces would have softened the heart of a Herod," and ends up by firing twice at the terrified children as they flee across the yard. Kane returns unmolested to his saloon.

A frightened tenderfoot scurries about inquiring anxiously where he can obtain a permit to carry a gun. When no one is willing to grant him authority, he consults a lawyer and is advised to arm himself with anything at hand—tent stakes, iron pins, or preferably a shotgun—and "never to go out after nightfall without at least one carefully loaded six-shooter in each pocket, and if molested by anyone, to shoot lively."

A shot rings out. A crowd collects before the Little Church Casino, where "Slim Jim" Bruce has just shot "Brownie" Lee to death in a quarrel over spoils from a confidence game. The crowd scatters as coaches of the two rival stage lines come charging up Chestnut Street, with passengers inside and out shrieking curses at one another and wildly firing revolvers. Along Tiger Alley, Hattie Garlock and Minnie Pillsbury, both stark naked, are sprinting in a spirited race for a bottle of whisky. A policeman passes by with the "first really insane person to be arrested in Leadville," charged with spending "all his time in prayer and religious exhortation." Newsboys are crying the *Chronicle* through the streets:

SICKENING ACCIDENT AT THE CRYSOLITE. Miner Overcome by Gas and Smoke Falls From Bucket Down the Shaft. A miner who ventures to the rescue is also overcome and shares his fate—

SMELTER HAND FAINTS AND FALLS INTO BOIL-ING SLAGPOT.

DANCE GIRL TRIES TO ARSENIC HER WAY FROM LEADVILLE.

GOSPEL GUIDE. Where Our Local Divines Propose to Hang Out Tomorrow—

PERILS OF THE STREET. The unknown man who was run over by the stage died at the Sisters' Hospital this morning—

PRICE OF PROVISIONS LOWER.

NEW STRIKE IN STRAYHORSE GULCH.

TELEPHONE SERVICE OPENED. It talks like a charm—

BUSH PLANS A NEW NEWSPAPER. The Evening Times *will employ a full corps of mounted reporters, all in black uniforms. The horses will all be black and fleet of foot—*

WANTED: FIFTY WAITER GIRLS! Pay in Gold Promptly Every Week. Must appear in SHORT CLOTHES or no engagement.

BULLETS AT THE BON TON. An Attempt to Clean Out the House. N. M. Alexander and Officer Morrissey Shot—

In the Police Court some thirty men are booked on sundry charges, "with Americans still in the lead." At this time a Negro gambler is sold into slavery to pay court costs, the successful bidder obtaining his services for three months at a price of $2. A few prisoners are fined $50 for indiscriminate use of firearms. Many more are fined the usual $10 for being "d.d."—i.e., drunk and disorderly. But the majority pay $5 for being simply "d."

From a room adjoining the court come sounds of revelry. A grand jury has just finished a fortnight's labors and is frolicking about a barrel of beer. One after another, jurors are bound and thrown on the floor to have the beer "administered through pipes and funnels." Sheriff Tucker has his "nicely starched shirt bosom nicely dyed a nut-brown color." City Treasurer Zollars is "floored and bathed in beer," while County Clerk Wells, loudly protesting as a temperance man, has the "limpid liquor poured all over him, from the rim of his paper collar down to the soles of his high leather boots."

The police force is called together "to have the Riot Act read to them by Alderman Moore, chairman of the Committee of Police, who made the rounds at a late hour last night, and to his surprise found only two of the eight policemen on their beats."

When the alderman has finished, the City Council convenes to wrestle with many serious problems inherited from the Tabor regime. Tabor's successor is William H. James, a Welsh watchmaker, who came west in the Pike's Peak rush of '59, settling in Nevada Gulch above the Gregory diggings. Here James erected a stamp mill which netted him, he later said, just $13.85. He moved the mill down the gulch without increasing profits, returned to Nevadaville as a watch repairer, and was then wiped out by fire, subsequently drifting from camp to camp as a foreman and superintendent of mines. Here in Leadville he joins the swelling ranks of bonanza kings, amassing a large fortune from a sampling works founded in partnership with Edward Eddy, a graduate of the South Kensington School of Mines, London, one of the few trained mining engineers in camp.

Although a far more able and energetic administrator than Tabor, Mayor James fails to achieve any marked success in the almost insuperable task of establishing order. In the first place, the city treasury is empty. Although they owe thousands of dollars in taxes, owners of mines and real estate stubbornly refuse to pay up until assured that neighbors are contributing their share. This is impossible for the good reason that everyone is evading any and all tax levies.

The police are disaffected, grumbling because their salaries of $100 a month are far in arrears, protesting at the same time that it is too much to expect eight officers to patrol the boisterous sprawling camp.

Money or no money, Mayor James makes a desperate effort to remedy the increasingly dangerous condition of the town. The police force is increased to thirteen officers, with a captain and a marshal, Mart Duggan retaining the latter post. Cabins standing in the middle of streets are removed. Harrison and Chestnut are graded and paved with slag from the smelters, to remove the bog holes in which several drunken men have had a narrow escape from drowning. A commission "to lay the terrible dust on our streets" is given to old Abe Lee, already through his second fortune, who loads several barrels on an old wagon and ladles water into the street with a saucepan as he moves slowly forward. Periodically he goes about collecting what he can from householders along his route.

Tabor comes forward to organize and obtain a franchise for his Leadville Water Company. He obtains another for his Leadville Illuminating Gas Company, and the Lake County Street and Horse Railway, a $500,000 concern with Tabor as president and George Fryer as treasurer. The latter is not a success, for on the steep grades the three large wooden cars prove to be too heavy for horses.

Against the determined opposition of property owners, hesitant steps are taken for the "removal of the garbage which threatens to depopulate the city." The camp reeks with terrible stenches from filth and dead animals lying in streets and alleys.

"At present we can do without water works and gas works," exclaims one citizen as the *Chronicle* applauds, "but we cannot afford any longer to allow the offal and filth of the whole town to accumulate, as it is now doing, in the rear of dwelling houses and hotels. Today I saw ton after ton of decaying meats and swill collected in the rear of some hotels. Others have dug open holes, some eight or ten feet deep, to throw offal and filth from the houses into. Owners of property should be compelled within the shortest time possible (what although it does cost highly; they have been reaping the harvest) to have the rear of their premises cleansed and purified. The City Fathers should have this done, no matter what the cost."

Prodded to action by the mounting death rate, the Council decrees that "manure in the rear of stables and barns be not allowed to remain more than a week," and threatens to fine property owners who fail to keep their premises "reasonably clean." But now citizens in the lower wards begin to complain that all of the town's garbage is being dumped at night in their front yards. This matter is no sooner remedied than others protest that "the City Fathers are straining at a gnat and swallowing a camel in allowing the smelting works to remain in our midst. These works poison the atmosphere with deadly gases more deleterious than the heaps of carrion lying on the corners of every street."

But this the Council cannot even pretend to remedy, for the smelters and mines are Leadville.

In a desperate effort to raise money, the Council instructed the police to give no protection to those who refused to pay their taxes, provoking a great outcry led by the *Chronicle*.

"This is the first bill of outlawry ever passed in the United States," it shouted, adding that it gave roughs and criminals a free hand to despoil delinquents. Existing laws were sufficient for the purpose, the *Chronicle* contended, in spite of the admitted fact that the administration, after the most strenuous efforts, had managed to collect less than $5,000 of the $32,000 owed the treasury.

The order was rescinded and a $4 poll tax substituted which ex-
acted as much from the poorest miner and homeless vagabond as
from Tabor himself. There was another loud outcry, though not
by the *Chronicle*.

"Gentlemen," wrote an indignant miner, protesting that the tax
equaled two days' pay, "have you ever for a moment considered
that many—very many—poor men have not a place to lay their
heads and are necessarily compelled to sleep in chairs in order to
go to work next day to obtain an honest livelihood?"

The poll tax was now abandoned for a system of high licenses
not only on saloons, gambling houses, billiard halls, variety theaters, brewers, and brokerage offices, but also on lumber yards,
transportation companies, door-to-door peddlers, second-hand
stores, restaurants, and boarding houses. As brothels and dance
houses were not included, protest waxed louder than ever.

"There are many cheap boarding houses and small restaurants
that cannot afford to pay such a senseless and outrageous license.
It will close up at least fifty or more places where the miner, la-
borer, freighter, and other transient people may obtain meals at
reasonable prices, and throw all custom and profit into the hands
and pocketbooks of the proprietors of the largest hotels and restaurants. Can the keeper of a modest house or restaurant, who
sells meals at twenty-five cents and liquors at a nickel, be expected
to pay as large a license as a hotel or restaurant which charges
fifty cents, seventy-five, or one dollar per meal, and fifteen and
twenty-five cents for cigars? If city revenue must be raised, for
heaven's sake don't raise it *all* from the pockets of the poor man.
Scale it at least."

But the aldermen were at wits' ends, and the licensing system
continued, with an abrupt command to the gambling saloons to
pay up or shut up shop. When none came forward, a few were
closed by the authorities, but the whole matter was soon forgotten.
A few months later the *Chronicle* found that not a fourth of the
many saloons in town were licensed.

As much as anything else, Leadville feared a general conflagration, and for three weeks in the summer of '79 a pall of smoke hung over the valley from a terrific forest fire raging through the timber just behind camp. With white ashes dropping like snow in the streets, destruction seemed almost certain. The fire cut across upper Harrison Avenue, razing Capitol Hill and blocking all roads but that to Malta. "The only hope for the city is the wind," warned the *Chronicle*. "If it should veer to the north, Leadville will be in ashes before uptown folks have time to eat their suppers." Fortunately, the wind held from the west, and the fire went roaring up the gulches, destroying the shaft houses of the Iron Silver and scores of mines on Carbonate and Iron hills. But danger threatened again as the fire crossed into Iowa Gulch and swept round to the south. The Mayor issued a proclamation ordering all citizens to assemble whenever an alarm was sounded by ringing the bell on the Methodist Church. This provoked an outcry that the whole town dared not answer the call until a force was recruited "to protect property and citizens from the ravages of the army of cutthroats and thieves in our midst while citizens are fighting the flames." A guard was detailed for just such an emergency.

The camp entirely relied upon three volunteer fire companies—the Harrison Hook and Ladder Company, the Tabor Hose Company, and the W. H. Bush Hose Company, with young Maxcy Tabor as social president. "The color of the [Bush] officers' hats is straw, with a pink frontpiece. The others have a black frontpiece, red ground, and white letters." Tabor had presented his company with a "four-wheeled, crane-necked, nickel-plated carriage," admired by all and pronounced a "perfect beauty."

Even as the City Council sat deliberating, the bell on the Methodist Church began to toll. In an instant the streets were filled with frightened people. The forest fire had not crept closer, but there was a great blaze in Chestnut Street. From the Coliseum, a large wooden theater and dance house, rose a great column of flame blown by the wind against adjacent frame buildings. Firemen rushed for their hats and soon had their apparatus on the street. It proved to be woefully inadequate. Firemen were greatly hampered by drunken volunteers who had to be rescued from the flames time and again. A strong wind was scattering sparks and burning ashes over half the town. Suddenly the wind turned upon itself and all but blew the fire out. Three firemen had been seriously injured, but the camp was saved. Fires occurred almost daily but never lighted a general conflagration.

Tabor now organized the Leadville Fire Insurance Company.

Two lady barbers from Chicago had established a shop on Chestnut Street, and above them Dr. Mary Barker-Bates was treating nervous disorders in an electric chair equipped with a "$300 Galvanic Faradic battery, a wonderful and very beautiful piece of mechanism." Down the street was the office of a most versatile quack, Dr. Charles Broadbent—phrenologist, mesmerist, medicine man, and temperance lecturer. By examining the head— "Examination $2, and with chart, $3"—he could "tell you what kind of a lady or gentleman you should marry, and whether you are long-lived or not." His remedies included Inhaling Balm for catarrh, Dandelion Pills for dyspepsia and biliousness, Nephriticum for kidney and bladder complaints, and nothing equaled his Great English Remedy "for Loss of Memory, Lassitude, Nocturnal Emissions, Noises in the Head, Dimness of Vision, and Aversion to Society."

Up the street was Mr. Needles' "elegant art photograph shop," which greatly impressed the Carbonate Kings and their families. "The photographs decorating his parlor, the music from his organ, the brilliantly lighted room, all reminds one of New York City. Miss Needles, talented sister of Mr. Needles, is assisting, and also paints in oil, crayon, and water colors, natural as life." Tabor was one of those who decided to go elsewhere for his art, paying one Fishlin of Chicago $3,000 for an oil portrait, the first of a series painted during these years.

An "artist" in tattoo with a shop a few doors away was well patronized. "Ladies come to me every day to have a monogram or some loved one's initials inserted into their skin. The habit prevails principally among the fashionable fancy women, but also in some good circles of society which follow the fads of London and Paris." For monograms in two colors, the charge was $50. For separate initials, $15 for the plain—$25 for the more elaborate. For $200 and up, the "Professor" inserted plain or colored mottoes and heraldic devices "on the upper arm, where it may never be detected, or on the knee, or the side of the thigh, wherever the fancy dictates."

For recreation and exercise, the fashionable organized an archery club and a bicycle club, and there were many gay roller-skating parties. Bill Bush formed the Leadville Trotting and Running Association, which built just outside the camp a half-mile track, reputedly the best west of the Mississippi. Here, in August, occurred the great sporting and social event of the season. From all the surrounding country came the fastest horses and ponies to try their speed against the trotters and racers of the Carbonate Kings.

Riding and driving appealed to the reputable and disreputable alike. On Harrison Avenue almost every evening one could see the "Mayor and his lady behind their lively stepping blacks; Dr. Square and Miss James behind a pair of mottled bays; Chief of Police Kelley and lady in an open clarence; Rev. Dr. Uzzell, looking as stern and serious as a hard-shelled Baptist, reining his beautiful span of dark browns through the crowded streets with the skill of a Bonner or Henry Ward Beecher."

The women of the town went driving every evening as well, usually intoxicated and smoking long black cigars.

"HELL ON THE ROAD—FIGHTING ALL ALONG THE BOULEVARD," read the *Democrat* one morning. "Sunday is always an occasion for fast women, rapid men, and all the sporting fraternity to air themselves on the beautiful drive. Toward evening these cheerful souls got hilarious. Presently, some big double-decked rooster opened the ball by jumping at a small courtesan and smashing her nose. The matinee then began. One female armed herself with a beer bottle and created on the head of a well-known gentleman several bumps not down on his phrenological chart. He retaliated by taking a board and damaging her some. Scarcely was this over when another woman drew a revolver and began scattering galena around in a particularly reckless fashion, and was only induced to stop when her solid man seized her by her false hair and mopped up the boulevard with her. Her yells had barely died away when another circus performance opened.

"We regret to announce that nobody was killed."

As night fell, men of means began to take refuge in the hotels amid swarms of speculators and promoters. Here, many a worthless or salted mine was brought under the influence of Venus Meretrix and champagne. Valuable lots occasionally changed hands three or four times in an evening. Customers could even be found for gold bricks. Two of these, allegedly from a stagecoach robbery in the Black Hills, were bought by young Smith of the banking house of L. C. Smith and Son, and ultimately bankrupted the institution, to the great distress of many poor depositors.

At the Clarendon bar, their favorite resort, Tabor and Bush spent many pleasant evenings together, discussing their business and personal affairs. Tabor was occupied with scores of mines, his real estate, his water company, his gas company, his insurance companies, two lumbering companies, and a horse-car company. He had his Leadville Bank and had organized the Pueblo, Canon City, and Leadville Railway, with George Fryer as treasurer. He had established the Leadville Stock and Mining Exchange, with himself as president and Fryer, Bush, and Rische as directors. He has founded Tabor City above Leadville on the Ten Mile

Road. He had incorporated the Tabor Milling Company, and the Smelters' Supply Company, to buy and sell ore, bullion, coke, charcoal, and machinery.

All of these had done much to satisfy Leadville's more primitive needs, and now Tabor and Bush decided that what the camp most needed was an opera house.

XI

BEL ESPRITS
AND BUNKOSTEERERS

"Song, Dance, and Mirth, and Emotional Novelties . . ."

WHILE the Tabor Opera House was building, Leadville did not want for either social or intellectual life. It had its fashionable balls and dance houses, its saloons and temperance revivals, its literary societies, beer halls, theaters, brothels, and clubs by the scores—dancing, dining, gambling, musical, scientific, social, religious, and political.

"There is much good society in Leadville," remarked the local press. "Neighbors have hardly had time to get acquainted, but social life is rapidly assuming shape and rendering residence here more agreeable to ladies."

Women were few, and all were treated with marked respect. "Long lines of men waiting at the post office for letters will fall back from the window as quickly and politely to let a prostitute in ahead of them as a married lady."

Early in '79, at the first fashionable ball in camp, all the youth, beauty, and wealth of Leadville assembled "under the coal-oil" at the Grand Hotel. With the arrival of Madame Gallat, French dressmaker, the wives of the richer cast aside home-made and store clothes, and now appeared more fashionably gowned—in black and brown cashmere, for the most part. One also noted an "occasional swallow-tail among the sterner sex, but as a rule a broad-gauge, steel-track, solid-bed mining town can raise but a limited number of such garments, and these of different styles and patterns."

Both grace and elegance improved with the coming of Professor G. H. Godat, who essayed "to teach all the fashionable glide steps of eastern dances, etc., and to introduce to the good people of Leadville all the latest styles of dancing glide quadrilles, contra dances, etc." Saturday evening "hops" at his academy were always well attended, as were "Professor" Simon's periodic *Soirées Dansantes*.

Any number of private dancing clubs flourished, of which the smartest was the Assembly Club, apostrophized in a dull novel written here at the time by Mary Hallock Foote, wife of a local mine manager.[1] More than forty couples attended one of its earliest balls at the Clarendon—with all the gentlemen but one in full evening dress, and all the ladies "so gorgeously attired" that the reporter's pen failed him. With increasing prosperity there was a plethora of masquerade balls by such groups as the German Turnverein, Standard Club, Jefferson Avenue Social Club, Ancient Order of Hibernians, Hebrew Ladies Benevolent Association, Scandinavian Society, and Carpe Diem Club.

But the climax of the first social season came during the Christmas holidays with the Firemen's Ball, ecstatically described as the largest and most brilliant party in the history of the West. It was held on the upper floor of the Central Fire House, "elegantly decorated throughout with the national colors and the hose of the brave fire laddies." Promptly at nine, Chief Engineer Bill Bush stepped out to lead the Grand March, and dancing continued till dawn. Altogether it was a gay and brilliant occasion, with the "showing of jewels almost fabulous."

Leadville contained clubs enough to have embraced every lonesome person in camp. Here were Red Men, Woodmen, Masons, Sons of Michigan, Odd Fellows, Knights of Labor, Knights of Robert Emmett, and Knights of Pythias—"with an elegant lodge room on Chestnut Street over Herman Brothers' Clothing Store"

—a New England Society, a Texas Club, a Pacific Coast Association, the B'nai B'rith, and Deutches Casino. Pleasant afternoons of whist and gossip were enjoyed by the Racket Club ("for ladies only") and the Lady Forget-me-nots. At the Alhambra Alley Saloon, Negroes instituted a social and political group rather mystifyingly named the Monroe Supporters. Almost all citizens belonged to either the Republican or Democratic Club. But in protest against machine politics the miners in Big Evans Gulch formed the Elephant Club, which decreed that "any member caught voting at any city, county, or state election shall forfeit a keg of beer and be summarily expelled."

Among the more purely social clubs for gentlemen were the Clarendon Club, the Leadville Club ("to which none of the ignorant bonanza kings belonged"), and the Elk Club, a dining club composed of younger and more cultivated professional men—engineers, assayers, lawyers, and doctors. Two promoters from the East tried to interest Tabor and other Carbonate Kings in a fantastic scheme to build a Union Club to cost $50,000,000. "They have been going around among our monied men with plans and specifications, and are meeting with great encouragement. Certainly, nothing is more needed in Leadville than a club house for gentlemen that is thoroughly cosmopolitan in character." Fortunately for all but the promoters, the club remained only an ideal.

The camp, too, had its more intellectual groups—the Leadville Literary Society, and the Bel Esprit Society. The former appears to have been much given to soprano solos, though it boasted of "some of the best literary minds in the country, including one who wrote the most part of Dr. Horace Greeley's *History of the American Conflict*." But, on occasion, it enjoyed orations, debates, recitations, and lectures on Cleopatra's Needle, the Seven Wonders of the World, and the lives of Alexander Hamilton and Robert Raikes. Tabor was one of the "Bel Esprits" who, one evening, enjoyed this program: "Gray's *Elegy*, a song *Farewell*, a humorous parody *To Dig or Not to Dig,* another parody on *The Boy Stood On the Burning Deck,* a fine vocal solo entitled *Watching,* and a rendition of *The Death of Poor Jo.*" Even the bonanza kings at the Carbonate Club occasionally sat through a lecture but more often were pleased to hear Mr. Sullivan sing "Minnehaha" or laugh themselves sick as he and another variety actor parodied *Romeo and Juliet.*

A free reading and lounging room was established by the Y.M.C.A., but little used. Nor can it be said to have received much support from those most vocally concerned about the camp's moral tone. The superintendent of the Evening Star Mine, one W. S. Ward, contributed to the Central Fire Club yearly subscriptions to *Harper's Monthly* and *Weekly, Lippincott's, Scribner's, Puck, Scientific American, Atlantic,* the New York *Daily Herald,* New York *Weekly World,* New York *Weekly Times,* and the Chicago *Weekly Times.* As he continued these subscriptions from year to year, the volunteer firemen must have made some use of them.

Certainly, one of the most interesting documents of the time is the published interview in which a local bookseller declared that a surprisingly large number of miners were among his best customers. "There is no demand for the English classics," he confessed. "The demand for Dickens has fallen off greatly. Miss Braddon sells much better than Dickens. Charlotte Brontë and her sister are out of fashion, too. Another quasi-classic, Ouida, is falling off, considering the fact that some two years ago Ouida was all the rage." Translations from the French were far more popular—Alphonse Daudet, Alexandre Dumas, and Emile Gaboriau with his great detective, Monsieur Lecoq. "A select and rather superior little circle read Jules Verne." Only less popular than the French were Wilkie Collins, Charles Reade, and a certain Farjeon. The bookseller listed as unsaleable Thackeray and Disraeli.

For a time, Leadville had a publishing house, perhaps the first and certainly the last in Colorado to be devoted exclusively to books. "It is my amusement," explained its founder. "Some men like wine; others take comfort in horses. Others like to play with silver. I am printing books because it is fun."

If any volumes were published, no record has been found of them.

Social and spiritual communion was promoted by many church societies—the Ladies Relief Society, the Rector's Aid Society, and the St. George's Ladies Aid Society, which held a memorable bazaar with "fancy" tables, an apron table, a Rector's table, a floral bower, a witch's tent, an ice cream parlor, and a gallery of "the richest and rarest works of art." The sole event of its kind during these years, the exhibition included *A True View of Seventy-Six, Horse Fair, Paradise on Earth, Flower of the Family,* and *Five Points of New York.*

Lastly, there were the temperance and similar societies—notably, the Blue Ribbon Society and the Leadville Temperance Club. A few more earnest women organized a "Praying Orchestra" to parade from dive to dive and, if not forcibly ejected, "offer prayer and song for the salvation of surrounding sinners." The Y.M.C.A. resolved rather ambiguously that "fifteen minutes of each meeting be devoted especially to intemperance." An Anti-Treat Society, founded by the Reverend Mackay of the Episcopal Church, gave its members pledge cards to carry in their pockets "to protect themselves against the assaults of those with whom they refuse to drink." A Pastors' Union was formed to confer once a week on the camp's morals, and in a laudable desire for knowledge decided to beard the tigers and the harpies in their dens. Often in the saloons it was "nip and tuck between a temperance orator in one room, and a gambler in the next, to determine which could yell the loudest and attract the biggest crowd," as remarked by the local press, which showed itself most unsympathetic toward the crusading societies.

"Saturday night a party of four distinguished and extremely pious divines made the complete rounds of the camp. They visited the dance dangers, gambling shops, bunko-coolers, and May-Minnie unmentionables. It took these pious parsons almost all night to satisfy themselves, and when they walked solemnly into church the next morning, a good many ministerial admirers thought perhaps they had been peeling onions, their eyes were so red and watery. But now they know all about the night side of Leadville. If even a small portion of the stories afloat about town are true, these mournful-faced parsons rather enjoyed some of the wiles of the Wicked Hater of Men.

" 'Look here, young woman,' observed a local preacher who was making a night of it recently, 'you possess singular refinement of manners, considering your rude and shameful associations; you have every charm and grace of person which the Lord can endow anybody with—your face tells me that you come from a home of luxury and comfort; perhaps you were educated in some seminary where loving hearts and hands had placed you for your future welfare—why, then, are you here? Think of the opportunities you have wasted, the home you have desolated, the Christian life you might have lead—think of it!'

" 'Look here, old fellow, don't get sentimental, please. You gray-haired old men are the worst, but you can't play me for a sucker. I know what you're after.' "

A great many proved to be equally suspicious of and impervious to such moral influence. But if few new converts were made, the abstemious enjoyed some success in enrolling one another in their several societies, especially when under the emotional intoxication inspired by professional temperance revivalists.

"Colonel" Henry Howland came from Chicago to horrify the more sensitive with a speech that has fortunately been preserved. He first "reviewed the ravages of drunkenness all over the land, in all conditions of society, among all Americans without distinction of age, sex, or condition, in Congress and the White House, in all

professions—the bench, the bar, and the people, and presented a
sickening examination of drunkenness in Leadville, ending daily
in many deaths from pneumonia, diphtheria, and erysipelas, and
was heartily applauded by all.

"Many of you know what drink did to me," the Colonel concluded. "I know now that a sainted mother and loving wife never
ceased praying for me. And I want to ask—am I the only one
here present, who has loving friends thinking of and praying for
him in the old eastern home? Are there not firesides in New England and New York, Michigan and Illinois, at which mother, wife,
and sister are at this moment praying, God protect our loved one
from intemperance and vice! When you write, if you will but en-
close in the letter one of our pledges, with your name plainly written upon it, it will be to the heart of the dear one far away like a
sunburst on a midnight sky, and methinks that quick will come
back the answer, in sentiment, if not in these exact words, 'The
birds never sang so sweetly as they do this morning, and the flowers never bloomed so lovely.' "

The Colonel was followed by a certain Campbell, "a heavy
thick-set man of terrible power, who could convert a drunkard
or knock down an ox with equal ease," according to the *Democrat*. "One doesn't hear what he says, but feels it. His words go
flying through the hall like red-hot balls of fire. Everybody is excited." So excited, in fact, that six hundred took the pledge. But
backsliders were numerous, and the press continued hostile.

"All temperance lecturers take special delight in telling the rising generation how gloriously drunk they used to get," complained
the *Chronicle*. "They fill an hour's lecture with anecdotes of how
they used to cuff their poor wives about, break the hearts of girls
who loved them, dishonor the sacred name of mother, and send
her sorrowing to her grave. Very often these lecturers will tell
how they used to lie, steal, pawn their wife's wedding dress, kick
over the kitchen stove, drag their little daughter around by the
hair, and cut other capers for which, had the law done its duty,

they would be serving out a life sentence in some state prison in place of bragging about their crimes before really temperate young men and women." [2]

In camp one day appeared a Dr. Gibbons with his wife, both temperance revivalists. But as they had not been officially invited, the temperance societies suspected them of poaching and received them very coolly indeed. On their last evening in town the doctor and his wife entered a saloon and obtained permission to speak.

"I could speak better after hearing somebody sing," Gibbons began, "but none of the good temperance people of Leadville are here to sing. I'm alone with you, boys. (Cheers) There is no use mincing matters. I'm making this speech without my supper, and I don't know where I'll find my breakfast. I had $26.30 when I came here two weeks ago. I have worked hard day and night for the temperance cause, and now am just $26.30 worse off than when I came."

Three hundred miners dug down into their pockets and donated sufficient money to satisfy their hunger and start them on their way. No more was heard of them until this headline appeared in the *Chronicle* some months later:

THE LORD'S WRATH

Dr. Gibbons, the Great Temperance Apostle, Struck by Lightning.
Miraculously Escapes Death While Descending Pike's Peak.

When temperance lectures failed, a militant minority attempted to have the Sunday closing laws enforced. The idea, remarked a critic, was that "all sorts of games, fighting of roosters and dogs, chasing of buttered pigs, and highway robbery are to be prohibited within the corporate limits of the town on Sundays; citizens are only to be allowed to buy mines, swap burros, drink lager beer, sing sacred songs, and take all rational comfort possible without getting vicious."

The Blue Sunday agitation came to nothing.

"Tis the day of the Lord. The theaters, twirling casinos, concert halls, silver exchanges, and A-lafroganzas are all aglow. Down on State Street a female voice is shrieking murder."

Every night, Saturday and Sunday nights especially, pandemonium reigned almost from dark to dawn along State Street, a tumultuous half mile brightly lighted by great kerosene flares blazing before its dance houses, variety theaters, gambling hells, saloons, beer halls, and brothels. As it descended from Pop Wyman's Great Saloon at the corner of Harrison, the street grew steadily more disreputable until it ended among the pines on the sand flat in two dark lines of "cribs," notorious Coon Row and still more notorious French Row, a dangerous neighborhood into which many men innocently strayed to be seen no more. Behind French Row the *Chronicle* reported three "high joints," opium dens, where many another man had been done to death. Above State Street, and below, ran frightful alleys crowded with dark dens and tenements, harboring every sort of vice, depravity, and crime. The one above was fittingly named Tiger Alley, while the one below was known as Stillborn Alley for the many evidences of abortion and infanticide found there:

"Yesterday morning a small child, or foetus, was found in a garbage heap in the alley below State Street. As this sight is not an unusual one in that part of the city, it attracted but little attention."

Above French and Coon rows were the brothels of Mesdames Frankie Paige, Carrie Linnel, Minnie Purdy, Mollie Price, and Sallie Purple. The most fashionable of them, Mollie May's, stood by itself on Main Street. These bagnios were ever in trouble. First and most seriously, wayward girls of thirteen and fourteen were never turned away when they sought admittance here. Several small girls in camp had to be rescued time and again from a life of sin in these houses. Then, too, patrons frequently complained of being robbed. Also, shootings occurred often, not only within the houses, but between them. One midnight open warfare broke out between Mollie Price and Sallie Purple. Mollie poured volley after volley into her enemy's house next door. Sallie, her girls, and their patrons replied with a spirited fusillade. "Both parties are resting on their arms and awaiting daybreak to resume hostilities," reported the *Democrat* next morning. Mollie and Sallie, it appeared, had had a bitter argument about the relative merits of Tipperary and Connaught as a birthplace—a dispute in which Mrs. Purple finally triumphed with a particularly obscene remark.

Leadville soon had three breweries, which did much to lessen drunkenness, measurably diminishing indulgence in whisky, the only drink to be had for a time. No resorts were more popular than the larger beer halls. Each had a singer or two to render in a throaty voice, to suddenly hushed audiences, such old favorites as "Silver Threads Among the Gold," "Cottage By the Sea," and "Papa, Stay Home, Don't Leave Me Tonight." Frequently, in sudden outbursts of deep emotion, the men showered a singer with silver after a particularly affecting number, for, as one homesick miner remarked, "these poor despised beer hall singers were a sort of cropped angel after all."

Up the street, the fashionable Tontine was the scene of many gay parties. The gayest, perhaps, was the large champagne supper party at which George Fryer was host. Fryer quickly squandered a fortune of half a million and committed suicide. The Utah saloon near by offered entertainment by Professor Joseph Ives, who claimed once to have held the chair of astronomy at the University of Oxford. Every evening Ives wandered from saloon to saloon and was given all the drink he could consume by miners pleased with his stories of ancient mythology, readings from the Greek and Latin poets, and snatches from the great masters played on his old violin. Ives soon dropped dead in a Stringtown dive. Monahan's Saloon attracted custom with Sculley, "the great pedestrian, who has walked in Gilmore's Garden, New York, and in London, Philadelphia, Boston, Cincinnati, St. Louis, Chicago, and Omaha." But a number scorned this craze for "itinerant idiots," preferring Bill Nye's more sedate new saloon, pronounced the finest in camp. "Behind the bar the cutglass decanters, goblets, and so forth are tastefully and skillfully arranged beneath a mirror, the largest and finest in the city. The chandeliers and jets of cut crystal are elaborate, though chaste in their design."

A shot rings out down State Street and Jack Morrissey, a Carbonate King, falls in the street, seriously wounded. It is not robbery, as the crowds first surmise. One of his assailants is recognized as the suitor of the sixteen-year-old girl whom Morrissey has seduced and cast aside. The two Dillions come reeling down the street; both will return to the mines soon and ultimately die in poverty. So, too, will all but one of the Gallaghers, after spending their fortunes in saloons and dance houses along the street. At the Clarendon five men, all grown rich from a lease which has just expired, are celebrating with champagne. As cigars go round, one suggests that each tell what he proposes to do with his fortune. One intends to buy a home for his mother, a second to pay off the mortgage on his father's farm, a third to buy a herd of cattle, a fourth to try to enlarge his fortune by grubstaking prospectors, while the fifth, Ferdinand Van Zant, a young mining engineer, hesitates to talk, so the story goes, but finally declares that he intends "to go to London, rent a suite of rooms, get a complete outfit of fashionable clothing, go into society, and marry the richest and most attractive girl he can meet." He succeeds, marrying the daughter of Sir John Lubbock, afterward Lord Avebury. But Van Zant, like Fryer, ends with suicide.

"The town is full of old-time sports. There are eight to ten public saloons with all kinds of games, and I think all are making money," wrote a gambler at the beginning of the rush. "This is a good place for a small man with money to operate with. It is a gay place, and there is plenty of money here. One old sport arrived here with $3 a few months ago and is now owner of a frame house, for which he has refused $600 a month rent. Today, he received $25,000 for a fourth interest in a mine. You can't imagine the excitement going on here."

Everyone gambled—from the bonanza kings in their private clubs, to the little bootblacks who bucked the tiger in a shack on Carbonate Hill. Poker, keeno, chuck-a-luck, Australian poolo, rouge et noir, lansquinette, and paddle-wheel had their advocates, but faro was the general favorite because it less favored the house and was not easily "braced."

But many a tenderfoot foolishly preferred the nut-shell game—the old thimble game of earlier days. The operator employed a simple technique. With three half walnut shells in his fingers, he kept a small pea or rubber ball flying back and forth across the table and then, as if unintentionally, clapped down the shells in such a way that the ball was left exposed under one, offering to bet $100 that none could "spot" the ball. This bet was a "blind" and, if called, was evaded or withdrawn. Again the ball flew back and forth, to vanish suddenly under a shell. At this point the operator usually turned round on some pretext or other. While his back was turned, a "capper"—an accomplice in the crowd— quickly stepped forward, revealed the ball, and hastily replaced the shell, with a wink at the crowd. Once more the ball flew back and forth, and disappeared. The capper offered a bet of $5, which the operator scorned as too small.

"The difficulty is overcome by a green-looking tenderfoot, who produces another $5, and the shell is raised—but no ball!"

The ingenuous often paid from $50 to $100 to convince themselves, beyond all doubt, that the hand is quicker than the eye. No player ever won at this game—except when the operator thought it wise to revive a lagging interest.[3]

Somewhat more sporting was paddle-wheel. This required a large board with squares numbered from 1 to 100 and an upright wheel bearing the same numbers.

"Choose your square! Your money down in time and the wheel goes round!" cried the operator, spinning his machine. With astonishing regularity, the wheel stopped just short of, or passed slowly over, the number on which the largest stakes were piled.

Chuck-a-luck, the most popular of the dice games, was played with three dice and a board with squares numbered from 1 to 6. In placing stakes on any square, one bet the bank even money that one of the dice would show the number chosen. At the same time the game offered opportunity for the highest kind of play, for one could bet on any of the many possible combinations of numbers, at odds running as high as 180 to 1. It was traditional for chuck-a-luck operators to shake their dice in a "small churn-like affair of metal"—hence the expression, "tin-horn gambler," for the game was rather looked down on as one for "chubbers," and chuck-a-luck gamblers were never admitted to the aristocratic circle of faro-dealers.

Faro required a more elaborate layout than any of these—first of all, a large board with thirteen squares representing the respective value of the cards. Every dealer had his "case"—a small folding box about four inches high, usually silverplated, in which the deck of cards was placed face up. Across the top of the case ran thirteen wires, strung with four buttons each. A tally of every card played was kept on this abacus—one wire with its four buttons representing, for example, the four kings or the four aces. The case was carefully kept to determine betting odds and protect both player and dealer. The dealer ($5-7.50 a day) usually kept the case himself, but in more elaborate establishments a second dealer was hired as case-keeper ($3.50-5). Such houses also employed a "lookout" ($3-4), who sat on a high stool overlooking the board to watch for errors by the dealer, particularly when they went against the house.

The card on top of the deck as play began was known as the "soda," and paid nothing. The next card was a loser, the next a winner, and so through the deck to the last card, the "hock," which also paid nothing. When the dealer had proceeded "from soda to hock," he reshuffled his deck. Cards could be bet either way—if to win, by simply placing chips on any square on the board; if to lose, by "coppering" the pile of chips with a token such as a Chinese coin or checker. Workers and businessmen were known to operators as "producers" and usually played "straight up," betting on a single card to win or lose. But professional gamblers usually preferred to "copper the heel" by betting on several cards at once. Although not easily done, faro was sometimes "braced." Tiny holes were punched in the cards so that the dealer, if to the bank's advantage, could pull two cards instead of one, giving the wink to the case-keeper to arrange his part of the swindle.

A faro bank necessitated, according to the limits placed on bets, a capital ranging from $100 to $10,000 or more. "Banks in Leadville probably range from $500 to $2,000. The limit with a solid bank is usually placed at $25 a card. But there are banks in Leadville which have no limit, whether $10 or $10,000."

In most Leadville houses the minimum bet was a twenty-five cent white chip, sold in stacks of twenty for $5. In games where stakes ran high, a stack of twenty red chips cost $20; twenty blues, $50; and twenty yellows, $100, $200, or even $500. Whether they won or lost, players contributed to the bank, for all winnings were regularly discounted by the house. Faro banks made an average monthly profit of $1,000, according to the *Chronicle*, which estimated that $25,000 changed hands daily over the green cloth. One small faro bank on Chestnut Street reported a profit of $40,000 within four months.

The largest and best of the gambling hells were Jeff Winney's California Concert Hall, the Board of Trade Saloon, and the famous Texas House. At Jeff Winney's miners could buck the tiger in the agreeable form of Kitty Crawhurst, lady gambler, who had become a professional woman to spare herself a worse fate. The Board of Trade specialized in stud poker, which in size of stakes was exceeded only by faro. Many men won or lost as much as $10,000 at a sitting here. Until discovered and soundly thrashed, one man won thousands by using a "shiner"—a silver dollar with a tiny concave mirror which, when placed on a pile of notes or coin, revealed all cards dealt over it.

On Harrison Avenue, just above State Street, stood the famous Texas House, which took in "more money in a day than the Carbonate Bank," to the great profit of Bailey Youngston and "Con" Featherly, both of Galveston. The latter, a "debonnaire little fellow with soft slender hands," was known in the profession as a "mechanic." He could "operate" a faro box as occasion demanded. Youngston was less accomplished, having once been an interior decorator, and by his own efforts he transformed the gambling hell into a "palace of beauty."

A huge saloon with many highly polished bars occupied the entire ground floor. At a dozen or more tables faro was played continuously from one day to the next. The dealers relieved one another in eight-hour shifts. About the tables at all hours crowded "miners hoping to extend their stay in camp by increasing the remnant of fortune left by last night's debauch; furnace hands and charcoal burners, begrimed with smoke, who have stopped in on their way home from a day or night's work; young men about town with more ease than elegance, and more luck than sense, eager to provide for some new depravity in the dens of sin and shame; strangers stranded in their search of a carbonate mine or some other sinecure, and seeking means to take themselves hence; visitors endeavoring to learn the mysteries of the tiger's lair at a modest cost; and young clerks who frequently lose more than their salaries."

Play went on quietly and steadily, with bets on single cards limited to $25, and on "dubs" (doubles) to $50. Although regarded as penny-ante fellows while working at their jobs, dealers at the Texas House earned sensational reputations by their personal winnings at other houses during their off hours.

Mining and merchant kings of the camp were seldom seen in the main gambling saloon downstairs. For them, Youngston had provided a separate side entrance leading up a flight of stairs into "three gorgeously furnished apartments, a reception and reading room, a dining room, and a gambling room with a lavishly stocked buffet, at which a guest was invited to help himself ad lib." In every room was a piano, "with an experienced musician to play it." Over all presided John Pentland, "round-faced, suave, and good natured," a New York gambler, who had drifted into camp unheralded but quickly gained renown by winning more than $80,000 for the house within a few months.

"At one moment he is asking you, with an ecclesiastical flourish, to join him at the sideboard," wrote a dazzled guest. "One minute he is dealing a $500 card winner with a church-like composure, and the next is looking idly on from the lookout chair, and then goes bustling through the apartments to make sure that all accommodations and courtesies are extended to his guests."

Perhaps the greatest social occasion of all these years occurred here when Featherly and Youngston played host to the Carbonate Kings and all richer merchants, bankers, lawyers, and judges in town. Tabor, Bush, and Rische were among the selected guests, who are said to have represented a capital of $80,000,000. The occasion was a "Parisian banquet for forty men, all in dress suits." There were fourteen courses, half as many wines, finished off with cognac and coffee. After many brimming toasts and speeches, there was sporadic conversation, but no mention of cards until midnight, when the guests insisted on greater excitement. A game of faro began, "with ivory whites at $1.25 and no limit." Deal after deal went against the house.

"Well, if I don't win again," shouted an excited judge. "$1,000 on the king to win."

"Why of course, bet $10,000 if you wish," replied Pentland with a smile.

Play lasted less than an hour, and all the guests won, as perhaps it was intended they should. In any case, the loss of the house exceeded $30,000, the largest night's play in Leadville during these years.

Shootings at the Texas House were infrequent, but it was here that City Marshal Mart Duggan was shot down and killed in '88, presumably by a house gambler whose life he had threatened.

Early every evening, brass bands took their stand in crowded State Street before each of the seven variety theaters. Here they struck up to contend in friendly rivalry for an hour or more. Then, one by one, they marched off with a great roar of brass and pounding of drums to beat up the town, parading it from one end to the other, trailing "boys and banners telling of can-cans, female bathers, daring tumblers, and other dramatic attractions." An urchin carrying a "wide-awake" lamp trooped along at the side of each musician so that he could read his music.

At a stop in traffic one evening, a small lamp-bearer proudly turned about "to tell a newsboy about his father's playing in the band." His lamp, swinging round against the leader of the band, caught "in the tinsel trappings of his uniform and flashed up through his long curly hair, setting fire to his hat and burning his neck to a blister." The music stopped abruptly and the lamp dropped, as the boy darted through the crowd, hotly pursued by the maestro, who was blocked and tripped by the miners as they cheered the frightened boy.

After a turn of the town, the bands reassembled in State Street to play again till nine o'clock, when they repaired inside the wine theaters as curtains went up, not to go down again till three or four in the morning.

Here, at the top of the street, was the Grand Central, where Tabor and other Carbonate Kings had their private boxes. A large three-storied frame building, only recently risen from the ashes of the old Theatre Comique, the Grand Central advertised itself as the "Largest and Most Elegantly Appointed Theatre West of Chicago." Before its kerosene footlights it offered such attractions as *Around the World in Eighty Days*, straight from Niblo's Gardens, New York, "with real camels, elephants, etc., in the famous Necropolis funeral procession," and *Nana, the Lovely Blonde*, at prices ranging from twenty-five cents to $1, with private boxes at $5.

Song, Dance, and Mirth
and
Emotional Novelties

A Host of Talented Artists
and

BEAUTIFUL WOMEN

Four Hours
of Elegant Pleasures, blended with a voluptuous feast without coarseness, concluding with Harry Montague's Spicy, Sensational, Melodramatic Comedy,

entitled

THE

N A N A LOVELY *N A N A*

BLONDE

Or, the Miser's Pet

Adopted from material selected from Emile Zolos' intensely interesting novel of the same name.
AND terminating with a Quadrille D'Amour (love quadrille), in which Nana and her friends will illustrate

The Poetry of Motion *a la mode.*

At the Grand Central, early in '80, appeared Charles Algernon

Sidney Vivian, an English actor, who in '67 had founded the Jolly Corks, from which in time emerged the Benevolent Protective Order of Elks. Upon arrival in camp Vivian had ambitiously taken over a mammoth tent, a notorious pleasure resort, first known as the Great Western Amphitheatre and then as the Buckingham Palace, and converted it into the Vivian Opera House. He there presented *Oliver Twist* and similar plays, but the enterprise soon collapsed. After a period of idleness Vivian did a number of variety turns at the Grand Central until fatally stricken with pneumonia in March, '80. He was buried in Leadville, with funds raised by a benefit performance, and nine years later his body was removed to Elks' Rest, in Mt. Hope Cemetery, Boston.

Down the street from the Grand Central stood two other large theaters facing each other, the Gaiety and the New Theater, originally the Athenaeum. The Gaiety offered "Thirty Acts in Lightning Succession—No long waits." These included such typical fare as *Female Bathers,* a skit *Shot in the Eye,* and *Razulefrom,* an extravaganza so riotously funny that "two ladies and a gentleman" twice walked more than thirty miles to see it. Across the street James McDaniel, for years one of P. T. Barnum's agents, presented on occasion "Messrs. Homer and Holly, Emperors of Song and Dance; Miss Lola Cory, Fascinating Serio-Comic Vocalist; Miss Fanny Douglas, Charming and Vivacious Cantatrice; and a Sparkling Olio, including the acts, *The West Point Cadet* and *No One's Darling,* concluding with Lew Spencer's Great Act, *Who Stole Keyser's Dog?*"

"Enter the New Theater. Admission is free, but you must patronize the bar. We at once hasten upstairs to the first row of curtained boxes. We have barely time to cast a glance at the Negro performer on the stage, when the door opens and a girl enters. She is dressed for the stage in a short skirt, short sleeves, and low neck. She is decked out in all her war-paint and bedizened out of all reason with beads, flounces, feathers and spangles.

She closes the door behind her and trips over to the man nearest her and plants herself upon his lap without the slightest ado. We observe she wears tights.

" 'Well,' says she, 'ain't you going to say something?'

" 'Say what?'

" 'Why, the drinks.' "

One must drink copiously here, as at all wine theaters, to be welcome. One evening a gentleman entered with a guest, took a box, ordered two cocktails, and declined to order more. Girls came again and again, and finally two barkeepers, to order the men below. The host demurred, declaring that he would remain where he was. But he was mistaken, "for he went below so fast that he had a leg broken and his face bruised and battered."

"Within a few minutes our fairy returns with a tray of glasses —beer for us, and for herself a cocktail, with slices of pineapple. She raises her glass and nodding pleasantly to each of us, hopes we may live long and prosper. We ask the price and are charged fifty cents a glass for the beer, seventy-five cents for the cocktail.

" 'God, it's time for me to go,' exclaims the dancer, as she trips out and enters the next box, to repeat her performance there."

A riot suddenly breaks out below. A drunken ruffian has staggered in to amuse himself by "jerking chairs out from under members of the audience, blowing out lights, pushing over stoves, tearing down benches, and taking off doors." A shot rings out, and the bartender falls wounded. The ruffian, with smoking revolver in hand, runs out and "although hotly pursued by an angry crowd," soon loses himself in the throngs jostling their way up and down the raucous street.

At last the Tabor Opera House was ready, and all of Leadville society looked forward expectantly to a gala first night. The Opera House was not merely a theater, but served as an office building and an annex to the Clarendon Hotel, which stood next door. The ground floor was occupied by Phil Golding's Cabinet

Saloon, the "neatest in the city," where patrons of the drama could enjoy a drink or two, or even a hand of poker, between the acts. Up a flight of stairs, and to the front, were two vast apartments, each with a tremendous mahogany desk. Tabor sat at one, Bill Bush at the other, managing their many separate and joint affairs. The third floor was joined to the Clarendon Hotel by a bridge and had a number of bedrooms for guests.

Tabor leased the theater to Bill Bush, who chose as its manager-director Jack Langrishe of the old Platte Valley Theatre in Denver. Langrishe had traveled far since leaving Denver in '71, having trouped New England, Canada, the Middle West, the Pacific Coast, and Mexico. Joining a rush to the Black Hills, he was playing at Deadwood and other camps in the Bad Lands when Bush summoned him to Leadville.

After being many times postponed, the time drew near when Leadville could inspect for itself the "elegant brick Tabor Opera House, the most imposing structure in the city and conceded by all to be the finest theater west of the Mississippi." It seated 880, and was "handsomely frescoed and furnished with the celebrated opera chairs manufactured by Andrews and Company of Chicago," according to Tabor's announcement. "All appointments in this temple of amusement are first class in every respect; the scenery, artistic; and under the full flood of gaslight, the cosiest place for lovers of the legitimate drama to throw off the cares of life and yield to the fascinations of music and imagery."

The program announced for the opening night was *The Serious Family,* a comedy, and a farce *Who's Who,* the latter written by Langrishe himself for the occasion.

But the opening night on November 21, '79, was not the gala event anticipated, for just two nights previously the Vigilantes had struck, hanging two men from the rafters of the new city jail a few steps up the street. Their lank bodies and the menacing hand of the Vigilantes cast a black shadow over a frightened and suddenly sobered town. Retaliation by roughs and criminals was generally feared, and for several weeks all who could remained indoors.

Perhaps this explains in part why Langrishe, within little more than a month, tried out a score of melodramas, each followed by a short burlesque or farce: *Naval Engagements, Divorce, The Lady of Lyons, Life and Trials of a Factory Girl, The Dumb Boy of the Pyrenees, Colleen Bawn or The Bride of Garry Owen* ("with new scenery painted expressly for the play, including the famous Water Cave Scene"), *London Assurance* (with "none of the drawbacks incidental to the first presentations"), *Flower Girls of Paris, Ireland As It Was* ("with Mr. and Mrs. Langrishe in the great characters of Ragged Pat and Judy O'Trot"), *Self! or The Rich of New York, The Obstinate Family* ("given to a half-filled house, for the audiences, we regret to say, have not been as large as expected, or such as the company deserves"), and finally the renowned *Two Orphans*.

This last was so ill received that the *Chronicle* uttered a loud protest against the "ignorant dolts, who, not having the common sense necessary to appreciate the excellent and legitimate performance given by Mr. Langrishe and his most estimable company, must needs disturb others in the house by their senseless interruptions, loud laughter, and insulting remarks. It is a matter of sincere regret to all who feel a just pride in the intellectual and moral status of the community that legitimate drama should play nightly to empty benches when amusements questionable in character should draw crowded houses."

During this first season Bush and Langrishe undertook a daring experiment when in March, '80, they offered the camp a program opening with *Othello* and closing with the *Artful Dodger*.

"Greeted by one of the largest houses of the season, it is impossible to speak of the performance without indulging in lavish praise," read the critique in the *Democrat*. "It was a genuine success in all respects. Mrs. Thompson has a very pleasing face and well-rounded form, with a musical voice; her method of delivery is easy and her motions are graceful. As Desdemona, she gave entire satisfaction throughout. Mr. Thompson, as Iago, possesses a fine face and figure, which his neat and elegant costume displayed to advantage. Roche, as Othello, although still suffering from a rheumatic ankle, really astonished those who already knew of his talent. His Moorish costume was very picturesque. Mr. Sullivan, as Cassio, was the recipient of three rounds of applause during his repentance scene in the second act, for his elocutionary efforts. Mr. Norris acted Roderigo very nicely. This gentleman is conscientious in all he does and makes as much of his varied range of impersonations as the author allows. The Gilberts convulsed the audience with laughter in the farce of the *Artful Dodger,* which concluded a pleasant evening's entertainment."

An Othellian near-tragedy almost immediately followed the performance. At two in the morning, a boarding house on Main Street was awakened by screams of murder. A woman in night-dress burst from the door and ran shrieking down the street. In a fit of jealousy the "conscientious Mr. Norris" had cut his wife's throat with a razor, having observed her seated during the performance beside a "very prominent local gentleman," doubtless one of the Carbonate Kings, whose gallant attentions obviously flattered her. The *Democrat* had also noted the by-play, but added that the "gentleman's character is so entirely above reproach that Mr. Norris' jealous fears are groundless."

With a new Roderigo, *Othello* was presented a second time to an audience which filled the lower part of the house. But the gallery, "crowded to excess the opening night," was quite empty. Two evenings of Shakespeare seemed to satisfy everybody, particularly Tabor, and the company returned to more familiar fields with:

A Romantic Drama in 5 Acts
entitled
the
MARBLE HEART
or
The Sculptor's Dream.

Act I—Prologue
The Dream—The Studio of Phidias at Athens—A Reminiscence of Ancient Greece—The Power of Gold Gives Life to Marble.

Act II
The Play—The Artist's Retreat in the Forest of Fontainbleau.

Act III
A Sculptor's Studio in Paris.

Act IV
Fashion's Fortress in the Bois de Boulogne.

Act V
Realization of the Dream.

"False one of the past,
False one of the future,
Woe to him that loves you!
The Gold-bought smiles
Have ever been,
And ever will be,
Ministers of
Ruin, Misery, and Death."

Melodrama of this kind held the stage at the Opera House until the theater was temporarily closed for repairs and remodeling three years later. New columns had to be added throughout to support the building. Fallen plaster was replaced. The gallery was materially improved, "as well as the ventilation, which had heretofore not been what it ought to be. Improvements are also being made on the stage in regard to scenery, scene-shifting, and drop curtains, to obviate those ridiculous delays and hitches that have heretofore occurred."

Jay Rial's Ideal Uncle Tom's Cabin Company reopened the Opera House with an improved version of that classic, which was the hit of all these years. "There is more of action and less of dialogue, more of the absurd and comical, and less of the commonplace, in this version. It ends in a sensible way with the death of Uncle Tom, with the transformation scene added. Ferocious blood-hounds are introduced. Mr. Rial's blood-hounds are the largest and fiercest ever brought upon the stage, but they are not allowed to hurt the audience."

At long last, in October, '82, Leadville heard its first opera when Tabor presented the Emma Abbott English Grand Opera Company. Denied the great social event it had anticipated the evening the theater first opened, the community resolved to make this a memorable occasion by appearing in full dress to welcome the singers.

"Plug hats, heretofore a rarity in this region, suddenly appeared upon the heads of male bipeds. They also brushed their clothes thoroughly, and took their pants out of their boots, and blacked the latter; a few even ventured to put on kid gloves. The ladies thronged the millinery stores during the past week and came to the opera in full bloom; flashy dresses, white opera hats, and colors flying."

A society reporter noted a "white satin bonnet with a delicate spray of flowers and two tiny birds in the act of flying, with a trimming of ostrich feathers"—a Gainsborough hat of white beaver, with three little tips and one large plume—a handsome little red plush bonnet and one "too utterly pretty bonnet of pansies"—a fashionable "blushing bonnet" or two, equipped with springs pressing so strongly against the temples that they caused a rush of blood to the face, heightening the complexion. The Lily

Langtry coiffure, it was also remarked, had become very popular as it required little or no false hair.

King for a Day, Chimes of Normandy, La Traviata, Martha, and *Fra Diavolo* were offered from the repertoire of Miss Abbott, who was, above all, English and a lady. Devoted to the score of *La Traviata,* she objected to its libretto as immoral and rewrote it to remove every vestige of amorous passion. It was she who "conceived and executed the idea of singing 'Nearer My God to Thee' in the third act of *Faust,* who introduced Siberian bloodhounds into *Lucia di Lammermoor,* interpolated "Swannee River" in *King for a Day,* lugged a real live baby into *La Traviata,* had a trapeze performance in *Romeo and Juliet,* and a trained mule in *Il Trovatore.*"

Of the operas offered Leadville, *Fra Diavolo* was the most appreciated, but even in this the camp confessed to some disappointment.

"Only two shots were fired, and only one man killed, when everybody fully expected forty flashes of fire and at least half that number of elegant corpses laid out for the benefit of the theatrical undertaker. Then, the bed chamber scene in the second act wasn't all it was cracked up to be, because of Miss Abbott's prudent and prudish rendition of this little episode."

Emma Abbott and her manager were far more critical of Leadville, especially of its want of financial support, and both hurried away, vowing never to return.

Certainly, the stage at the Tabor Opera House was never trod by a more distinguished and exotic figure than Oscar Wilde, who arrived in '82 to talk to the miners on the future of art. Not met at the railway station by a welcoming committee, contrary to the camp's hospitable custom, Wilde slipped "quietly into the Clarendon Hotel by the ladies' entrance." A few hours later, reclining upon a couch as he panted for breath in the high altitude, he received a few of the curious. They found him to be "some six feet tall, with long hair reaching to his shoulders, with a languid far-away look in his eyes, and a mouth vying with Soldene's in size." To his visitors' obvious chagrin, Wilde was conventionally dressed in tweeds and not carrying either sunflower or lily.

Some local wits, so the rumor ran, proposed to attend Wilde's lecture in costumes intended to cast ridicule upon the speaker, leading the newspapers to protest that the miners should not prove themselves to be such boors as the students at Harvard.

"Whatever may be the value of Wilde's peculiar views," remarked the *Democrat,* "it is certain that he is a gentleman, and as such entitled to ordinary courtesy." Whatever Leadville's faults, Wilde was not insulted here as he was by fatuous wags throughout the East.

"I went to the theatre to lecture, and I was informed that just before I went there, two men had been seized for committing a murder, and in the theatre had been brought on the stage at eight o'clock in the evening, and then and there tried and executed before a crowded audience," said Wilde some months later in a series of stupid and almost incredibly naïve lectures to English audiences on his American visit.[4] "They [the people of Leadville] are miners—men working in metals, so I lectured to them on the *Ethics of Art.* I read them passages from the autobiography of Benvenuto Cellini, and they seemed much delighted."

A surprising number indeed attended Wilde's lecture, which was entitled *The Practical Application of the Aesthetic Theory to Exterior and Interior House Decoration, with Observations on Dress and Personal Ornament.* The majority no doubt had been attracted rather by curiosity about Wilde himself than by any interest in his "practical" aesthetics. For the reception of the "apostle of Beauty," Bill Bush had the stage at the Opera House "laid in a balcony scene and prettily adorned with bric-a-brac."

"Wilde stumbled on with a stride more becoming a giant backwoodsman than an aesthete, dressed in a suit of very elegant black velvet, which included a cut-away coat cut in circular form, knee breeches, low shoes, and black stockings. At his neck was a Byron collar with a flossy white neck-handkerchief, while from his snow-white shirt front glittered a single cluster of diamonds. His hair was very straight and very long, falling in a dark mass over his shoulders, and was parted directly at the equator. Without much introduction, he proceeded at once to business, pitching his voice at about middle C and inflecting only when tired nature asserted itself and compelled a rising inflection by a long-drawn breath. There was not a comma or a period in the whole hour, save when he came to a stop to take an unaesthetic drink."

Scant attention was paid to Wilde's address—and deservedly, if, as seems evident, his observations were fairly reported. He talked at great length of Beauty, nebulous and bizarre, and "said nothing but what has been better said by Ruskin and scores of others," as the *Democrat* remarked. "What he did say was in a dull, heavy, and uninteresting manner, in a monotonous voice, very much like a school boy reciting his lessons. As a lecturer, Oscar Wilde proved a conspicuous failure."

But Wilde was pronounced a "Prince of good fellows" by the miners, who were pleased to discover "no piousness in his nature." He in turn found them to be "very charming, and not at all rough." During his stay Wilde was invited to inspect Tabor's famous Matchless mine. He was dropped down the dripping shaft in a rickety iron bucket in which, so he said, it was "impossible to be graceful." At the bottom of the shaft his party was met by a dozen miners, each with a bottle. By invariable Western custom, every bottle had to make the rounds. Within a few minutes, everybody had had twelve "snorters." The miners without exception were rather dizzy, but Wilde remained cool, steady, and collected. He was loudly cheered and "voted a perfect gentleman."

After his lecture, Wilde asked to be shown the town. When he was led into Pop Wyman's Great Saloon, the largest and most popular of its day, his velvet coat and silk stockings caused some agitation among miners unread in art. But Wilde was soon drinking with them, and the evening passed quietly.

Wyman's Great Saloon was a complete pleasure resort—saloon, gambling hell, dance house, and variety theater, with luxurious rooms on the second and third floors for private parties of every kind. A short powerful man, florid of face, quiet in voice and manner, Wyman ruled his house with a firm but gentle hand. No drunken man was ever served at the bar, and no married man was allowed to play at the gambling tables, rules of the house which were strictly enforced by several special policemen. In his dance hall Wyman would have none but young and pretty girls possessed of some manners, and he treated them well as "Pop" (every keeper of a dance house was "Pap" or "Pop" to his girls). Orderly and well run, the resort witnessed few brawls and caused no public scandals. Perhaps no man in camp was more popular with rich and poor alike, for Wyman was kindly, affable to all, and genuinely good-natured, which can be said of few of his kind.

COME TO POP WYMAN'S TONIGHT!
Free Roll at 7:30
Everything Wide Open
Bible Reading by
T. Dewitt Talmadge of New York.

An "ecclesiastical yellow-back, a sort of religious Bowery Boy," as the newspapers stigmatized him because of his passion for cheap notoriety, Talmadge was delighted to read from the large Bible which Wyman kept chained to a mahogany pulpit just inside the swinging doors. All guests, from Paddy Ryan to Oscar Wilde, remarked on this pulpit, as well as the sign painted across the face of the clock above it, *Please Don't Swear!* In the dance hall, behind the saloon, Wyman had painted another sign above the orchestra, *Don't Shoot the Pianist—He's Doing His Damned-*

est! Wyman, too, had a flair for publicity of a kind and carried his small change in a purse fashioned from a human scrotum.

Wyman, some say, started life as a preacher, but the story is apocryphal. At one time or another he had been, in fact, almost everything but that. He began his career in Massachusetts as a friendly rival of Jim Fisk, subsequently Lord of Erie. Both peddled wares about the neighborhood from small wagons. Wyman was then shoemaker, mechanic, farmer, and auctioneer before coming to the Clear Creek camps to establish himself as a grocer. A lone horseman buffeting the snow, he rode into Leadville late in '77 as local agent of the Colorado State Lottery. This advertised itself as the "Grand Two Dollar Scheme," offering a first prize of $30,000. But the winner of this prize, curiously, could never be found. Such was the announcement in '78. When a similar announcement was made the next year, the *Chronicle* counseled the wisdom of finding the winner at all costs. "The public has an aversion to being humbugged twice in succession by the same party." Even before the Postmaster General suppressed this swindle, which by charter paid five per cent of its earnings to the State, Wyman opened a small saloon, which rapidly grew into one of the largest and most elaborate resorts in the West.

The Great Saloon paid him $45,000 a year, Wyman confessed, in spite of high wages to a large staff of barkeepers ($100-150 a month), gamblers ($5-8.50 a day), actors ($25-75 a week) musicians ($25-35), cooks ($15-50), waiters ($7-10), and dance house girls. Such girls were paid a wage never exceeding $10 a week and a small commission on all drinks sold to their partners. With rare exceptions, all had other sources of income ($10-25), which in the first days of the boom made many of them relatively rich.

Almost a lone monument to old State Street in the days of its shameless glory, Pop Wyman's Great Saloon still stands at the corner of Harrison and State Street, now a cheap frame rooming house, all warped and bent by sun and rain.

"The clock on the Grand Hotel points to one. Shots are heard from Carbonate Hill. The roar of revelry is on the increase. The streets are full of drunken carousers taking in the town."

So crowded are gambling hells at this hour every evening that tables are overturned and games interrupted. There is only standing room in the wine theaters, but the throngs are greatest in the dance houses—The Little Casino, Silver Thread, Dillon's, Tudor, Bon Ton, Red Light, and Odeon, among others. The last two stand side by side facing the Grand Central, lighted by its flares. The Odeon especially is notorious for its "forty-rod vitriol, its hat-rack females, its cheap faro brace, and general odor of degradation, attracting a case-hardened pugilistic crowd fit for treason, strategem, and spoils, particularly spoils."

Along one side of the Odeon runs a bar supporting a number of drunken men, all spoiling for a fight. Along the other wall are tables devoted to poker, faro, chuck-a-luck, rolling mustang, twenty-one, keeno, and paddle-wheel. Here grim, silent, unsmiling men "stake their all in the hope of bribing fortune for enough to buy a good-night slug of whiskey, a twenty-five cent bed, and a meager breakfast in the morning." A few win something perhaps, but most of the players slink away penniless into the night, some to drift down the street to the more disreputable dives below, the more desperate to prowl the back streets of the town in search of drunken prey.

At the far end of the Odeon is a small open space for dancing. On a dais here play three musicians. The fiddler is drunk, the banjo player has difficulty picking his strings, and the cornetist at the moment is carrying the tune. Several miners, either dead drunk or "bucked to death by the tiger," lie snoring in far corners.

"Gentlemen, get your partners for the next dance," shouts a

tall powerful man in shirt sleeves and red vest, edging his way through the crowd. He singles out a well-dressed tenderfoot and urges him to dance. The stranger hesitates, pleading that he has not been introduced. The "rustler" seizes him by the arm, leads him through the crowd, and all but hurls him into the arms of the nearest dance girl.

"Partner for you," he shouts at her and turns away. The dance is scarcely begun before it ends abruptly. The rustler collects fifty cents from each man on the floor and hands each girl a pasteboard check. The girl leads her partner to the bar to show her ticket, for a drink of bad whisky for both is included in the bargain. Dancing, if it can be so called, goes on till dawn.[5]

"Checks," calls the head barkeeper sleepily when the house has emptied. The girls hand in their tickets. Usually a little tipsy, the barkeeper slowly and methodically counts the checks of each, concentrating with rather painful effort until the task is done.

"You done good tonight, Em," he remarks at last, handing the girl $2.

XII

REIGN OF THE FOOTPADS AND VIGILANTES

"Footpads may rob a man in broad daylight on the most public streets, and there is no civil power in Colorado that can give the robbed redress."

RELATIVELY quiet in '78, Leadville became steadily more boisterous and lawless as the boom rose toward its height during '79. Among thousands of adventurers of all kinds, the new Eldorado attracted a large number of hardened ruffians from all of the older mining camps in the West. Violence and crime rapidly mounted to such alarming proportions that local newspapers soon styled the period the "Reign of the Footpads." There were also many complaints about playful promiscuous shooting in the streets. "It is getting to be a nuisance, this indiscriminate pistol practice from ten P.M. to daylight." The police, numbering only eight officers at the time, could do little as matters drifted from bad to worse.

Much criminal violence must be attributed to hunger and necessity. In March, '79, several minor bread riots occurred. Local newspapers suppressed the fact, but Governor Pitkin heard of it and promptly wrote Tabor to make a number of confidential and highly disingenuous proposals.

"The presence of so many people in Leadville, some of whom are idle and destitute, is undoubtedly an element of danger, and even a slight trouble, if not promptly checked, might soon become a serious matter." It might involve "not only the lives of good citizens but their property, including merchandise in the stores and money in the vaults of your banks."

The Governor suggested that "leading citizens take steps quietly to organize a military company, with membership limited to those only in whom the utmost confidence can be placed." He promised arms for a full company.

The Governor's allusion to the banks impressed Mayor Tabor, who next morning summoned a select few to a secret meeting. Among others, he invited Bill Bush, August Rische, George Trimble of the Miners' Exchange Bank, Phil Golding of the Cabinet Saloon, and City Marshal Duggan. Mart Duggan at the moment was suspended from the force on complaint of a barkeeper at the Tontine, who testified that when he made the usual discount on a "trade" dollar offered him by Duggan, the Marshal "became violent and abusive, drew his revolver and, threatening my life, came behind the bar, knocked me down, called me all kinds of bad and dirty names, and denounced the owners of the Tontine as thieves and robbers." Duggan was exonerated at a hearing before Mayor Tabor a few days later.

So nervous were richer and more respectable citizens that they recruited not one, but many military companies. All were ostensibly organized to suppress any outbreak of the Ute Indians, long ago driven far over the Continental Divide. In reality, the companies constituted the private armies of the Carbonate Kings, who armed and equipped the several companies—the Leadville Guards, Carbonate Rifles, Wolf Tone Guards, and the Tabor Highland Guards. Tabor's company mustered sixty-four men, all handsomely accoutered in "black doublets, with royal blue and red cord and facings, kilts of royal Stuart style, and stockings dashed with red and green." Each also wore a "sporan of white goat's hair with silver tassels and mountings, a Prince Charlie bonnet ornamented with silver buckle and plume, a royal Stuart shoulder plaid with silver buckles and *cairn gorn* jewels, and every man carries a *skein dhu* in his stocking."

But his Highland Guards neither quieted Tabor's fears nor satisfied his growing taste for splendor. Soon the Tabor Light Cavalry, beautifully mounted, came clattering along the crowded streets in red trousers, blue coats, and shiny brass helmets—very like the German *pickelhaube*. The company mustered fifty fighting men, commanded by three line and five staff officers.

"The staff officers, including General Tabor, wear black felt hats with a black plume and gold cord, and flashing steel scabbards on belts mounted with gold, and having gold buckles with the monogram of the company. The General's belt is of Russian leather, embroidered in gold by hand. The price of this article is $50. The sword is a straight one. The blade bears on one side the inscription, *General H. A. W. Tabor, C.N.A.*, and on the other, *Tabor Light Cavalry*. The General's epaulets are mounted with a silver star and ornamented with three-ply genuine gold fringe. The spurs of the privates are plainly formed of brass with steel wheels, while those of the officers are plated with gold. The uniforms of the officers are blue broadcloth, trimmed with gold. Their pants are of light cloth, with broad gold stripes running down the legs."

Tabor provided the squadron with stables, club rooms, and an armory, which was dedicated with a grand ball. The hussars wore "their tasteful uniforms to a man, with General Tabor in the full attire of commander as the central figure." In one of her few public appearances Augusta attended "in an elegant black silk, with white lace and magnificent diamond jewelry." Altogether, it was a brilliant affair, with the wives of the Carbonate Kings in "expensive white and wine-colored satins, light blue brocades, black velvets with white bunting, black silks with carmine bows and lace."

It cost Tabor $10,000 to become a general and immediately he led his men in an impressive demonstration to awe the lawless and hungry. The military companies in full regimentals, the police in their new uniforms, the Harrison and the Bush fire brigades, the

Tabor Hose boys with their nickel-plated carriage—all paraded up and down the town, trying to look their most martial when passing the vicious dives along State Street. But footpads, burglars, highwaymen, counterfeiters, lot-jumpers, mine-jumpers, road-jumpers, bunkosteerers, and ruffians in general—none appear to have taken General Tabor very seriously.

"HELL LET LOOSE," read the *Chronicle* headlines a few days later, "Bloodiest Night on Leadville's Calendar—Murderous Attack upon a Kokomo Freighter—Assault and Robbery on Harrison Avenue—A Tenderfoot Garrotted on Capitol Hill—Daring Robbery of a Man at the Comique—Arrest of a Notorious Confidence man."

Two murders were committed by "Big Ed" Burns, leader of the roughs and bunkos. Indicted for one, he was promptly discharged "for want of evidence." A member of his gang, one "Keeno Bill," wanted for murder, returned boldly to town, precipitated a drunken row, shot twice at an officer who attempted to interfere, furrowing his scalp, and again escaped—only to return shortly. "Slim Jim" Bruce, another of the gang, first shot down a "greenie" who objected to being swindled in a confidence game and then killed "Brownie" Lee in a quarrel over the spoils. Officer Townsend was shot to death by a prominent young lawyer in a quarrel over constable's fees amounting to ten or fifteen cents. City Clerk Murphy, removed from office for drunkenness and many gross abuses, openly threatened the life of Alderman Kavanaugh, who on two occasions barely escaped assassination at his hands. The owner of a dance house murdered a miner for slapping one of his girls and was acquitted.

Desperados jumped the Ten Mile Road and erected toll stations to levy tribute upon travelers. Several attempts to jump the Malta Road, the main highway, were forcibly repulsed. Lot-jumpers continued their assaults upon isolated individuals. In quick succession mine-jumpers attacked the Buckeye Bell, Black

Prince, Panhandle, Grand View, and Highland Chief, with several fatalities. The attack on the Highland Chief was led by City Marshal Duggan and Charles Frodsham, who posted a guard of sixty blacklegs to repulse any counterattack. Warrants were issued, but only Frodsham was arrested, to be dealt with shortly by the Vigilantes. When the Park mine was jumped, it was stormed and recaptured by the Miners' Guard, which then placarded the town with a warning to all mine-jumpers "not to repeat the performance upon pain of having their necks stretched."

New crimes made their appearance as the rush increased. Pickpockets plied their skill profitably in all public places of resort, finding their fattest wallets in the crowded lobby of the Clarendon. Rich ore was stolen in daring raids on shaft houses and dumps. To "ore agents" were added others specializing in horses, stoves, shoes, and groceries; the bold thefts of a clever "oyster-champagne agent" caused much concern. The school was raided time and again by sneak thieves who stole all of the children's apparel from the cloakrooms. Timber thieves were cutting their way through claims of others in the mountains, and many a brisk skirmish was fought among the pines. Ghouls robbed the dead not only of jewelry, but of their coffins. The armory of the Pitkin Light Cavalry was looted of arms and ammunition. Coffee Joe's, largest of the Negro gambling saloons, and the house of Judge Pendery, a Carbonate King, were dynamited. In a drunken fury Kate Armstead, Sioux-African queen of the quarter, fired and destroyed Coon Row. At least two attempts were made to burn the town in hope of plunder during the excitement.

"A person would naturally suppose that real silver is found in sufficient quantities about Leadville to make it unnecessary to make spurious articles or import them from abroad. However the supposition may stand, the facts show that a considerable amount of counterfeit halves and quarters are afloat in the city."

"There is a gang of ruffians in a frame shanty on Fifth Street who are constantly on the watch for unprotected females, whom they insult with foul propositions and filthy epithets. . . . The police should keep an eye on this gang."

"Last night about eight o'clock five men armed with revolvers and shotguns came bursting into the Long Branch Saloon on the Big Evans Road in great excitement. They said they were looking for the man who had attempted to outrage the daughter of Mr. Welsh, who keeps a saloon in the neighborhood. The little girl is only three years old."

Every night men were assaulted by footpads, not only in the lonely dark side streets, but on the principal thoroughfares. Many a jaw was broken, and many a skull fractured, in murderous attacks with sandbags, metal pipe, clubs, stones, iron wagon pins, hatchets, and axes. So many known footpads and bandits openly walked the streets and prowled the surrounding highways that stage companies practically refused to transport coin and bullion by raising their rates to prohibitive heights. Again and again the *Chronicle* gave warning of twelve "road agents" hiding in California Gulch, from which they planned to swoop down on the stagecoaches and raid the banks some noontime. The *Chronicle* had made the most alarming discovery, but did not yet dare be too specific.

Many men disappeared and were never seen or heard of again. It is no doubt true that in the restless chaotic camp many were reported missing who merely drifted away unnoticed. But it is also true that a number were secretly done to death—crimes practically impossible to detect, according to the *Herald*, because "victims could be buried in the cemetery without a certificate from the coroner, or even from a physician." Three well-to-do visitors, the *Chronicle* announced in June, had been missing several weeks. "They were taking in the sights, got separated from their friends, and have been seen no more. Their friends know these men were murdered. They were hustled into some dark alley— every alley is dark—or into one of the five hundred dark dens in these dark alleys, killed, robbed, put into a box, and perhaps taken to the City Cemetery and buried in an unmarked grave."

Yet hired pamphleteers and local boosters could attempt at this very time to represent that Leadville was as orderly and almost as quiet as the "most Puritanic town in New England." Reports of crime and violence, they asserted, were grossly and maliciously exaggerated. Certainly, that was not the opinion of the local press, which frankly admitted that the reports were "false" in a quite different sense—that the reality was far blacker than they painted it.

"Not one-twentieth part of the depredations committed by the several scores of well-known bunko thieves and highway robbers in the city ever find their way into print. None of the local papers desires to deter capital and enterprise from seeking this camp. They report only the most glaring crimes that are publicly known."

Although good citizens were clearly in a majority during even the worst of the Reign of the Footpads, they were disorganized and powerless. Nor could they place any great reliance upon the police for protection. In fact, the police themselves became increasingly suspect—and with good reason. Riddled with politics, the force was notoriously inefficient. "A man with influence gets himself appointed, is numbered and branded with a star, and turned loose. From this time on, he runs wild, as it were. He has no instructions what to do, and what not to do. He makes arrests when he feels like it, and sometimes tries and discharges his own prisoners. There are citizens who, owing to the murmurings of an approaching Vigilante storm, would be glad to see this matter changed."

Secondly, the police, from Mart Duggan down, were as violently lawless as any desperado. On duty one evening, Officer O'Connor entered a saloon and offered to set up the house. The Negro porter asked if he were included. "For reply O'Connor knocked him down, and kicked him in the head and groin." When O'Connor was arrested, a party of seventy-five men collected near the jail, "all armed with shotguns and six-shooters, the latter being frequently discharged." Led by ex-Officer Kelly, a desperate character constantly in trouble, the gang demanded O'Connor's release. A magistrate was awakened and hurried to the jail to free O'Connor on bail. "After the release, the crowd quietly dispersed and returned to its State Street headquarters."

Lastly and worst of all, many of the police appear to have been in league with criminals and bunkos. When honest men complained of being robbed and assaulted, they themselves were often arrested and long held in custody, ostensibly to assure their presence as witnesses in the event, always remote, that their assailants were brought to trial. One naive citizen, still bleeding from a savage attack, pointed out a notorious desperado as the offender, was himself arrested and thrown into the single small cell of the jail. At the moment it contained forty-four hardened criminals, including the offending footpad and many of his confederates. These pounced upon the robbed citizen and beat him almost to death. When he screamed to the jailer for help, the latter growled "Oh, hell, let them give it to you. Who cares?"

"There is a general feeling," remarked the *Chronicle* in reporting this incident, "that every man must be his own bodyguard, and be prepared to shoot down anyone who attempts to invade his personal or property rights"—dangerous doctrine no doubt, but inevitable under the circumstances.

Robbed on State Street in broad daylight, a miner gathered witnesses and followed the culprit as he walked boldly up the street. Upon meeting a policeman, all identified the thief and demanded his arrest. "The thief conversed with the officer for a short time and then handed back to Mr. Devins his two $20 bills. The officer and the thief smiled, and Mr. Devins, the man robbed, fortunately escaped being locked in a felon's cell."

As the summer of '79 advanced, considerable activity among both good and bad citizens became apparent.

"The respectables are busily organizing a Vigilance Association to hang the bunkos by the neck till they are dry. The bunkos, who complain of dull trade on account of the opposition of the respectables, are actively engaged in preparing to hang all those who have or may hereafter interfere with their profession. They consider themselves sufficiently strong to take charge of the city, choose their own mayor and city magistrate, and appoint their police force. There is a third party, consisting of highway practitioners, road agents, put-hands-up and stand-and-deliver professionals. An attempted fusion between this last party and the bunkos has fallen through. With these three parties in full operation, about every man in Leadville can make arrangements to pull hemp about four days after the ball opens."

But first, a preliminary skirmish under legal auspices occurred between the bunkos and the respectables. Caught red-handed, a desperado was indicted and brought to trial. All his confederates turned out in force to intimidate the court and swear mightily to the prisoner's preposterous alibi. With the explanation that "men look so near alike in Leadville that it is difficult to tell one from another," the jury acquitted the cutthroat.

"The bunkos positively, unequivocally, and without the least reservation of mind or matter, have things all their own way in Leadville," so the *Chronicle* concluded from the trial. "Footpads may rob a man in broad daylight on the most public streets, and there is no civil power in Colorado that can give the robbed redress."

Matters came to such a pass that Alderman Kavanaugh seriously offered a resolution that the mayor "be empowered to discharge the entire Police Force, Fire Warden, City Jailer, Street Commissioner, Deputy Clerk, and City Engineer." Mayor James spoke in favor of the motion. As every ordinance was flaunted and juries refused to convict on the clearest evidence, there was "no use wasting time, paper, ink, and light in discussing and passing ordinances for the good government of the city," he declared, adding ominously, "I have lived under no law and am prepared to do so again."

The motion was lost after long debate, and the usual formal processes of government continued to function feebly as the camp slowly drifted under the arbitrary law of Judge Lynch. In a last desperate effort to strengthen the forces of law and order, Mayor James appointed a private detective under his immediate command to spy less upon criminals than upon the police whose lawlessness and neglect of duty became daily more flagrant.

Storekeepers united to organize and support a private police force of eight men to stand duty from sunset to daylight. They were "to try doors, watch for burglars and other bad characters, convey messages, collect letters, answer calls, and make themselves useful to the public generally." The manifold activities of the Merchants' Police were reflected in their report for December, '79. Altogether, they answered more than five hundred calls. They picked up thirteen starved or inebriated men lying in the streets and rescued them from freezing. They discovered and helped to extinguish three fires—one from a lamp explosion, the other two bearing every mark of incendiary origin. They made fourteen arrests themselves and assisted the "Metropolitan" police to make sixteen more. They escorted seventy helpless or frightened citizens to their homes after dark, and quelled twenty bloody brawls and riots in the streets.

With the rush continuing from day to day, matters moved rapidly toward a crisis during September and October as cold, hunger, and crime increased together. The *Chronicle* announced that it was "keeping a list of those robbed every night until the Vigilance Committee starts giving hanging bees." Again next day, the editors returned to the subject.

"It is not generally known that there is a Vigilance Committee

in this city in full working order. A large proportion of their number is so eager to begin operations that they are out every night
watching for prey. It is the determination of the Committee, many
of whose members have been compelled to hold up their hands
and deliver, to burn the first highwayman they catch over a slow
fire until he is dead."

But threats of Vigilante violence impressed bunkos and bandits
as little as fire and militia companies on parade.

THEY'VE COME

First Appearance of Road Agents in
Leadville

They Bounce a Coach within Sight
of the City

Alarm knew no bounds next day when the *Chronicle* let slip
what it had long known—that California Gulch harbored none
other than that already legendary figure, that prince of highwaymen and bank robbers, Jesse James himself. In his party were
the two Ford brothers, Charlie and Bob, the latter of whom
treacherously shot James in the back three years later and was
himself shot down here in Colorado in 1892, at the boom town
of Creede, where he was running a saloon.

Although James and his gang were living quietly and working
hard on the claim they had staked in California Gulch, they were
suspected of the stagecoach robbery, but none dared move against
them. A few weeks later, when two other coaches were held up
almost on Chestnut Street, a great howl of indignation swept the
helpless baffled city. Jesse James was again suspected—most un-
justly, for all three robberies were soon laid at the door of John
Fraser, Captain of Police.

Lynch! Lynch! Lynch! cried the press.

Lynch! echoed the judges, one of whom naïvely remarked that

"every policeman in the city is anxious to have a hanging." An organized mob was now ready to move, but no one quite dared take the lead. It remained for a little German barber to precipitate the crisis.

Held up on State Street one November midnight, Carl Bockhouse shot one footpad dead and wounded the other, who managed to escape. Several hours later a youth of twenty was found bleeding and freezing to death in a doorway near by. Suspected as the wounded robber, he was arrested but stoutly denied his guilt, protesting that he had been wounded in a saloon brawl, as he might well have been. No one ever charged the youth with being a professional footpad, and he convinced many of his innocence. But whether innocent or not, a question that was never to be determined, he can have been only the clumsiest kind of an amateur in crime, as proved by the disastrous holdup itself. At worst, he was no more than one of many poor unfortunates driven to robbery by hunger and cold.

But the populace was not interested in extenuating circumstances, or nice questions of evidence. Everybody was jubilant that someone at last had dared resist criminal violence. Next morning Bockhouse, in his barber's chair, was raised on the shoulders of the mob and paraded in triumph through the streets, "with the wildest cheers and waving of banners." The celebration ended at a jeweler's, where the barber's admirers presented him "with a gold watch and chain costing $250, to acknowledge his valor and courage."

The morale of the respectables markedly improved until on November 19th, a few nights later, the Vigilantes struck under cover of dark. City Jailer Caldwell, so he testified later, was relieved of duty early and sent home. A heavily armed mob collected on the outskirts of camp, descended upon the jail about midnight, overpowered the turnkey with a show of force, unlocked the single cell, chose its victims, and dragged them forth. Somehow word of the proceedings had leaked out. All respectables but those in the mob remained apprehensively at home. All bunkos and bandits went into hiding. The streets were strangely quiet and deserted, remaining so throughout the night.

Those abroad early next morning discovered two lank black forms dangling from the rafters of the new City Hall under construction on Harrison Avenue. There, for all to see, they swung in the wind for many hours before they were cut down. Upon their backs the Vigilantes had pinned lists giving the names of some eighty undesirables who were to leave town before sunset. Below, appeared a warning that the Vigilantes had their eyes on many more whose names they did not happen to know.

The lynched were readily identified as Stewart, the boy suspected of robbery, and Charles Frodsham, arrested with Mart Duggan for an attack on the Highland Chief mine. The coroner returned a verdict of death "at the hands of parties unknown." But the coroner was alone in his ignorance, if it was real and not feigned, for all in camp knew the facts.

There were two active vigilante committees in town. One consisted of "Gentlemen Vigs, organized among the more wealthy portion of the community." As their ultimate aims were already rather suspect, another committee had been recruited "among the mining and laboring element." The *Chronicle* had good reason to know that the city was "indebted to the former association for the work done at the jail a few mornings since."

Why the Gentlemen Vigs chose only Stewart and Frodsham when any number of known murderers and notorious ruffians were roaming at large, notably Big Ed Burns and his gang of desperados, is rather difficult to understand. Perhaps they were restrained by the same fear of reprisal that so long held the *Chronicle* from specifically naming Jesse James as an object of suspicion. Stewart was not to be feared, for he was alone and without confederates. Frodsham commanded a crew of lot-jumpers, but they were really not desperate characters. Neither Stewart nor Frodsham had taken life. To many the choice of the

Gentlemen Vigs seemed so partial and ominous that poorer people generally, led by working miners, promptly organized themselves into an armed body seven hundred strong.

For weeks after the lynchings a cloud of gloomy apprehension hung over a subdued and strangely sober camp. Who would strike next, and where? Business was virtually abandoned. The military companies were ordered out to patrol the streets day and night. Roughs and criminals went into hiding, or withdrew. Big Ed Burns led his gang down the canyon to Buena Vista, the terminus at the time of the Denver and Rio Grande Railway, which was pushing on toward Leadville. Burns and his ruffians took the town by storm and terrorized it for several weeks. But the freighters and workers there rose in force, "selected a stout piece of rope," and set out to overpower the desperados. Unused to such open and spirited opposition, the bunkos fled in all directions. Leadville breathed a sigh of relief when word came at length that Big Ed had been lynched in Arizona for murdering a deputy sheriff.

During all this time Jesse James and his followers, although suspected of many villainies, lived quietly and unmolested in California Gulch. A year later, when he departed, one of his gang confessed that their exemplary conduct had not been as innocent as it seemed. Upon carefully looking over the ground, they had decided against action, he declared, because the roads of escape were too few. If true, Jesse James feared and respected local authorities far more than hundreds of almost anonymous gunmen whose brazen deeds, far from spreading their fame over the earth, earned them no more than a passing notoriety in an evanescent boom town.

Gradually alarm subsided, and the town began to talk of other things than the lynchings. By Christmas, some noted "evidence that a feeling of confidence is returning to the city, for simple drunks are again approaching their former average." But unhappily, as confidence returned, so did the bad men. Again the familiar faces of bunkos, footpads, and murderers were seen on the streets. All set to work with a vengeance, until in October, '80, crimes of violence reached almost incredible totals for even the most turbulent camp of 30,000 people. Within this month five were arrested for assault and battery, twenty-eight for assault with deadly weapons, and forty for murder—ten times the homicide rate in Chicago in 1929.

Another hanging occurred in Leadville in March, '81, but under legal auspices. Gilbert and Rosencrantz were publicly executed in the streets for several particularly brutal slayings.

Of the many hundreds of murderers in jail or at large in camp during the boom, these two alone paid the extreme penalty for their crimes.

But if the Gentlemen Vigs had little success in suppressing crime, they succeeded rather better in breaking a strike, apparently a more serious crime than murder. As early as June, '79, miners began to talk of organizing a union. At the time there were eight thousand of them working twelve-hour shifts at an average wage of $3 a day—a high money wage but, during the inflation of the boom, a low real wage. The authorities and Carbonate Kings both frowned upon the proposed union as dangerous and revolutionary. As the miners themselves proved to be lukewarm, each yet hoping to strike it rich and become a bonanza king, the union made no headway.

The first labor difficulties in camp occurred at the Malta Smelter, where furnace-keepers ($3.50 a day) and their helpers ($3) struck for an eight-hour day and the installation of a few fundamental safety devices. Within two weeks, three men had died of frightful wounds at this one smelter. Growing faint from the terrific heat and the fumes of the furnace, they staggered back against the boiling slagpots, to be burned alive under a flood of white lava. All were forced to work twelve hours a day and fre-

quently long periods of overtime, which, "in the poisonous atmosphere of the tanks, is enough to kill a horse," as even the
conservative *Chronicle* protested. Supported by almost the entire
community, the strikers obtained concessions.

Late in '79, encouraged by this, the miners began to agitate for
an increase of wages to $3.75 a day. They complained, too, of un-
necessarily dangerous working conditions. Many mines, the Little
Pittsburgh and Crysolite conspicuously, were paying such huge
monthly dividends that no money remained for safe or even economical development, resulting in great ultimate loss to investors.
More seriously, it caused the death of many miners from falling
rock in shafts and tunnels inadequately timbered. The nature
of the ore resulted in so much serious sickness that an attempt
was made to establish a hospital to treat miners for lead poison-
ing. Miners died by the scores of pneumonia contracted during
long exhausting hours in cold, wet, and unventilated mines. But
agitation among the miners at this time was checked when Gentlemen Vigs, fresh from hanging Stewart and Frodsham, accused
the miners' leaders of being "Molly Maguires" and forcibly
escorted them from camp, with a warning not to return.[1]

Late in May, '80, the miners struck. The immediate cause was
an order issued at the Crysolite that anyone found talking or
smoking underground was to be instantly discharged. Rather than
carry out this order, the shift bosses resigned, declaring that the
men worked hard enough as it was. The Crysolite miners selected
one Michael Mooney as their spokesman and under his leadership
marched from mine to mine. All men walked out, and by afternoon only a few carpenters and timber-haulers were working at
the shafts.

Next morning the miners at a great mass meeting on Carbonate
Hill formulated their demands—eight-hour shifts and a wage
increase from $3 to $4 a day. Then, some four thousand strong,
drawn up four abreast, led by Mooney on horseback and a band,
the miners marched through town to Fryer Hill. They marched

in perfect silence, and the community was awed. There was not a drunken man among them, and the best of feeling prevailed, according to the *Democrat*. A committee was appointed to confer with the mine managers, but as these had been instructed by their companies to concede nothing, they walked out of the conference and threw heavy guards about the mines. The Crysolite and Little Chief in particular resembled military camps, with pickets, outposts, and breastworks.

At another mass meeting on Fryer Hill the miners first pledged themselves to refrain from destroying property and then sent an embassy to ask that the armed guards be withdrawn. The delegation returned to report failure.

"Stop the damned pumps," roared the crowd. But Mooney advised peace and order, and turned the energies of the meeting to organizing a Miners' Co-operative Union.[2] A hat was passed to raise funds, but less than $10 was collected. Altogether, remarked the *Chronicle*, the meeting was "as orderly as could be expected with the thermometer nearly at zero, and with flakes of snow cutting the faces of the audience."

Shopkeepers, feeling the pinch from want of customers, called a combined meeting of businessmen, mine owners, mine managers, and strikers. The Reverend Mackay entered the lists with a hysterical appeal to the miners: "Look across the ocean to poor starving Ireland, to the working men of England, to the downtrodden of Russia; and I ask you, are you justified in the course you have taken?" Businessmen talked compromise and seemed on the point of triumph when George Daly, superintendent of the Little Chief and mouthpiece of the mine owners, made a most unconciliatory speech. Prophesying violence and bloodshed, he walked out of the meeting.

After a week of inactivity Daly resolved to open the mines and resume work at all hazards. The miners made no announcement, but it was rightly suspected that they would resist. Now the county commissioners, the Sheriff, and the editor of the *Chronicle* issued a proclamation calling upon all good citizens to stand behind the authorities in the assault they planned upon the miners. Such pressure was brought to bear that Mooney felt compelled to sign a pledge that the strikers would not interfere with miners desiring to return to work.

"From the moment Mr. Mooney relinquished the right to prevent men from working for less than $4, the strike became harmless. . . . Thus ended the great strike at Leadville," the *Chronicle* complacently announced.

But that night and throughout the next day there was rapid and continuous firing all up and down the gulches, with the Little Chief and the Little Pittsburgh as the chief targets. Miners returning to work were roughly handled. The Sheriff mustered the Carbonate Rifles to disperse the strikers, several of whom were shot and wounded. Two companies of militia were dispatched from Denver. Meanwhile, those rushing in to steal the miners' jobs proved to be so inefficient, and in their ignorance of mining so destructive, that most managers dropped all pretense of operating. They were infuriated at their inability to hire trained workers, asserting that most of these were being intimidated by a few dozen strikers.

"The authorities and managers are using every means to ferret out the men who are doing this work and giving them warnings, with the commendable idea of making short work of them and setting an example that will have a salutary effect upon all offenders of this class."

But nothing was accomplished and matters drifted along for another two weeks, with beggary and robbery on the increase, with Strayhorse and Big Evans gulches echoing every night to rifle fire.

The Carbonate Kings now frightened the community by threatening to close down the mines for six months. This threat appears to have been part of a calculated attack upon the City Treasury.

Abetted by the local clergy and press, which daily shrieked commands at the miners to return to work as the strike was hurting business, the Mine Owners' Association intimated through the *Chronicle* that citizens had signally failed in their duty and that the least the City could now do was to assume full responsibility for the armed thugs guarding the mines, including payment of their salaries at $10 a day. This was an especially brazen piece of business, for the mines had violently and successfully resisted every effort to tax them on anything more than surface improvements. One mine owner carried out the threat, ordering his superintendent to stop operations until November, remarking that it would then be possible to get "all the labor we want at $2 a day."

The threat failed, however, for the authorities dared not manifest their partisanship so openly. Increasingly angry, Carbonate Kings and shopkeepers now met in Tabor's vast apartment at the Opera House to organize a Committee of Safety, "patterned after the famous San Francisco Vigilance Committee." Pinkerton detectives were hired to watch the strikers. Arms for additional military companies were ordered. Next morning every store was closed at ten o'clock as shopkeepers, leading their clerks, marched them to the police station to enroll their names in the several military organizations. These were now organized as a regiment, with Editor-owner C. C. Davis of the *Chronicle* as commander-in-chief.[3]

At this point a demonstration in force was decided on. Trailing a large number of mine guards, the regiment marched through town, armed with revolvers, shotguns, repeating rifles, clubs, axe handles, and other weapons. Tabor made a martial address from the balcony of the Opera House. It shocked the *Chronicle* to report that the regiment had been greeted with hoots and catcalls by the street crowds, which seemed to be largely in sympathy with the strikers. It displeased Editor and Commander-in-Chief Davis even more to note that the miners remained "exasperatingly quiet."

Five days later the Carbonate Kings petitioned Governor Pitkin to proclaim martial law. The Governor agreed and Sheriff Tucker forthwith issued a remarkable proclamation commanding the miners to dissolve their unlawful organization and go back to work. A ten o'clock curfew law was established. Saloons were ordered to remain closed day and night. All without means of support were to be arrested as vagrants and made liable to a fine not exceeding $100. More than four hundred, including a number of strike leaders, were jailed.

Fortunately for the honor of Leadville and Colorado, which was thus spared an earlier Cripple Creek and Ludlow, Pitkin entrusted the high command to David J. Cook, the terror of all outlaws since the days of the Reynolds gang. From City Marshal of Denver, he had risen to become Major General of Militia.[4] Cook arrived, according to his own report, to find a fatal collision imminent. He discovered mine owners, businessmen, and property-holders arrayed against the miners, with a large lawless element playing one side against the other in the hope of plunder during the conflict and confusion.

Dispossessing General Tabor and establishing himself in his private apartment at the Opera House, Cook immediately sent reliable men among the crowds to learn what was afoot, especially on the part of the Committee of Safety. He quickly learned that the Committee was plotting to arrest Mooney and five other leaders, deliver them into the hands of military organizations friendly to the Committee, which would spirit them away and lynch them. Cook early discovered that the local military companies were not to be trusted to preserve order. From their ranks he carefully selected three hundred men and sent them out to report any suspicious gatherings, and to arrest all defying the curfew order. At midnight he learned that a mob had collected and was only awaiting his retiring for the night to seize the miners' leaders and hustle them away to their deaths. Cook met the challenge decisively with his usual fine instinct for fair play.

"I sent for Captain Murphy and Lieutenant Mart Duggan of the Tabor Tigers, a company formed principally of sporting men, who were opposed to hanging on general principles, arguing that it was something that might happen to anybody. On being questioned as to whether their men could be trusted to round up 'stranglers' or not, Murphy replied: 'Now you're shoutin'. If there's anything in the world these boys are dead sore on, it's stranglers.' " By squads the Tigers were sent out to patrol the streets, with orders to arrest any group of three or more, whether militiamen or civilians. Several arrests were sufficient to avert the storm. By daylight all was quiet.

Two days later the saloons were allowed to reopen. Next day the Governor decided to end the reign of martial law, but a large part of the camp protested.

"We request you to leave the matter of military law in this country in the hands of Major-General Cook. It is for the best interest of all," telegraphed the miners.

A few days later the strikers declared their willingness to return to work at their former wages, but insisted on eight-hour shifts. But the mine owners and managers refused even to discuss this, serving formal notice "that their right to regulate the affairs of their mines is absolute, and that they will not submit to any dictation as to hours of labor or rates of wages from any person or association."

Discouraged and exhausted by hunger, the miners capitulated, and three nights later the victors celebrated with a grand military ball at the Clarendon. In the view of the "Radical bonanza kings of the Carbonate Camp," as even the conservative *Rocky Mountain News* of Denver protested, "laborers have no rights. If they assert any, they ought to be hanged by the Vigilance Committee."

But if the Carbonate Kings won the strike, their triumph also marked the end of the boom, for it brought to light the fact that Leadville's largest and richest mines were nearing exhaustion from hasty and reckless exploitation. The Crysolite had actually been borrowing money to pay phenomenally high dividends. When this was discovered, its stock fell sharply from $46 to $3.75 a share. A similar state of affairs existed in the Little Pittsburgh and the Little Chief. The Little Chief should never have paid dividends of more than $50,000 a month, according to the mining engineer, George Daly, leader of the Carbonate Kings' forces during the strike. Instead, it continued to pay double that amount up to the day of its premature collapse. There were charges that the stock in all these mines had been manipulated by insiders, with the result that Eastern investors began to look askance at the camp.

"The year of '80 has been one of mingled prosperity and melancholy, of gladness and vicissitudes. The wild and reckless career of unchecked prosperity, the great boom with which 1880 opened, received a violent set-back early in the spring," as the *Democrat* declared late in the year, "and from that time on, all through the summer and fall, it was an incessant struggle with adversity, with widespread distrust, with undeserved obloquy and loss of confidence."

Although the peak of production was reached in '82, when the mines produced more than $17,000,000 of bullion, the camp in other respects slowly began to decline. In '81 it was remarked that the variety theaters and sporting houses were much less crowded and prosperous than a year or two before, and much less champagne flowed. Millions had been spent in these resorts, and "yet not one manager can be pointed out today as the possessor of a handsome independence," remarked the *Chronicle* at the time.

One after another, the banks failed, impoverishing many. The Grant smelter burned and was rebuilt in Denver. Fires broke out with startling regularity. The Windsor Hotel and the Palace of Fashion, the camp's largest department store, burned and were not rebuilt. Many fires, obviously, were of incendiary origin, but only one merchant was convicted of arson committed to obtain insurance on his stock and building. Tabor abandoned Leadville for Denver in '81, and was followed by other Carbonate Kings. The decline of Leadville was not rapid during the next decade, but continued steadily from year to year.

"The Leadville of '79 is now a thing of the past," wrote one who knew it then and came to revisit it in '89. "The omnipresent six-shooters that used to outnumber the men of the mining camp ten years ago are rarely seen here in public. If men carry pistols, it is in their pockets, and the shoot-the-lights-out ruffianism of the old frontier days rarely shows even a symptom of revival."

XIII

DIES FAUSTUS

"Lightning has struck Tabor again; he has made more money in four years than a man ever made."

B Y '81, as the Leadville boom subsided, Denver had established itself beyond challenge as the capital of all the surrounding plain and mountain country. It was no longer the wild, bleak, straggling settlement it had been during its early years. The railroads had come to make it an important distributing center. Increasing tribute was paid to it by farmers tilling fields along rich river bottoms and by cattlemen who had carved out great ranches on the Plains and in mountain parks. It had profited, too, from the great silver flood from Fryer, Carbonate, and Iron hills, and drew revenue as well from the Clear Creek camps, which were enjoying a renaissance. Senator Hill had built a large smelter here, and now Grant came from Leadville to build another. As the Magic City began to decline, it was Denver, "Queen City of the Plains," which attracted Tabor and other Carbonate Kings with the hope that here they might increase their fortunes and perhaps enjoy a few more of the amenities of life.

In comparison with Leadville, Denver was almost sedate. Already it had the veneer of civilization which it has never since lost. While not remarkable for either convenience or design, its buildings began to be less obviously makeshift. It could boast, as it did, of a number of large houses surrounded with lawns and trees.

"The distinguishing charm of Denver architecture," a contemporary noted, "is its endless variety. Almost every citizen is laudably ambitious to build a house unlike that of his neighbor, and is more desirous that it shall have some novel feature than that it shall be surpassingly beautiful."

In '82 Denver held a Great Mining and Industrial Exposition, with Tabor to the fore in erecting a large fair building south of the city to exhibit Colorado's products and resources—ores of all kinds, grains, vegetables, fruits, factory goods, and art. Gold and silver medals were awarded for the best exhibits of each, together with "a handsomely engraved certificate suitable for hanging." Any number of special prizes were offered—a plush piano stool for the best display of silk-worm eggs and cocoons, an accordion for the best portrait in crayon, cold cash (by Tabor and Bush) for artistic floral designs. The art gallery at the Exposition was remarked by the press, with the comment that "it is high time for our gentlemen of wealth to begin to encourage taste and show it in their houses."

As Denver grew larger and more circumspect, an odor of "moral" reform began to taint the air. The Denver Citizens' Protective Association was formed to prevent "ladies from killing themselves with tight lacing." The police closed all brothels except those on Holladay (formerly McGaa, later Market) Street. "Cigarette smoking is rapidly becoming a national curse," declared other messianic cranks; "no person can smoke them habitually without serious injury to health." Women of the town were forbidden to go driving along Exposition Road on the Sabbath, while a Law and Order Association concentrated its energies upon forcing all stores and saloons to close on Sundays, even objecting to the movement of trains. Led by Dean Hart of St. John's Cathedral, parsons thundered against the gambling house of Bat Masterson, old gun-fighter, and especially against the Palace, famous gambling saloon and variety theater kept by Ed Chase, owner of the Progressive of earlier days. Dean Hart pronounced it a "death-trap to young men, a foul den of vice and corruption."

But the popularity of the Palace was little affected. Among his "almost nightly visitors" at this time, Chase entertained Tabor, Edward Wolcott, and Tom Bowen, all soon to be Senators.

"I always took good care of them," said Chase later. "All of them liked to josh the girls and some of them would play strong, especially Wolcott and Bowen. Wolcott was at the same time the finest gentleman and the biggest loafer I ever saw." Chase was soon devoted to a new and most charming client, Eugene Field, just arrived to become city editor of the local *Tribune*. Sensing the beginning of a moral crusade, Field began to promote the cause in his own way in occasional paragraphs later collected and published as the *First Primer:*

> *This is a Bottle. What is in Bottle? Very bad whisky. It has been sent to the Local Editor. He did not buy it. If he had Bought it, the Whisky would have been Poorer than it is. Little Children, you Must never Drink Bad Whisky.*

> *What is this Nasty looking Object? It is a Chew of Tobacco. Oh, how Naughty it is to Use the Filthy Weed. It makes the teeth black and Spoils the Parlor Carpet. Go quick and Throw the horrid Stuff away. Put it in the Ice Cream Freezer or in the Coffee Pot where Nobody can See it.*
> *Little girls, you Should never Chew Tobacco.*

Tabor, approaching the zenith of his career, was the man of the hour, and his enterprise the talk of Denver and all Colorado. He established his son Maxcy as partner of Bill Bush at the new Windsor Hotel with its quantities of red plush, its sixty-foot mahogany bar, its charming Ladies' Ordinary, Grand Banquet Room, Russian and Turkish baths. "These oriental ablutionary parlors," they advertised, "are elegantly fitted up and handsomely furnished throughout in white marble."

Tabor talked of building a hotel of his own—"such a one as Denver never heard of or even dreamed of," he informed Bush.

On Larimer Street he spent $325,000 to build the Tabor Block, "something new in Colorado architecture." As Colorado granite would not do, stone was imported from Ohio, even for the sidewalks. "Each stone was chiselled and fitted ready for place. Thus was reared, like Solomon's Temple, a magnificent six-story building, with brownstone front, ornate but tasteful. Over the front arch are engraved the words, *Dies Faustus."*

Happy day indeed for Denver. And now it, too, was given its Tabor Opera House, which was to be as impressive as money could make it. With Frank Edbrooke, local architect, Tabor journeyed through the East making notes on all larger and handsomer theaters. Edbrooke was sent on to Europe to continue his studies there. In the end, however, Tabor was "practically his own architect" in designing "that matchless specimen of modern architecture, with its perfect plan and arrangement of detail, the auditorium with its graceful curves, its grand columns, exquisite carvings, and luxurious appointments, the stores opening on the streets, and the furnace, pumps, and artesian wells in the basement."

A five-storied office building of red pressed brick with white stone trim, "an oddity of architectural originality," the general style of the Opera House was perhaps most aptly described as "modified Egyptian Moresque," a phrase coined for it by Eugene Field, who would never be more amused than by Tabor during the next few years.

The theater proper, so Tabor announced, was "designed upon the selected features of the Covent Garden Theater, London, and the Academy of Music, Paris, and combines the beauties and excellencies of both." Italian marble was imported for pilasters, wainscoting, and lintels. Throughout, the theater was finished in red cherry from Japan, and the woodwork everywhere was richly carved and upholstered. Heavy silk fabrics from the looms of France lined the boxes rising in three tiers, with a rare Italian tapestry stretched as a canopy over each.

In the beamed ceiling was a large dome of cathedral glass, from the center of which hung an immense chandelier of cut crystals partially concealing many hundreds of gas jets. Two massive cherry columns supported the proscenium arch. Above, was a mural depicting Hector in the act of comforting Andromache as he sallied forth to battle.

The stage itself was large and well equipped, with an elaborately invested Green Room and many large dressing rooms below. Tabor spent a "small fortune on the curtain alone," giving the commission to a Robert Hopkin of Detroit, recommended to him as "essentially an artist in temperament, and as an executant especially strong and effective in marine compositions." But the curtain of the Tabor Grand, famed in the West from that day to this, did not present a seascape, but the ruins of an old Roman city, its former grandeur departed, with great marble buildings tumbling to the ground on every hand—a scene of melancholy desolation.

As the opening night approached, a heated and acrimonious debate raged on the question of whether it was to be a "full-dress swallow-tail affair" or not. Both the *News* and the *Tribune* devoted many long editorials to the issue. Tabor insisted upon the proper formality and was roundly abused.

This, as the *Tribune* (Eugene Field) protested, "does not furnish good grounds for an assault. The wearing of a dress coat has never been regarded as a crime, even in Colorado. A man who will not wear a dress coat on a dress occasion is a snob. . . . When Tabor is before the public as a politician, he is legitimate subject for criticism. When he is before it as an enterprising citizen, he is not."

Tabor had installed Bill Bush as manager of the theater, and for the opening the latter secured the Emma Abbott English Grand Opera Company, which explains Miss Abbott's visit to Leadville. Programs for the occasion were printed on gorgeous white silk. The railways offered low excursion rates from all points within several hundred miles.

On September 5, 1881, an evening long remembered, the Tabor Grand celebrated its opening. A drizzle was falling, unfortunately, as the fashionable and the curious departed for the theater. There was an annoying scarcity of hacks. Disregarding the rain, a large crowd had collected in the street to see the more eminent drive smartly up in their own carriages and alight under the bright marquee. A red plush carpet ran across the sidewalk and up the steps and into the lobby. Here, to one side, was a luxurious reception room where the women doffed their "cloaks of snowy plush" and arranged their jewels and costly gowns—"heavily-embroidered silken crapes and exquisite combinations of cashmere and swan's down, satin-lined."

The men improved the interval in the large and highly-polished saloon opening off the other side of the lobby.

Cheers went up in the streets as Tabor drove up and pushed his way into the bright and animated lobby. He was delighted with all he saw there—all but a portrait on the wall. Calling Bill Bush aside, he pointed at the portrait and, so the story goes, inquired:

"Who's that?"

"That's Shakespeare."

"Who the hell is he?"

"Why, the greatest author of plays who ever lived."

"Well, what has he ever done for Colorado? Take it down and put my picture up there!"

Denver society slowly jostled its way inside, to find the auditorium everywhere garlanded and festooned with flowers, with any number of floral pieces designed to spell "Tabor." It was a gay and exciting scene. Tabor's box, lined with white satin and sumptuously furnished, was wholly filled by a great horseshoe of flowers.

In time, the lights grew dim. Conversation dropped to almost breathless whispers as the curtain slowly rose to reveal—Bill

Bush, bowing and smiling, who was pleased to announce that Miss Abbott would now sing the mad scene from *Lucia*. It was received with thunderous applause, and "honest little Emma" was called back to be presented with a tremendous floral harp with the compliments of Tabor and the management.

An unknown gentleman then appeared upon the stage to ask if Governor Tabor was in the house. After a few moments, Tabor emerged from the wings, obviously nervous and flustered. With his stumbling gait more pronounced than usual, he crossed the stage to great applause, the audience rising to its feet time and again to cheer him.

This, unquestionably, was the high moment of his life, though Tabor himself may have preferred an evening two years later in Washington. But this evening of popular acclaim deeply moved him. It took away the bitterness of those long lean years of poverty and obscurity in the mountains. His present position of splendor and honor was brighter because of them. The audience rejoiced with him and bore him, for the most part, only good will.

But many asked about Augusta, who was conspicuously absent.

The gentleman on the stage at last made himself heard and, at the conclusion of a long eulogy, asked Tabor to accept an album containing the autographs of all who had participated in building the theater. Then, in behalf of the citizens of Denver, another speaker presented him with a gold watch and a gold fob, "engraved with the milestones on his road to wealth and fame," and inscribed with the motto: *Labor Omnia Vincit*.

Genuinely moved by the ovation, Tabor could only mutter a few words of thanks and acknowledgement, which dropped unheard as the audience rose to its feet to cheer him again.

The three acts of *Maritana* that followed were anticlimax.

A large audience, though not in evening dress, attended the second night and all through the two weeks that Emma Abbott remained. At her last performance she received many handsome presents—a huge star of tuberoses and geraniums from Tabor. The Tabor Grand then presented a week of Gilbert and Sullivan, followed by Lawrence Barrett in *Hamlet, Othello,* and *Julius Caesar.* The Madison Square Players came to offer *Hazel Kirke,* "doubtless better known to theater-goers than *Hamlet.*" Rafael Joseffy, Hungarian pianist, failed "to draw even a moderately full house." At the conclusion of the season Bill Bush announced that the undoubted favorites were Emma Abbott, Leavitt's Minstrels, and Hasenwinkle's Ideal Dramatic Company in *Uncle Tom's Cabin.*

Early the next year Oscar Wilde arrived. Eugene Field made a plea that he should be received politely, "if not as a lecturer, then as one who may yet rank among the strong English poets, for his first volume certainly holds out such hope." Denver was somewhat more impressed with Wilde than Leadville, saying that he "taught no bad doctrine and advanced no startling innovations. He simply said that the gentle and beautiful are pleasant in life and worthy of consideration. If aesthetes are fools, it is because they have a higher opinion of our powers of intellectual evolution than they should have."

But Denver, like Leadville, found that Wilde, as a lecturer, "never stirred his audience but in the direction of the door." After his address, when Wilde returned to dine in his suite at the Windsor, many visitors came pounding at the door, including Tabor, who gave Wilde a pass allowing him to visit the Matchless mine while in Leadville. "Mr. Wilde expressed himself delighted, saying that of all things, that which he desired most was to visit a mine."

This same year the great Modjeska, Christine Nilsson, and young Minnie Maddern appeared at the Tabor Grand. "Miss Maddern is bright, talented, and earnest, and it seems a great pity that her youth, beauty, and talents should be handicapped and hampered by such a conglomeration of dramatic rot as *Fogg's Ferry,*" wrote Field with fine critical appreciation. In later years

Miss Maddern returned as Mrs. Fiske to surpass Field's first estimates of her gifts.

Up to 1900 the stage of the Tabor Grand was trod by Booth, the Salvinis, Irving, Jefferson, Drew, Mansfield, Forbes-Robertson, Mary Anderson, Clara Morris, Lily Langtry, Ada Rehan, and many another famous player.

Though profits were relatively small, amounting to a mere $31,000 the first year, Tabor was delighted with the popularity of his opera house. Now he began to talk of building opera houses throughout the country. When certain of his mines in New Mexico promised more than any of his Colorado strikes, it was "openly stated that if they pan out, the Governor will enter upon the erection of opera houses in New York, Chicago, Kansas City, and San Francisco. Tabor has long had this scheme in view—in fact, his intimates say it is his pet ambition. He has divulged it to Eastern managers and they have encouraged him in it. All are to rival the Tabor Grand in splendor, the New York edifice to cost $2,000,000."

But Tabor, now at the zenith of his career, was too occupied elsewhere to realize his dream. His millions multiplied from year to year. His income from his mines alone at this time cannot have been less than $4,000,000 annually, according to Hook. The crash of the Little Pittsburgh Consolidated and the Crysolite had not affected his fortune, for he had disposed of his stock in both before the collapse. The Matchless continued to pay him $2,000 a day, and scores of other mines helped swell his purse. His milling, lumbering, real estate, insurance, gas, and water companies were still profitable. And he struck it again in the Tam O'Shanter and the Henrietta, the latter valued at $1,000,000.

From day to day Tabor expanded his operations. As old mines played out, he bought new ones—in Colorado, New Mexico, Arizona, and Texas. He purchased the Colorado Fire Insurance Company to merge it with his own. He bought patent rights to the cyanide process of extracting gold and spent $100,000 to erect a large mill in West Denver. He bought almost a half interest in the prosperous First National Bank of Denver, controlled by Chaffee and Moffat. He plotted with others to corner the wheat market. He speculated in corn as well. For $1,200,000, he bought a controlling interest in the Calumet and Chicago Canal and Dock Company, which owned a stretch of shore along Lake Michigan some ten miles south of the Chicago River; here Tabor planned a harbor and manufacturing center to rival Chicago itself. Finally, he organized the Tabor Investment Company, with agencies in New York, London, Amsterdam, and Paris, "to buy and sell mines, and fill orders for capitalists in all parts of the world." The company bought more mines—in Utah, California, Mexico, and South America. It bought a great tract of 460,000 acres in southern Colorado, and by a master stroke obtained a concession in Honduras of almost four hundred square miles, a vast empire rich in minerals and mahogany.

"In fine," remarked a New York financial journal after this coup, "the combined interests, mining and otherwise of Mr. Tabor, will make him the richest man in America in ten years. It is almost staggering to hear him talk of millions as glibly and unconcernedly as other men talk of hundreds. Mr. Tabor is far from being visionary. He does not look like a man whose head would be easily turned if the course of events should lift him to the highest pinnacle of fame in the councils of the nation or make him the greatest moneyed king of his day."

Tabor, in fact, had long had his eye on the highest councils of the nation. As lieutenant-governor, he had hoped to advance a step nearer his goal by succeeding to the governor's chair, but abandoned his aspirations as premature, realizing that more preparations were necessary to become a statesman. He had since been ingratiating himself with the leaders of his party. At the most casual hint, his purse flew open to forward the Republican cause.

"Tabor is going to have the senatorship or know the reason why money has lost its potency. He has more of that excellent senatorial qualification than any one or two of the balance of the Republican crowd," remarked the Denver *Tribune,* itself a Republican organ. But it added, "Tom Bowen's gold is a very nightmare to other aspirants."

Tabor had every reason to fear Bowen, another bonanza king, once a carpetbagger in Arkansas, where he had ultimately risen to a seat on the Supreme Court Bench, later becoming Governor of Idaho Territory during Grant's administration. Returning to Arkansas, he ran for the U.S. Senate and was defeated. As native Arkansans were coming into their own, Bowen chose Colorado as a new field of endeavor. For a time he drifted from town to town, practicing law, gambling heavily, running deeper and deeper into debt. At last he succeeded in having himself elected as a district judge in the San Juan Valley, in the southwestern corner of the state. There he struck the Little Ida, a rich gold mine, which soon yielded him several millions. Bowen was more suave than Tabor and an even better poker player.

A seat in the Senate fell vacant in '82 when Senator Henry Teller of Colorado was named Secretary of the Interior by President Arthur.[1] There was a great flurry in local Republican circles. Bowen announced his candidacy, and Tabor his. As a "moral man," according to the *Tribune,* Governor Pitkin objected to both, and the power of making the temporary appointment to the seat lay in his hands. Tabor annoyed the prim Governor further by publicly boasting, upon being told that Pitkin was cold to his pretensions:

"H'm, I've started for it, and you bet I'll get there."

All Leadville united to boom Tabor. All the San Juan camps favored Bowen. Leadville supporters obtained five thousand signatures on a petition urging Tabor's appointment. The San Juan camps presented one quite as long. At a great mass meeting in Leadville, Tabor announced that he would "use only fair means to obtain the seat." Next day a large number of prominent citizens, both Democrats and Republicans, journeyed to Denver in a body to argue Tabor's qualifications.

Within the week Pitkin announced the appointment of George M. Chilcott, lawyer and a Colorado Congressman, "certainly not brilliant but generally regarded as an eminently respectable politician."

Both Tabor and Bowen were hurt and indignant. One obstacle to Tabor's appointment is said to have been his refusal to promise not to run for the seat at the next election. Bowen blurted out, "Pitkin knows I am not such a scalawag as some fellows try to make me appear."

Both Tabor and Bowen plotted revenge, for Pitkin also aspired to the Senate. Tabor allied himself with the notorious Jerome Napoleon Chaffee, banker and speculator, charged with much sharp practice, to say the least of it—charged particularly with the crash of the Little Pittsburgh. Chaffee had served in the Senate and was suspected by all but Tabor of seeking to serve again. Eugene Field remarked the curious alliance:

> Chaffee had a little lamb
>   Who wore a fierce moustache,
> And people wondered how that lamb
>   On Chaffee made a mash.

> What makes this Chaffee love the lamb?
>   Incessantly they cried.
> The lamb has got a golden fleece,
>   The knowing ones replied.

Even friendly critics pronounced Tabor's ambition ridiculous: "He must know that he is not the man for the office and that his supporters will rest under suspicion." By all he was proclaimed a dupe: "It will be worth a great deal of money to Mr. Tabor to tumble to himself, even if it is necessary for the opera house to fall on him to bring about the desired result."

But Tabor entertained no apprehensions, confidently announcing to the Associated Press that he was certain of election. When the *Tribune* remarked that "this method of doing it costs very little, but is unsatisfactory, because not lasting," Tabor took the rebuke to heart and, according to Field, this colloquy ensued:

> *Are you pretty well up on geography? asked H. A. W.*
> *Waal, ya-as, said Chaffee.*
> *The reason I ask is because I am curious to know where in hell Phillipi is.... You see I met Governor Pitkin this after-noon, and says I to him, in a humorous way, Fred, says I, what do you think of my campaign now? Ain't me and Chaffee agoin' to scoop in the Legislature next winter as easy as rollin' off'n a log? Never mind, says he, we will meet at Phillipi.*
> *Maybe it's some little town down in the San Juan Valley, you know Pitkin is powerful strong down there.*
> *No, there's no such town in Colorado.... We must investigate this Phillipi affair, said H. A. W.*
> *Of course we must and if Phillipi hasn't been fixed yet, you'll have to draw a check and I'll see that it's solid at the proper time.*

In January, '83, the State Legislature met in Denver to elect two senators—one for a full term of six years; one for a term of only thirty days, to fill the seat temporarily occupied by Chilcott. Not only was Tabor confident of winning the long term, but the public in general and gamblers in particular shared his opinion. The latter offered bets of $1,000 on Tabor against the field but could find no takers, for it was almost officially stated that Tabor in his campaign had more or less judiciously distributed $200,000. Not altogether trusting Chaffee, he had also made a deal with Bowen, who was to throw his support to Tabor on the first six ballots. If not then elected, Tabor was to support Bowen on the next six.

On the first ballot for the long term, Pitkin received twenty-one votes, Tabor ten, and Bowen five in the Republican caucus. Day after day the balloting continued, with Tabor still the favorite. Once, Tabor received twenty-four votes on a ballot on which Bowen received three—enough to have given Tabor a majority if Bowen's men had supported him. Tabor was furious, tossing a note to the leader of his henchmen, "Bowen in bad faith. Adjourn."

Bowen now got up in joint legislative session to confess the deal and deliver countercharges of treachery. Accusations of chicanery and treachery flew thick and fast, and a motion was passed that votes in caucus were to be cast *viva voce* so that all could see how each man voted. "This probably prevented Tabor's nomination," according to the *Tribune*, "for Pitkin's followers were open to seduction." Finally, on the ninety-seventh ballot, Pitkin's men swung to Bowen and the prize was his.

Republican leaders now waited on Tabor to offer him the thirty-day term, unanimously. Tabor did not immediately reply, but finally accepted.

"It is not always that one who goes in for a big prize is put off with one seventy-second part of it as I have been," he remarked, "yet I am thankful and satisfied."

At the Windsor Hotel that night occurred a "regular old Wild Western celebration." Bowen's four-room suite was packed, and a half dozen bellboys were "kept busy opening the best brands of champagne." In the center of the crowd stood Bowen, "shaking hands and being hauled about pretty much as if at a dance in a mining camp." Tabor came in from his suite opposite, but soon withdrew. Later that night, he departed for Washington.

Augusta was not with him.

Indeed, they had just been divorced.

Late in '79, Augusta went home to Maine for a long visit. After her return, she and Tabor were seldom seen together. This caused no particular comment, for Tabor had long been accustomed to taking his pleasures without her. But day-by-day relations between them became increasingly strained. Augusta had developed a sharp tongue and may have become somewhat cantankerous with the years. When gentlemen of the cloth descended upon her to argue the merits and comforts of their several faiths, Augusta caustically remarked, "I suppose Mr. Tabor's soul and mine are of more value now than they were a year ago."

Angular and spare, now almost fifty, Augusta was certainly no beauty in the blue glasses she now had to wear to protect her eyes. But what moved Tabor to anger and disgust was her stubborn refusal to set up as a grand lady. She refused to entertain as lavishly as Tabor wished. Frankly disliking his parasitical friends, she was at no pains to conceal her contempt. She made it a practice of inviting the servants in to hear music, no matter what bonanza kings happened to be present. She insisted on dressing simply in her own restrained way. Tabor felt thwarted and frustrated by her want of any adequate idea of splendor.

Although few knew it, Tabor had deserted Augusta in January, '81, which explains Augusta's absence at the opening of the Tabor Grand. A few months after Tabor's triumph on that occasion, all Colorado was scandalized when Augusta charged in a suit of complaint against Tabor that he had contributed nothing to her support for almost two years, forcing her to support herself "by renting rooms in her place of abode and by keeping boarders."

Tabor had the suit quashed on the grounds that the Denver court did not have jurisdiction. But little more than a year later Tabor reversed himself and actually forced Augusta to sue for divorce, for he was in a very delicate position—just how delicate only he knew.

The trial occurred in Denver in January, '83, just as the state legislature assembled for the senatorial elections, and not three weeks before Tabor departed for Washington. The trial proceeded swiftly and smoothly in spite of almost incredible evidence of fraud and perjury on Tabor's part. His counsel blandly admitted that some months previously Tabor had journeyed to Durango, a small town in the far southwestern corner of the state, and had there obtained a divorce from Augusta, quite without her knowledge, for no papers had been served on her. Then, to keep the fraudulent and illegal matter secret, Tabor found means of persuading the clerk of the court to paste together the incriminating leaves of the record. Unfortunately, an election soon occurred, resulting in the appointment of a new clerk. Noting the strange state of the record, the latter unpasted its leaves and notified Augusta, who vehemently protested.

But now, under the heaviest kind of pressure—the reasons would soon become apparent in a lurid scandal—Augusta was persuaded to accept the inevitable. Tabor took the occasion to announce that the property settlement exceeded $1,000,000. The court record more conservatively placed it at $250,000-$300,000, including the Tabor house. At the conclusion of the trial, when presented with papers to sign, Augusta turned toward the judge and asked somewhat hysterically:

"What is my name?"

"Your name is Tabor, ma'am. Keep the name; it is yours by right."

"I will; it is mine till I die. It was good enough for me to take. It is good enough for me to keep. Judge, I ought to thank you for what you have done, but I cannot. I am not thankful. But it was the only thing left for me to do. But, Judge, I wish you would put in the record, *Not willingly asked for.*"

Augusta rose to leave the court, striving to control herself. But before reaching the door, she broke down, sobbing through her tears, "Oh, God! Not willingly, not willingly!"

Tabor arrived in Washington preceded by a story which, true or false, made him an object of ridicule throughout the country, for the newspapers circulated it widely. Tabor was becoming a national figure, if only for a day. On the train to Washington, according to the story, Tabor had ordered the porter to make up his berth early. "A gorgeous velvet cap, elaborately decorated, was first produced and hung on a hook for all to see. Next followed a magnificent ruffled nightshirt, half smothered with costly point lace of the finest quality, which the Senator said was worth $250."

Sworn in on February 3, '83, Tabor came forward to take the oath of office, dressed in black, with an immense diamond solitaire on either hand and large gold cuff buttons set with diamonds and onyx in checkerboard arrangement flashing above them. One Senator was heard to exclaim, "G-r-e-a-t God!" But the general impression was that he would "do at least as well as Chilcott, who won golden opinions by his silence and promptitude in voting as directed by his party. But he must shoot that diamond ring. If any burlesque actress should happen round, it might get him into trouble. It did once before, as will be remembered."

Tabor, it must be said, took his honors easily and attempted to adapt himself to Washington society "by relinquishing some of the splendid diamonds which, not out of place among the further western peoples, made him unnecessarily conspicuous here." But Tabor, as a "Wild Western Senator," was considered fair game by every scribe in Washington, and they made the most of their opportunity—often with poor taste and feebler wit. But their raillery stung the Leadville *Herald* and other local newspapers to reply with some heat that the "people of Colorado do not feel that they have any reason to be commiserated with on their representative in the present Senate."

But the scowls of local patriots failed to silence Eugene Field, who relentlessly goaded Tabor. Almost every day the *Tribune* carried fictitious accounts of the Senator's activities, many containing just enough fact so that they were not altogether fanciful.

According to the *Tribune,* Tabor said of his first day in the Senate that "already he had set in with the boys on the tariff game and proposed to stick it out until either the pot was gone or other hands were drawn." Next day, he was introducing a bill for the suspension of gold coinage: "Tabor, having obtained the floor, kept the whole Senate at bay for three hours, delivering the most powerful address heard in the Senate since the great French Arms debate. He analyzed the bill to the dregs, and was at times ferociously satirical."

And now President Arthur had asked him to join the Cabinet, and it became "definitely understood that the Administration will hold up all appointments until Senator Tabor gives the word to go ahead." A few days later he was on his feet to raise a question of privilege, saying "his attention had been called to a late copy of the *Wet Mountain Pilot,* in which occurred a paragraph designating him (Tabor) as an anomaly. He had determined when he started out on his political career to pay no heed to the utterances of his enemies. . . . But here was an instance where the libel was so unprovoked, so wanton, the slander so malicious, and the charge so appalling, that he felt impelled to notice it. How and at what time had he committed the offense? Who was his accessary to the deed? Honorable Senators would observe absolutely no specifications; why had his slanderers neglected to draw up a bill of particulars? He would tell the Senators why; the charge was unqualifiedly and ignominiously false! (Applause)"

During his thirty days in the Senate, Tabor made no address, seconded one motion, and introduced two bills of his own. One asked an appropriation of $100,000 to establish a military post in Colorado; the other, a similar sum for the preservation of the forests of the West, "for I don't see," said Tabor, "where railroad ties are going to come from unless something of this kind is done."

But the Carbonate King was not always at his desk, or in his study. Chilcott returned to Denver with the news that Tabor had been warmly received and was finding all the poker he desired, but still thought that "he was played low down and feels quite sore about the matter." And Eugene Field, in his generous way, had the Senator enjoying many a pleasant evening in the highest society:

"Tabor spent Sunday in New York as the guest of the Honorable Roscoe Conkling. 'Tabor,' remarked Conkling to a New York *Herald* reporter last evening, 'is a charming fellow. He is full of anecdote and *bon mots,* and quicker at repartee than any man I know. As we sat at table this afternoon, Vanderbilt, who is something of a wag, was inclined to banter Tabor for cracking nuts between his teeth, instead of using the silver implements provided for the purpose. "What has become of your crackers, Horace?" said he. Quick as a flash, Tabor retorted, "I ate them in my soup an hour ago!" Ha, ha, ha! a merry fellow—full of jest and song and mirth when occasion demands.' "

But Tabor actually had his social triumphs, one of which was the talk of Washington for days.

On March 1, '83, less than two months after his divorce from Augusta, Tabor was married at the Willard Hotel, "amid a fairyland of flowers," to Elizabeth Bonduel McCourt, of Oshkosh, Wisconsin.

The bride, just turned twenty-two, was golden-haired and blue-eyed, "a blonde of rare personal attractions, with a full fine figure and of charming manner, with vivacious and entertaining conversational powers."

Miss or Mrs. McCourt, as she was confusingly addressed at this time, was not unknown in Colorado as "Baby" Doe, the divorced wife of Harvey Doe, son of an Oshkosh lumberman. After their marriage they had come west to live at Central City for a time. About a year later Mrs. Doe obtained a divorce on the grounds of non-support. Where Tabor first met his bride is a matter of conjecture and the subject of many stories. Bill Bush later declared that they had first met in New York in '82, publicly and specifically denying the gossip that Tabor had known her in Leadville and "had fitted up a magnificent suite for her at the Windsor in Denver." Certainly, others had known her in the "Magic City," where she had danced for a time in one of the State Street wine theaters.[2]

With her own hand the bride addressed the invitations to the wedding, each with quarter-inch silver margins and engraved superscription, also in silver. President Chester Arthur received one. So, too, did Secretary and Mrs. Teller, Senator and Mrs. Hill, Senators Sawyer and Chaffee, General Charles Adams, Bill Bush, Tom Bowen, young Maxcy Tabor, and all of the bride's family. The McCourts were numerous, as Tabor was soon to learn to his cost. There were fourteen of them, "Lizzie" being the fourth daughter. Their father, old Peter McCourt, had come from Ireland and once been a prosperous clothier at Oshkosh, but was living in greatly reduced circumstances until his new son-in-law aided him, generously providing him with a comfortable house and a fortune of $150,000.

At nine in the evening the wedding party assembled at the Willard. The bride, gowned in heavily brocaded white satin, wearing white gloves, and carrying a bouquet of white roses, was attended by her father and mother, two sisters, two brothers, and two brothers-in-law. As the family was in mourning for the death of another brother-in-law, all were in black, though the ladies' funereal robes were "relieved by ornaments of diamond and onyx." The bride was a blaze of sparkles in a $90,000 diamond necklace, the latest of her many gifts from the groom.

In a few minutes Tabor appeared with his attendants—Bill Bush and Tom Bowen, the Senator's rival, who is said to have exerted his utmost powers in finally persuading President Arthur to attend.

In one of the larger hotel parlors the bride and groom took their place before a table richly draped in cardinal red, bearing a "candelabrum with ten tapers, shedding a subdued light over all." The ceremony, an abbreviated nuptial mass, was performed by the Reverend P. L. Chappelle, D.D., of St. Matthew's. Upon its conclusion the bride was "fittingly congratulated by the President, her husband and family, and attending friends," and the party pushed "through the folding doors to the collation chambers," profusely decorated for the occasion.

In the center of the room, standing six feet high upon a great basin of blossoms, rose a "massive wedding bell of white roses, surmounted by a Cupid's bow, with an arrow on the string, tipped with a heart of violets, the rest being composed of various hued roses." At either end of the huge table stretching the length of the parlor, was a "colossal four-leaf clover in red and white roses and carnations." A canopy of flowers with trailing foliage provided a bower for the separate table required to support the huge wedding cake, "chaste in design." Sweet-smelling violets were strewn about everywhere, even on the floors. Flowers appeared on "each dish of dainty viands," and were garlanded about the champagne buckets.

"The collation ended, the party engaged in general conversation, the President paying particular attention to the bride. Just before he left he expressed a wish for a rose from her bouquet, which she quickly handed to him. At 10:45, President Arthur took his departure. He was followed by the other guests, and by midnight the gay reception room was deserted."

XIV

BACK TO THE EARTH AGAIN

"Trusting to God that something will be done for me . . ."

TABOR was elated by his social triumph and at no pains to conceal his pride in himself and his young and beautiful bride. On his last day in the Senate, she sat prominently in one of the balconies, sparkling with diamond necklace, earrings, and bracelets, attired in one of her trousseau costumes, a brown silk with a snug bodice, "accentuated by a bejeweled girdle in the form of a serpent, with diamond eyes, ruby tongue, and a long tail of emeralds." As Tabor went from desk to desk collecting autographs in a large album, he pointed out his wife to his colleagues. And with that, though he could never have believed it at the moment, Tabor took leave of public life.

"Special advices from Washington agree that yesterday was the most exciting day ever witnessed in the United States Senate," Eugene Field romanticized. "It terminated the Honorable H. A. W. Tabor's career in that august body. . . . Early in the day the streets were alive with people hurrying to the Capitol. Flags were hung at half-mast. . . . The galleries were filled to overflowing with the most beautiful and accomplished ladies of the Republic and the floor of the Senate was crowded with eminent persons.

"When Senator Tabor entered the room, bearing a new patent-leather grip-sack and wearing a superb trousseau of broadcloth and diamonds, the vast crowd was as hushed as the grave. Senator Sherman admitted a series of resolutions lamenting Tabor's departure. It was unanimously adopted, Senator Tabor maintaining his characteristic modesty to the last and abstaining from voting. The Senator rose to speak. As he proceeded to recount his services, love of country, and devotion to the public weal, men groaned in speechless agony and whole platoons of police were kept busy carrying insensible ladies from the galleries.

"At night there was a torchlight parade in ex-Senator Tabor's honor. It was an imposing affair, numbering 12,000 persons in line and the entire American Navy on wheels, and was gorgeously illuminated. The crowning feature of the procession was a huge papier-mâché yacht, representing the Ship of State and manned by forty-one beautiful young girls, representing the States and Territories, from Oshkosh."

On this day, however, the Tabors provided a real sensation. Father Chappelle, who had officiated at the wedding, publicly complained of being imposed upon and returned the $200 fee given him by Tabor. Had he known that both Tabor and his bride had been divorced, he would never have married them against the canon of the Catholic Church, said Father Chappelle, adding that he had taken every reasonable precaution to satisfy himself of the eligibility of the couple to receive the marriage sacrament. When the bride's father had been asked if he knew of any impediment to the marriage, he clearly answered that he did not. "To say all in a few words, I was shamefully deceived by the McCourt family," declared the priest, who threatened to have the marriage declared illicit by carrying the question to the highest authorities in the Church.

To this Tabor replied, through the press, that "Father Chappelle did not ask either me or Miss McCourt whether either of us had been divorced or not."

Next day, there was an even greater sensation when the news leaked out that the Senator and his "bride" had been man and wife for some time, having been secretly married at St. Louis six months previously—three months before Tabor had secured a legal divorce from Augusta. It now became plain why Augusta had left the courtroom crying, "Not willingly, not willingly!" She had sacrificed herself to spare Tabor a trial for bigamy just as he was preparing to scale the heights.

A final shudder ran through Washington, so the New York *Tribune* reported, when the Senator announced that he liked the Capital so well that he proposed to build a large house there in which to entertain and spend his winters. "There has been nothing so picturesquely vulgar as this gorgeous hotel wedding of a pair married months already," as several exclaimed. But some were inclined to look upon the Carbonate King's exploits rather more tolerantly.

"If he wants to marry a wife, and Mrs. Teller and Mrs. Belford refuse to come to the wedding, he can get on just the same. Still, it is sure to be mentioned. When a man steps out into the public square and has a band play behind him, he must expect people to look and listen. The man who insists upon Tabor's sort of a good time must take it and be content without honors or office." [1]

Returning to Denver, Tabor and his wife established themselves in a large suite of rooms at the Windsor, being welcomed by few but the members of two German Athletic societies, who gave them a serenade upon arrival and carried them off to a banquet at which the Senator was honored as one of the first Americans to identify himself with a movement which "aims to educate our youth not only in physical, but also in moral development." Tabor and his bride, on a visit to Leadville, were received by the Tabor Light Cavalry and the Tabor Hose Company, which escorted them to the apartment prepared in their honor.

Shortly, the peace was disturbed again. A most scandalous public quarrel broke out when Bill Bush was supplanted as manager of the Tabor Grand by the bride's brother, Peter McCourt. Tabor brought suit against Bush on a charge of embezzling $2,000.

Bush was acquitted and replied with a terrific blast. In a deposition laid before the Supreme Court, Bush claimed that Tabor owed him $100,000 for various curious services rendered. He demanded $5,000 for time and influence employed in helping Tabor "emerge from the obscurity of California Gulch into the realms of statesmanship." He asked the sum of $10,000 for securing testimony and witnesses for Tabor's fraudulent divorce at Durango and for persuading Augusta at last to bring suit and unravel the bigamous tangle. He asked a larger sum for "aiding him in effecting a marriage with the said Mrs. Doe, commonly called Baby Doe." He asked $1,547 for bribes paid to legislators during the senatorial election, in sums ranging from $5 to $475.

The quarrel between Tabor and Bush was never mended. But Bush remained a friend and partner of young Maxcy Tabor, who sided with Augusta after the divorce. With her financial aid, the two leased the large Brown Palace Hotel, perhaps still the finest in Denver, upon its completion in '91. Augusta lost most of her investments during the panic of '93, and two years later she suddenly died while on a visit to California, having lived virtually as a recluse since the day of the divorce.

The sight of Tabor and Bush quarreling publicly and scandalously alienated many of the Senator's friends and delighted his enemies. The smelter king, Senator N. P. Hill, his most outspoken enemy within the Republican party, seized the occasion to deliver Tabor what he hoped was a death-blow, and even the once friendly *Tribune* scathingly attacked the Carbonate King.

"Tabor is an utter disgrace to the State; he disgraced it in private life; he disgraced it as a public officer; he made it the jeer of the country during his brief but petty career in the Senate. Essentially a vulgarian of doubtful antecedents, he strove to buy his way into political position. To a small extent he succeeded. He bought the cheap creatures of the Legislature for the first place in its gift, but did not buy them in sufficient number, and when this failed, he begged his way into the second position.

Society in Denver gave its verdict on his course when it recognized the kindly old lady whom, in his gulch ignorance, he put aside. He is a social and political outcast in all senses of the word."

Even the Leadville *Democrat* protested against this savage editorial. But no one hurried forward to defend "Ex-Senator Night Shirt" by attempting to justify his course.

Shortly after his return to Denver, Tabor announced his intention of building a great mansion of solid mahogany to be imported from his immense concession in Honduras. Too involved in business affairs to carry out this project, he soon abandoned it and bought a city block in Denver's fashionable quarter, remodeling the large house which stood on it into a tremendous Italian villa. It impressed all with its lavish proportions and great lawn, on which sported iron dogs and deer. Greek statuary and a hundred strutting peacocks were later added.

Tabor presented his wife with a magnificent carriage in black and pale blue enamel, upholstered in azure satin. Four black horses richly caparisoned drew it through the streets, with two Negroes in scarlet liveries perched solemnly on the box behind. Tabor continued to shower his wife with diamonds and jewelry of all kinds, and of a painter named Heyde ordered five oil portraits of her, each in a different pose and costume.

Though the Tabors entertained many distinguished people of the theater and a number of visiting celebrities, Denver "society" shunned the house. Augusta Tabor was always formally correct, bowing but never speaking when she chanced to meet her former husband and his new wife. Then one evening, in Tabor's absence from the city, the doorbell rang and, to the consternation of Baby Doe, Augusta was announced.

"Good evening, Mrs. Tabor," she said. "I have come here with the greatest reluctance. But it seemed to me that if I called, others might follow." After a desultory conversation of several minutes,

Augusta departed. None followed her example, as she had hoped, and the two women never met again.

Two daughters were born to Baby Doe. The first was named Elizabeth Bonduel Lillie, and began to attend the theater regularly from the time she was six weeks old. The baby seldom cried, it was remarked, and as she grew older, amused herself "by capering all through the play in her father's box." She was said at the time to be the most photographed baby in the world, "always posing herself without assistance," and as the child of his later years was her father's idol.

When three months old, "Baby" Tabor was taken to Oshkosh to be christened in the church attended by the McCourts. Her robes for the occasion "were marvelously fine, being of the most costly point lace, the two flounces on the robe costing $500 apiece. They were covered with a cloak of white embroidered velvet trimmed with point lace and marabou feathers. Her tiny French felt hat was heavy with marabou tips, each one of which cost not less than $10. The baby's wardrobe at the present time consists of fifty lace robes and dainty velvet gowns of the richest description. She has a profusion of jewels of rare and unique designs and of great value, presented by her father and by friends everywhere, even from Europe; and every pin placed in her clothes is garnished with a diamond."

In '89 a second daughter was born and named Rose Mary Echo Silver Dollar Tabor. She, too, enjoyed her triumph in an $800 christening robe, but she was not to know many years of splendor.

Tabor, little affected by sharp and general criticism, still hoped to be returned to high office. Politically, he was only half ostracized, as it were. His party was always willing to accept his contributions to its funds but persistently denied him any customary reward. Tabor sought the governorship in 1884.[2] He spent $75,000 on his own campaign, donating an additional $40,000 to the party's coffers. But another received the nomination in spite of all promises given him by party leaders. Two years later he poured out money to secure the senatorial nomination and was defeated. Again in '88 he sought to be governor. It is an interesting speculation how long Tabor would have continued spending money for the ultimate benefit of enemies and rivals in his party, had he not now begun to lose battles on the main front.

Investing injudiciously and speculating wildly, indulging his extravagance by purchasing a yacht in New York, Tabor was in financial difficulties as early as '86. Indeed, when Tabor had been making his only successful campaign for the Senate in '82, one responsible newspaper attacked him solely on the grounds of insolvency. The attack was no doubt premature, but certainly Tabor was soon hopelessly involved.

One by one, his mines "petered out." He bought others, only to spend hundreds of thousands in vain attempts to make them profitable. Not only did income from his mines dwindle, but his capital funds began to vanish rapidly. He lost a half million on the Calumet Dock project along Lake Michigan, and another half million speculating in the grain pits. His copper lands in Texas proved to be valueless. His realty, lumber, gas, and water companies at Leadville paid smaller dividends and then became a liability as the camp declined. His life and fire insurance companies had to be dissolved. He had literally thrown away millions in politics. Although he had long been an excellent poker player, now card sharpers preyed on him. Stories of his heavy losings at this time are many and too circumstantial to be altogether ignored.

Pressed for money, Tabor first mortgaged his beloved Matchless, the only one of his Leadville mines that continued to run a trickle of silver. Soon Tabor had little income but that from his Denver properties, and now he had to mortgage these, one after another—finally, the Opera House.

At this time Tabor might easily have liquidated his unprofitable enterprises, according to friends, and left himself in secure possession of a considerable fortune. But he was determined to hold all, still having faith in "Tabor Luck," at which he himself had so often smiled. Unfortunately, he delayed too long in attempting to salvage something from his crumbling empire. He cherished illusory hopes not merely of restoring but of increasing his fortune up to the very day the great panic of '93 struck the West to close twelve strong banks in Denver within three days. The panic here and in the mountains was intensified by the repeal of the Sherman Act. Suddenly, the Federal government ceased buying for coinage purposes 4,500,000 ounces of silver a month. Throughout the world the price of silver dropped sharply. What little activity remained in the silver camps abruptly ceased.

Tabor strove desperately to hold on. With the last of his capital, increased by some small loans, he obtained an option on the Phil Sheridan and Free Coinage groups of mines in the new Cripple Creek gold field, lying just behind Pike's Peak and in its day the richest in the world. Here, in Poverty Gulch, almost incredible treasure had been discovered in 1891 by "Crazy Bob" Womack, a cowhand on the Broken Box Ranch, who celebrated by riding into town to go on a roaring drunk, galloping up and down the streets of Colorado City, accepting $500 for a claim that soon produced $5,000,000.[3] Tabor had no luck here. His stake was soon used up, and he had to relinquish his options at a loss. The mines almost immediately began to yield millions to their new owners, but Tabor had not yet lost hope of striking it rich in a new Little Pittsburgh or another Crysolite.

His sole remaining hope—ironically enough—was the Eclipse, up Boulder Creek, which seemed to be a fair prospect. Being quite without funds, Tabor journeyed to Colorado Springs to see an old acquaintance, Winfield Scott Stratton, the carpenter-prospector whom he had hired not so many years before to erect the huge Silver Dollar symbol on the roof of his now defunct Bank of Leadville. Stratton was now one of the bonanza kings, having recently unearthed fabulous golden treasure in his Independence mine at Cripple Creek after vainly prowling the mountains for more than twenty years.

"Senator Tabor! Sir, I am honored," exclaimed Stratton, warmly greeting the bewildered old man, for Stratton, though eccentric and often cruel in many things, never forget anyone who had done him a favor in his less fortunate days. To a man who had once given him a dollar when he was hungry, he promptly sent $1,000 out of his first profits.[4]

Tabor hesitantly explained his mission, saying that if he had money to develop the Eclipse, he could get along and perhaps might be able even to reopen the Matchless:

"You know, Mr. Stratton, there still is silver in the mine, and I always say to Mrs. Tabor, 'Hang on to the Matchless!' "

"Now, Senator, don't say another word," interrupted Stratton, reaching for a pen. "You know how deeply I appreciate this honor. Will this be enough to get started on?"

Glancing at Stratton's check for $15,000, the only substantial aid he received during all these tragic years, Tabor flushed, partly from surprise and excitement, partly from embarrassment. Protesting that he could accept the money only as a loan and not as a gift, he offered as collateral a deed to a mine in Arizona, which Stratton knew to be worthless. Accordingly, a ninety-day note was drawn up, and with a pathetic flourish it was signed, "The Tabor Mines and Mill Company, by H. A. W. Tabor."[5]

The $15,000 was soon exhausted, and in a frantic effort to save at least the Opera House, Tabor wrote Senator Henry Teller a most naïve and moving letter:

> *Senator Teller*
> *My Dear friend*
> *To fully let you know the status of affairs relative to the blocks, I will tell you what Mrs. Smith told me this week. She told me a party told her he had the money in hand to loan her to pay off the North Western [Insurance Company]*

but that he would not talk to her about it until she was in possession. I today tried to get a thirty days option from her and she flatly told me she would not take less than four hundred thousand dollars, but of course if we can establish it as a mortgage in the upper Court she will have to accept three hundred and thirty thousand dollars ($330,000) the amount at which she bid it in at. She was very hard on me this morning and was very determined to get this buildings. If she gets possession it will cost me many thousands of dollars on account of her management, therefore we must leave nothing undone to defeat the same. On account of my being such a strong advocate of Free Coinage *it is at this time impossible for me to make a loan. I feel that the Judges of this silver state should protect me until after the elections for then there will be no trouble to make a loan. But now Senator you know that it is exactly the same as in a time of actual war and the Judges have power to issue any order that will protect their own and I feel that I belong to them for my funds were always freely used for the good of the party and country. and if I have it again it will be the same and all I want is to keep what belongs to me and lead a quiet home life. And I feel that if you will go now to the supreme court or court of appeals and ask them to issue an order to Judge Johnson restraining him from giving her possession until my time expires for redemption with the North Western which would leave her three months to secure a loan if I failed she being a Judgement creditor I feel senator that the judges will not refuse you but that they will recognize that there is an actual war. It will not only save me but it will help our silver cause and such an act will be admired by the toiling masses. Senator I believe if you ask Judge Johnson to make an order that the assignees stay in possession for both parties the full time of my redemption with the North Western giving Mrs Smith all the money over and above running expenses because the*

*assignees are economical and trustworthy that he will do it
for you and the silver cause. But I feel sure that the upper
court will do it for you alone. The case comes up before Judge
Johnson at ten on Monday next. Trusting in God that something will be done for me I remain*

> *Very sincerely your friend*
> *H. A. W. Tabor*

Senator Teller failed, if indeed he tried, to persuade the United
States Supreme Court to declare a state of war in Tabor's behalf.
Now the Tabor Grand passed from his hands, and Colorado's first
great bonanza king was penniless. His carriages and stables, his
Italian villa, his and his wife's and his daughters' diamonds—all
had been sold over the block.

An old man, approaching seventy, utterly crushed and bewildered, Tabor set out alone into the mountains to go prospecting,
working many futile months up Boulder Creek at the Eclipse.

In January, '98, after a year of hardship, Tabor confessed himself "stunned at the information" that his former generosity to his
party had been recognized and rewarded at last. Experience
gained during the long lean years in California Gulch now stood
him in good stead. Senators Teller and Wolcott had used their
influence in his behalf to secure for him an appointment in Denver. At a salary of $3,500 a year, "sufficient to rescue him from
penury," he again became a postmaster.

In the curiously complete cycle of his life, Tabor was back
where he began.

A year passed, with Tabor and his family living in one small
room at the Windsor Hotel. He had abandoned all hope of re-
gaining fortune. He was again as quiet and resigned as on that
day just twenty years before when those two strange prospectors,
Hook and Rische, had walked into his store at Slabtown. What he

thought or dreamed of during this year, what memories of triumph he had or what regrets, will never be known.

On the morning of April 10, 1899, after a week's illness, Tabor passed quietly away at the Windsor. His wife and daughters were at his bedside. Shortly before the end, Maxcy Tabor was sent for, though he had been estranged from his father for years, ever since the divorce from Augusta. But he did not arrive until Tabor had sunk into the coma from which he never awakened.

In a grave marked by a small granite stone, on which appeared only the name "Tabor," the greatest of the Carbonate Kings was buried with simple ceremony in the presence of a few mourners at Mt. Prospect Cemetery, "Jack O'Neill's Ranch" of earlier days, another of the Larimers' hopeful but disappointing real estate promotions, long since a neglected patch of brambles and weeds.

In its personal aspects Tabor's tragedy had its roots less in his vices than in his virtues, for he was "confiding, charitable, generous, and merciful to an extreme," as even his enemies testified. "These attributes proved his financial undoing. No man ever went to him for a favor when he had money and came away empty-handed. No man ever forgave his enemies quite so cheerfully or testified so willingly to the sincerity of his forgiveness by afterwards aiding them. . . . He made many mistakes during the days of his prominence and prosperity but, his surroundings and opportunities considered, carried himself as well as any of his contemporaries."

But, in larger part, Tabor's tragedy must be attributed to his misfortune in outliving his era. Businessmen and financiers with their studied methods of systematic exploitation had already won the West. Tabor and others of his kind had nothing to oppose to their refined techniques and fell an easy prey to them. Bluff and usually straightforward even at his worst, Tabor boldly blundered ahead where shrewder and more sophisticated men of fundamentally less integrity felt their way along cautiously and cunningly toward success. His sudden complete loss of fortune is inexplicable unless, as seems likely, he really never understood the forces he strove to master. His ways were the simple and naïve ways of the Frontier which had already passed before his death—"in the Southwest with the capture of Geronimo in 1886-8, in the Dakotas among the Sioux with the totally needless murder of hundreds of women and children at Wounded Knee in 1891-2, and throughout the whole West in 1893 when the world panic of that year enabled the Eastern money-lender to foreclose on the overborrowed West and pull the frontiersman—now gray-haired—from his saddle," as many an aging pioneer bitterly lamented.

"That ended the Frontier, ended the frontiersman; in came rapidly woman suffrage, prohibition, anti-gun laws, . . . and the Frontier was gone—gone into history."

Only the Matchless was saved from the wreck of Tabor's fortune, again through the generosity of Stratton.[6] But the Matchless was now exhausted. Within two months of Tabor's death his family was actually destitute, living in a small brick house, old and dingy, standing just off Larimer Street with its dilapidated buildings of earlier days. Having meantime quarreled with her brother Peter, Tabor's general manager, who had managed to survive the crash with a sizeable fortune, Mrs. Tabor stubbornly refused to accept any aid from him.

Taking her daughters with her, one an adolescent girl, the other a child of ten or eleven, Mrs. Tabor soon quit Denver and went to Leadville to settle down there in an old cabin beside the shaft of the Matchless, up Strayhorse Gulch, a mile and a half above the town. Around her, on the slopes of Fryer Hill, were the unsightly dumps and long-abandoned buildings of other great bonanzas—the New Discovery, Robert E. Lee, Little Pittsburgh, Little Chief, Crysolite, and Maid of Erin. Imbued with a deathless faith in the Matchless, Mrs. Tabor donned overalls every day and made the rounds of the mine, taking out sample ores, inspecting old machinery and rusted ore buckets and cables, frequently making a dangerous descent of some three hundred feet into the bowels of the earth to determine how high seepage water stood in the shaft and flooded tunnels. Down there, she was convinced, there was another fortune if she could only manage to get at it.

Within a few years, tragedy struck again. Life on the dump of the Matchless was drab and dreary. Tired of poverty and hardship, having none of her mother's faith in the mine, recalling perhaps her early triumphs and the silks and laces she had enjoyed as "Baby" Tabor, the elder daughter Lillie—or "Golden Eagle," as she was sometimes called—was restless and rebellious. After many bitter quarrels she left home, going to live with Grandmother McCourt in Chicago. She soon married and removed to Wisconsin, breaking all bonds with her family, turning her back on all the Tabors. Her hard-pressed mother, now in her forties, never heard from her again.

In this heart-breaking defeat there was one solace, one ray of hope, and Mrs. Tabor bore up. She still had her favorite with her to cheer her spirits and lighten her burdens, her beloved "Honeymaid," as she liked to call her younger daughter. Warm and impulsive, with dark hair like her father's, Silver Dollar was an attractive girl, with gay and winning ways, happy to share with her mother their desperate struggle against adversity. Time did not improve the situation and some years later the girl, now twenty, began to contribute bits of verse to local newspapers to earn an occasional few dollars. To her father she dedicated a song "On President Roosevelt's Colorado Bear Hunt," which brought some local notice, and her mother's eyes brightened with pride and hope that the Muse might perhaps help them mend their shattered fortune. Silver published other pieces on "Love and Lillies," "Spirits," "In a Dream I Loved You," and the "Outlaw Horse," one stanza of which reads:

And the Wild West goes,
And the civilized grows
  All in progression's course,
But there's still a flood
Of the dauntless blood:
  That goes for the outlaw horse.

The girl then tried her hand as a newspaper reporter, going to work for the old Denver *Times,* sending home to her mother each week a large part of her wretchedly small salary. Still courting the Muse, Silver soon resigned and sat down to write a lurid short novel entitled *The Star of Blood,* sentimentalizing the exploits and *amours* of a notorious local criminal. In a final literary effort the desperate girl founded in Denver the *Silver Dollar Weekly,* a society tittle-tattle sheet, of which only one or two issues were published.

A few years later, defeated and discouraged and now past thirty, Silver informed her mother that she planned to enter a convent, soon drifting away to be gossiped about occasionally until, in 1925, she was found dying under rather mysterious circumstances in a disreputable part of South Chicago. Terribly burned and scalded, she expired a few hours later, insisting to the last that her injury was an accident, that she had slipped and toppled over upon herself a tub of boiling water. But in the shabby room was found a man's photograph with a notation on it that if anything happened, he would know all about it. The original of the photograph, one Jack Reid, a former saloonkeeper, was held for questioning but soon released by the police.

Mrs. Tabor happened at the moment to be visiting Denver and in the evening, hearing the news shouted in the streets and not having in her purse the few pennies needed to buy a newspaper, she trudged several miles to the Denver Public Library. It was late, and the reading rooms were being closed. But at her insistence one of the staff, noting her strange tattered costume and perhaps sensing who she was from the intensity of her manner, relented and agreed to let her glance at the evening newspaper. On the front page appeared a picture of Silver Dollar and the sordid details of her death. Slowly, never lifting her eye from the page, Mrs. Tabor read to the end.

"Silver!" she sighed, choking back her tears, and in her ill-fitting miners' boots shuffled out into the night.

After a few days, when no one claimed the body, neighbors began collecting money to bury "Ruth Norman," the latest of Silver's aliases. In the end Peter McCourt sent $300 for funeral expenses. It was reported at the time that Mrs. Tabor had succeeded in obtaining funds to attend the funeral. But she was not present when the last rites were performed. Mrs. Tabor later declared, and to the end of her life maintained the fiction, that the prematurely old and wasted woman who came to such an unhappy end in Chicago was not her daughter—that Silver Dollar, her darling "Honeymaid," was alive and well in the convent to which she had once announced her intention of retiring.

Secretly nursing her sorrow, Mrs. Tabor returned to Leadville, now bereft of everything a woman holds dear, her heart a graveyard of vanished hopes and fears. The props of her life, one by one, had given way. She had lost much, but there was always the Matchless, still a shining beacon in the night as the shadows closed in. Many times the mine was almost wrested from her, but always she managed to retain it by supreme efforts of her own or by the generosity of friends and even strangers touched by her heroic willful fight against absolutely hopeless odds.[7]

Down the years she strove desperately to make the Matchless once more pour forth treasure, becoming a legendary figure in the mountains, commanding more and more respect, for all the vagaries of Fortune and the cruelest decrees of Fate had never broken her spirit. Nor had they embittered her soul. Though suspicious of strangers, reporters, and gaping tourists, as she had reason to be, she had her small circle of friends, and they were much attached to her for her gentle ways, her wit, and her stout heart. She was never heard to complain of her lot or express envy of the good fortune of others, not even of those who had battened on Tabor's *largesse* and then snubbed and betrayed her in her hour of need. Having made her choice, she never wavered or looked back, manifesting a fierce pride in trying to get along on her own resources. Though enduring the bitterest hardships, at times being reduced to wrapping her feet in gunnysacks in want of shoes, she scorned gifts sent to her by those whom she rightly suspected of pitying her and acting in a spirit of condescension. But when the miners of Leadville, hearing of her difficulties from time to time, clubbed together and sent up a box of groceries, she was pleased to accept and deeply grateful.[8]

One day two lawyers insisted on seeing her, saying that she should bring a suit of libel for something written about her and the Tabor family, and that she could easily get a substantial judgment—perhaps as much as $50,000—which was not unlikely. Mrs. Tabor patiently heard them out, and then dismissed them.

"I am not interested in lawsuits," she said. "I am interested in mining."

The buried treasure in the Matchless had become an obsession with her, and to the day of her death she lived and toiled there on bleak Fryer Hill, almost on the crest of the Rockies, just a few hundred feet below timberline. Nothing could persuade her—not even the unanimous opinion of experts—that the mine was altogether barren and exhausted. But the Matchless, it is obvious, had become something more than a mere mine in her eyes. It was, in truth, her life—part of the very fiber of her being. It was the thread tying together all that she had known and enjoyed and suffered—all of her early dazzling triumphs and her later tragic sorrows. When all else had vanished, it remained a symbol of the golden days of her youth when she was rich and gay and beautiful.

Early in March, 1936, with the temperature hovering around zero after more than a week of fierce and blinding blizzards, the skies suddenly cleared and Mrs. Tabor's closest friend and nearest neighbor, Sue Bonnie, a former waitress who lived about a half mile below, noted with some anxiety that no smoke was coming from the cabin up on the Matchless.

Mrs. Tabor had not been seen for almost ten days, not since she had come stumbling into a Leadville grocery, covered with ice and mud, having cut her way through heavy snowdrifts piled up between her isolated cabin and the road down in Strayhorse Gulch. In town she bargained for her usual meager supplies— as many loaves of stale bread as she could obtain for $1, and a few pounds of the most inexpensive "plate boil" (brisket of beef). As she was leaving, the delivery boy offered her a lift in his truck, which she smilingly and graciously accepted, for whatever her tastes may once have been, she had seen quite enough of the shams of the world and now liked plain, kindly, unpretentious people.

Becoming alarmed as she watched the cabin up on the Matchless for some sign of life, Sue Bonnie went for another of Mrs. Tabor's close friends, Tom French, an old prospector. Together, they pushed their way along the icy road up Strayhorse Gulch, climbing to the cabin by means of the stakes and ropes set up by Mrs. Tabor as a guide to her door when she was out in fearful winter blizzards. Peering through the window, they saw Mrs. Tabor lying on the floor, partially clothed. In the one-room shanty, with its lean-to, there was some wood and even some coal heaped in a corner, but the stove had long been out. It seems probable that Mrs. Tabor had become ill and, in getting up from bed to tend the stove, had fainted and slowly frozen to death on the floor.

In a far corner, with a crucifix on the wall above it, was a rusty old iron bed, with a tumble of gray blankets upon it and a decrepit old rocking-chair near by. A battered oil lamp stood on the small table which had a leg missing and was supported at one corner by a wooden box. Cheap net half-curtains, repeatedly mended with coarse twine, hung at the windows. Wooden and cardboard boxes served as shelves around the room, and all were decorated with branches of evergreen, which were nailed in bunches along the walls as well, doubtless a survival of Mrs. Tabor's effort to make her cabin as gay and bright as possible for Christmas.

One whole end of the room was filled with old trunks, heaps of yellowed newspapers with articles on the Tabors, batches of letters, and a litter of boxes, large and small, gifts sent to the lonely cabin from all parts of the world. Many of these contained shoes and warm clothes, candies and delicacies, but most of them were unopened.[9] In the dusty litter was found a large crushed cardboard box, tied with a string, and obviously cherished for many years. On the cover was written a note in pencil, undated, a haunting echo of happier days:

"God bless her. In this box was the beautiful, soft, blue and white bathrobe my darling child, Honeymaid Silver, sent me."

The news of Baby Doe's death spread quickly through Leadville, and her passing was genuinely mourned by her few friends and by the working people of the town, to whom she was a familiar figure in the streets and who knew from their own experience what a bitter struggle she had managed to survive for so long. Whatever she once had been in the few short years of her splendor, she had long since become one of them, and they responded to her unfailing courage in the face of ill luck and utter catastrophe of every kind. Talking of her death, a graybeard of the town remarked, and this might well be her epitaph:

"She was one of the old prospectors," he said—and there were now so few of them left.[10]

It was first planned to bury Mrs. Tabor in Leadville, and a grave was dynamited in the rocky, deeply frozen soil. Later, through one of her brothers, arrangements were made for burial

in Denver, and a handful of the curious were present at the railway station when her remains arrived. Some of the more crass
took occasion to come forward and attract attention to themselves with large talk of raising funds by public subscription to
buy a solid silver casket in which to bury Mrs. Tabor.

Fortunately, better judgment prevailed, and she was spared
this final mockery, being quietly laid to rest in Mt. Olivet Cemetery, her long travail ended. Whatever her sins, she had paid for
them many times over, without a whimper, asking no favors. In
her own way she was as strong a character as Augusta Tabor, and
as brave and loyal.

Little remains of Tabor's Leadville though the town still has a
spirit and charm of its own. Late in the '90s, a few years before
Mrs. Tabor's return, the camp enjoyed a boom when gold was discovered deep under the exhausted carbonate veins and created
new bonanza fortunes—notably, those of John F. Campion and
James J. Brown, who was best known perhaps for his wife, the
"unsinkable Mrs. Brown," an heroic survivor of the *Titanic* disaster, who had a frankly wonderful time in crashing society in
Denver, New York, Newport, London, and Paris.[11]

But the boom did not approach that of earlier days, and since
the turn of the century Leadville has steadily declined except for
flurries of activity during war years. Today, it is not a tenth as
large as it was in '79, sheltering some three to four thousand
people.

Many long streets of frame houses and cabins are altogether
deserted. Chestnut Street, once so crowded and loud with riotous
bustle, lies in ruins. Long boarded up, Tabor's old Bank of Leadville and the Clarendon Hotel have been razed in recent years.
The Tabor Opera House still stands, but no drama has been presented upon its stage for many years. In 1905 the building passed
into the hands of the Elks, and the huge apartments in which
Tabor, assisted by Bill Bush, once managed his millions and re-

ceived visitors in almost regal state, are now used as lodge and club rooms. State Street, in its day as wild and drunkenly boisterous as any in the world, is a waste. All of its large gay resorts have burned or been torn down. There is nothing here but the old Pioneer Saloon and a short line of cribs, occupied largely by Mexican and Spanish-American girls, who sit rocking behind large plateglass windows, boldly exhibiting their charms, some with a coyote chained beside them.

Still less remains of Tabor's Denver. The mansion Tabor bought for Augusta and the other he rebuilt for his new bride are both gone. The Tabor Block, in which he took such pride—"reared like Solomon's Temple, a magnificent six-story building, with brownstone front, ornate but tasteful"—still stands on Larimer Street, but for years it has been known as the Nassau Block. In the stone over the dingy entrance, however, one can still make out the words, *Dies Faustus*, inscribed there by Tabor as he rose to the heights.

A sole monument to his memory, the Tabor Grand Opera House still bears his name though its days of glory have faded, and plans have been announced for its destruction.[12] Today, after some years of cheap melodrama and cheaper vaudeville, it is a second-rate movie house playing blood-and-thunder mysteries and bad Westerns. It has been considerably altered and stripped of almost all of its former splendor—its bright silks and satins and red plush, its huge crystal chandelier, its Italian marble and elaborately carved woodwork of Japanese cherry, the large portrait of Tabor that once graced the lobby.

But it retains its famous curtain, hanging high in the flies, which is still to be seen on occasion. Time has not dulled the scene painted there so many years ago—a once-proud Roman city falling to ruin, its elaborate palaces and beautiful temples of marble tumbling to the ground. Only a few broken columns remain standing. Lions and other fierce beasts of prey lurk in the shattered ruins soon to vanish under a tangled mass of vegetation. Below this melancholy scene appear these lines of Kingsley, their irony growing more pointed with the years:

> *So fleet the works of man*
> *Back to the earth again,*
> *Ancient and holy things*
> *Fade like a dream . . .*

Perhaps it was at Tabor's insistence that the stanza was left incomplete, with the omission of the concluding line:

> *And the hand of the master is dust.*

NOTES

1. Very little has been written about this first American gold rush. For the bare bones of the story, see (American Guide Series) *Georgia: A Guide to Its Towns and Countryside* (Athens, Georgia, 1940).

2. For Colonel Sutter and the California Gold Rush, see *Sutter* (New York, 1934) and (Rivers of America Series) *The Sacramento: River of Gold* (New York, 1939), both by Julian Dana; *California* (New York, 1939), in the American Guide Series, which contains the best short and complete account; Erwin G. Gudde, *Sutter's Own Story* (New York, 1936); and Archer Butler Hulbert, *The Forty-niners* (Boston, 1931). See also Mark Twain, *Roughing It* (New York, 1872) and *Autobiography* (New York, 1924); and *Letters of Bret Harte* (Boston, 1926).

3. See Josiah Gregg, *Commerce of the Prairies: The Journal of a Santa Fe Trader* (New York, 1844), a classic of the early West, reprinted in Thwaites' *Early Western Travels;* and R. L. Duffus, *The Santa Fe Trail* (New York, 1930).

4. See that other classic of the early West, Francis Parkman, *The Oregon and California Trail* (New York, 1849), available in various reprints; also, W. J. Ghent, *The Road to Oregon* (New York, 1934), and (American Guide Series) *The Oregon Trail* (New York, 1939), which contains a definitive map of the route, with many fine old illustrations and photographs.

For both the Oregon-California and the Santa Fe Trail, see that brilliant study of the great historical forces shaping the Mexican War and the first great westward rush, *The Year of Decision: 1846* (Boston, 1943), by Bernard De-Voto.

"It was Parkman's fortune to witness and take part in one of our greatest national experiences, at the moment and site of its occurrence. It is our misfortune that he did not understand the smallest part of it," writes DeVoto with penetrating insight. Parkman's "trip to the prairies produced one of the exuberant masterpieces of American literature; it ought instead to have produced a key work of American history."

5. For this first Spanish exploration of the Rocky Mountain West, see George P. Winship, *The Journey of Coronado, 1540-42* (New York, 1904).

6. See Herbert E. Bolton (ed.), *Spanish Explorations in the Southwest, 1542-1706* (New York, 1925).

7. See Zebulon Montgomery Pike, *An Account of Expeditions to the Source of the Mississippi, and through the Western Parts of Louisiana* (Philadelphia, 1810), the relevant part of which appeared as *Arkansas Journal* (Philadelphia, 1811). Pike gave added currency to the notion that the western prairies and high plains were the "great American Desert," virtually uninhabitable, and that they were of no value save as a sort of natural *cordon sanitaire* between the westward-moving Americans and the Spanish settlements in the Southwest, thus obviating conflict along the ill-defined frontier.

8. For the Major Long expedition, see Edwin James, *An Account of an Expedition from Pittsburgh to the Rocky Mountains* (Philadelphia, 1822-23). The scientists in the Long party agreed with Pike that the trans-Missouri country was good for nothing but a "range for buffaloes, wild goats, and other wild game." See the excellent chapter entitled "The American Approach to the Great Plains" in that

revolutionary study of the settlement of the West, *The Great Plains* (Boston, 1931), by Walter Prescott Webb.

9. See John Charles Frémont, *Memoirs of My Life* (Chicago, 1887); Allan Nevins, *Frémont: The World's Greatest Adventurer* (New York, 1928); and Irving Stone, *Immortal Wife* (New York, 1944), a fictionalized biography of the explorer's wife and able publicist, Jessie Benton Frémont, a volume which gingerly skips around much damaging evidence and throws the best possible light on the exploits of the "Pathfinder" and his many dubious ventures. See also, *The Year of Decision: 1846* (Boston, 1943), by Bernard DeVoto, who blasts the pretensions of the "Pathfinder" —scores of Mountain Men, including the explorer's mentors, Kit Carson and Tom ("Broken Hand") Fitzpatrick, had known the western wilderness by heart for twenty years before the vainglorious Frémont appeared—but points out that "the myth of the Great American Desert went down before this literary man's examination . . . In the book he wrote, Frémont deserves well of the Republic."

10. South Park, still one of the most beautiful spots in the Rockies, was known to the Mountain Men as Bayou Salade, so named for its salt and alkaline marshes. The Georgians may have been led here by reading Zebulon Pike, who reported that at Santa Fe, in 1807, he had met an Indian trader, James Purcell of Kentucky, who claimed to have found gold along the headwaters of the South Platte. Though the Georgians made no discoveries, there was gold here in considerable amounts, as discovered the next year when the camps of Tarryall, Fairplay, Buckskin Joe, and Montgomery were established. For a fascinating account of South Park in the days of the Mountain ·Men, see *Life in the Far West* (London, 1849), by young George Frederick Ruxton, lieutenant in Her Majesty's 89th Regiment, who wandered all about this country in the early days.

Other graphic, first-hand accounts of life in the Pike's Peak country in the years before the gold rush appear in Thomas J. Farnham, *Travels in the Great Western Prairies* (Poughkeepsie, N. Y., 1841); George Frederick Ruxton, *Adventures in Mexico and the Rocky Mountains* (London, 1847); Francis Parkman, *The Oregon Trail* (New York, 1849); Rufus B. Sage, *Rocky Mountain Life* (Boston, 1857); and Lewis Garrard, *Wah-To-Yah* (meaning "Breasts of the World," the Indian name for the Spanish Peaks in Colorado). This last is perhaps the best book of the period, though still largely unknown.

CHAPTER II

1. Erected in 1853, this was the third and last fort built up and down the Arkansas by the Bent brothers—William, Charles, Robert, and George. The first (1826) stood close to the mountains. Two years later, at the suggestion of the Indians with whom they traded for peltry, the Bents moved some eighty miles down the river, well out on the Plains, to be in the heart of the buffalo country. Here, near the mouth of the Purgatoire (later corrupted to Picketwire by cowmen and originally from the Spanish, *El Rio de las Animas Perdidas en Purgatorio,* or River of the Souls Lost in Purgatory), stood Bent's famed Old Fort, solidly built of adobe, in its day the most important post on the American frontier, for years the rendezvous of the Mountain Men. Kit ("Little Chief") Carson, related to the Bents by marriage, was employed at the fort as a hunter for eleven years, until 1842, when he piloted Frémont on his first expedition into the Rockies.

In the early 1850's, with the decline of the fur trade, Colonel William Bent, the sole surviving brother, offered to sell the Old Fort to the Federal Government. When negotiations got snarled in red tape, the Colonel quickly lost patience. Collecting his goods, he loaded them on twenty large wagons drawn by many yoke of oxen, blew up the fort, and moved down the river some forty miles to build the last of his forts here at Big Timbers.

In 1859, a year after the Larimers stopped here, Bent leased the fort to the Federal Government upon being appointed Indian agent to the Arapaho and Cheyenne, with whom he had been intimately associated for so many years. The fort was subsequently renamed Fort Fauntleroy, Fort Wise, and finally Fort Lyon, in honor of the first Union general to fall during the Civil War.

For the colorful life at the Old Fort in its heyday, see George Frederick Ruxton, Francis Parkman, and Lewis Garrard (*supra*); Stanley Vestal, *Kit Carson* (Boston, 1928) and *Dobe Walls* (Boston, 1929), a romance of the old Southwest centering on Bent's fort; and G. B. Grinnell, "Bent's Old Fort and Its Builders" (Kansas State Historical Society Collections, Vol. 15).

2. The Spanish had built a temporary settlement here as early as 1673, and it was on this spot that Zebulon Pike's party camped for five days in 1806 while the commander himself set out to the north in an unsuccessful attempt to scale the "Highest Peak," subsequently named for him.

Jim Beckwourth (see below, Chapter VII, Note 7) and other Mountain Men established a trading post here in 1842, constructing "an adobe fort sixty yards square," wrote Beckwourth, ". . . and we gave it the name of Pueblo." Francis Parkman visited it four years later and was not impressed, saying that it was "nothing more than a large square enclosure, surrounded with a wall of mud, miserably cracked and dilapidated." The main apartment was a "small mud room, very neatly finished . . . and garnished with a crucifix, a looking-glass, a picture of the Virgin, and a rusty horse-pistol. . . . There was another room beyond, less sumptuously

decorated, and here three or four Spanish girls, one of them very pretty, were baking cakes at a mud fireplace in the corner. . . . Passing out the gate, we could look down the little valley [of the Fontaine qui Bouille] to the Arkansas, a beautiful scene. . . . Tall woods lined the river, with green meadows on either hand; and high bluffs, quietly basking in the sun, flanked the narrow valley. A Mexican on horseback was driving a herd of cattle towards the gate. . . ."

Parkman found here a vanguard of the Mormon migration that had just arrived in their prairie schooners from the Missouri. They built cabins among the cottonwoods, where they lived until they pushed on to Salt Lake the following year.

Here, in 1853, another of the great Mountain Men, "Uncle Dick" Wootton, established a ranch and did a thriving business swapping fresh oxen for footsore and broken-down animals, at a ratio of one to three or four. Put to pasture, the lame animals quickly recovered, and Uncle Dick was ready for some more swapping. Here, he also made one of the first attempts to establish a buffalo farm, capturing young calves on the Plains and pasturing them with his cattle, but the scheme did not work out.

After the massacre here on Christmas Day, 1854, the fort was abandoned, being avoided by the Mountain Men who believed it to be haunted by headless Mexican women.

3. More than twenty years earlier there had been a strong trading post some thirty miles down the Platte, Fort Vasquez, built in 1836 by two of the Mountain Men—Louis Vasquez, later the partner of Jim ("Old Gabe") Bridger, and Andrew Sublette. The latter was one of four brothers in the fur trade, the best known being William ("Cut Face") Sublette, who established on the North Platte the post first known as Fort William, subsequently renamed and renowned as old Fort Laramie on the Oregon-California Trail.

In building their fort here, Vasquez and Sublette were working for the Rocky Mountain Fur Company, rival of John Jacob Astor's American Fur Company, and for a time they employed Jim Beckwourth as a trader. Though it is to be taken with a grain of salt, for Beckwourth liked to dramatize himself and told the tallest yarns of the day, there is a good account of the methods and ruses of the Indian trade in the *Life and Adventures of James P. Beckwourth* (see below), pp. 290-312 (in the 1931 edition).

After four years of prosperous trade with the Arapaho and Cheyenne, Vasquez and Sublette sold the post to other traders in 1840. Two years later, Arapaho raiders stormed and looted it, and it was soon abandoned. An interesting, full-sized replica of Fort Vasquez now stands on its old site, near the town of Platteville, Colorado.

4. The log cabin, apparently so natively American, is actually a "furriner." The first settlers at Jamestown and Plymouth did not build log cabins for the good reason that they did not know how. Rather, they erected English types of shelter. The log cabin was brought to our shores by the Swedes and Finns who settled along the Delaware in the 1640's.

5. See Herman S. Davis (ed.), *Reminiscences of General William H. Larimer and of His Son William H. H. Larimer* (privately printed, Lancaster, Pa., 1918).

CHAPTER III

1. The material in this chapter and the four following is largely from manuscript, pamphlet, and newspaper sources in the Colorado State Historical Society and the Denver Public Library—the former under the direction of Dr. LeRoy R. Hafen, the latter under that of Mr. Malcolm Wyer. Both deserve the highest praise and tangible encouragement for their tireless and far-sighted efforts in saving priceless old documents and building up splendid collections of indispensable source material on the history of the Rocky Mountain West.

For further details on the rush of '59, see LeRoy R. Hafen, *The Colorado Gold Rush: Contemporary Letters and Reports* (Glendale, Calif., 1941); *Pike's Peak Gold Rush Guide Books of 1859* (Glendale, 1941); and *Overland Routes to the Gold Fields, 1859* (Glendale, 1942).

2. See Henry Villard, *Past and Present of the Pike's Peak Region* (reprinted by Princeton University Press, 1932).

CHAPTER IV

1. For old Fort Laramie, see Francis Parkman, *Oregon Trail* (*supra*); LeRoy R. Hafen and Francis Marion Young, *Fort Laramie and the Pageant of the West* (Glendale, Calif., 1938); and Bernard DeVoto, *The Year of Decision: 1846* (*supra*).

2. See Horace Greeley, *An Overland Journey from New York to San Francisco in the Summer of 1859* (New York, 1860).

3. As a matter of fact, the conception of the Pullman sleeping car—local tradition to the contrary—was not born in some overcrowded cabin along Gregory Gulch, though it might well have been. See the *Colorado Magazine*, May, 1940, for an authoritative article on "George M. Pullman and the Colorado Tradition," by Peter D. Vroom, assistant editor of the *Pullman News*.

4. The next year, on a visit to the town, President Grant stayed at the Teller House and enjoyed a very lively reception. Descending from the stagecoach after a breath-taking drive up Virginia Canyon, Grant was ceremoniously escorted along a pathway of solid

silver bricks laid from the middle of the street to the entrance of the hotel as boys on the roof of a neighboring livery stable tossed snowballs at his plug hat. Grant was shown the handsome bar and then led to his suite several flights up. Gazing out the front windows, he seemed to be in an eagle's eyrie and could see for miles. Going to the back windows, he found himself at ground level. Scratching his head, he is said to have wondered aloud whether it was the liquor at the Teller bar or in his own bottle that was so deceptive.

Another hostelry famed far and wide in its day was the Hotel de Paris (not Pa-reé, but Pá-ris, and no nonsense). It adorned the neighboring camp of Georgetown and was presided over by one of the most fabulous characters in the mountains, Louis du Puy, the last of many aliases assumed by Adolphus Francois Gerard (1840-1900), born to wealth and position at Alençon, France.

Du Puy has been well characterized as "an innkeeper who hated his guests, a philosopher, and a poet who left no written record of his thought, a despiser of women who gave all he had to one, an aristocrat, a proletarian, a pagan, an arcadian, an atheist, a lover of beauty, and, inadvertently, the stepfather of domestic science in America" —through the influence which his learned disquisitions on food and wine had upon Dr. James E. Russell of Columbia University, who first gave domestic science academic and professional status.

After a fantastic career which included service in and desertion from many armies, Du Puy appeared in Georgetown as a miner in 1869. Seven years later, after a serious accident in the mines, he opened his hotel. Built largely with his own hands, it was a two-storied brick structure with a brown stone façade. A *cheval-de-frise* of gilded spikes ran around the roof. Gilded lions guarded the gates. A gilded

statue of Justice surveyed the town from the cornice. Inside, there was more gilt on the chairs, mirrors, paintings, and sculptures of nudes— "heathen images," snorted the pillars of church in the town.

Over this lavishly Parisian establishment, Du Puy ruled like a feudal lord. If the appearance of prospective guests did not please him, he shooed them out the door. Even registered guests occasionally found their baggage in the street if they offended Du Puy's sensibilities. Most women did, as a general rule, but if they came with one of the host's favorite friends, they were admitted, no matter what their marital or non-marital status. As a consequence, there was always a rush to Du Puy's doors, for it was regarded as a great privilege to be allowed to eat his food, drink his wine, and talk with him about everything under the sun, from Napoleon to his own highly individualistic and almost anarchic ideas.

"If you are a college man," he once said to Dr. Russell, "surely you know that no gentleman invites himself to be the guest of a stranger. This is my house. If I want guests, I invite them."

5. Since 1932, with the reopening of its opera house after many years of disuse and neglect, Central City has enjoyed a short but brilliant theatrical season each summer, a series interrupted by the war but now to be resumed. The town has been hailed as the "summer theater capital of the world" by metropolitan critics not ordinarily given to extravagance, attracting serious play-goers, professional first-nighters, and bibulous sensation-seekers from as far away as New York and San Francisco.

Dark since 1910 and falling to ruin, the old opera house had passed into the hands of Peter McFarlane of Central City, one of the original contractors, and in 1931 his heirs presented it to the University of Denver with the hope that it might be saved from rot and slow destruction. Its roof was falling in. Its walls were black with mold and dirt. But its four-foot walls of granite, mined in the neighboring hills, were sound and intact.

Thanks largely to the initiative and imagination of Ida Kruse McFarlane, Edna James Chappell, and Anne Evans, daughter of old Governor Evans of Territorial days, a campaign got under way to save the opera house and restore it not merely as a museum—there is no want of these—but in its own proper function, a far more interesting and creative idea.

Restoration was financed by the sale of memorial chairs in the house, each bearing the name of some Argonaut of '59, or some other local worthy—or anyone at all, for that matter, who had family or friends to pay $100 for the purpose. Some 250 seats were thus sold, and the Central City Opera House Association was formed.

The roof was repaired. The old frescoes on the grimy walls were uncovered and skillfully restored by Allen True, of Denver. The interior was refinished, and the stage facilities were enlarged and improved. The original handmade chairs, which had fortunately been preserved, were put in place again. And they were chairs—not upholstered seats—good solid chairs of hickory, with nothing to cushion the angularities of the spare or rest the spreading amplitudes of the rotund, almost enforcing strict attention to the business on the stage.

The auditorium is beautifully proportioned and seats some 750 on lower floor and small balcony. Decorated simply in Empire style, the restored opera house is one of the most charming and impressive small theaters in America—"a perfect gem," as it has been described.

The first offering was Lillian Gish in *Camille*, followed in 1933 by Gladys Swarthout in *The Merry Widow* and by Walter Huston in *Othello* the next year. Up to 1942, when the play festival was suspended for the duration of the war, the theater had presented memorable productions of *The Gondoliers*, Ibsen's *Doll House* in an English version by Thornton Wilder, *Ruy Blas*, *The Yeoman of the Guard*, *The Bartered Bride* by Smetana, *The Barber of Seville*, and Gluck's *Orpheus*. All were well received, without exception, by critics and audience alike.

First night at "Central" is always a gala affair, a high spot in the lives of local socialites for hundreds of miles around. Some of the more enterprising take houses here for the two or three weeks of the festival and lavishly entertain a succession of guests from near and far, gracing their tables with whatever visiting celebrities can be corraled. Competition among the local lion-hunters is sharp and severe, and not infrequently precipitates a good old mountain feud. But as our modern Hatfields and McCoys have laid aside their squirrel guns and six-shooters, hostilities seldom rise above a rather low verbal plane—though spirited and amusing enough at times, especially when rounded off with some bold unblushing phrase reminiscent of better days.

The old Teller House, standing just below the theater on steep Eureka Street, has been acquired by the Opera House Association, which has refurbished it, polished up its renowned Little Kingdom Bar, and added a night club and roof garden. With gambling saloons running wide open in a sedate way, with Morris dancing in the streets and square dancing under professional direction at Williams' old livery stable, with Louis Spies working manfully with his accomplished staff at the Teller House bar to meet the clamorous demand for regular potions and such specials as "Camille Catastrophes," "Doll House Detonators," and "Ruy Blas Bombshells," there is a good deal of forced gusto and rather self-conscious roistering on the part of those who are, in normal course, plain and even bleak respectable citizens. The restoration of the opera house has made it necessary to rejuvenate the old town jail, too, for the proper reception of some of the "visiting firemen," though in the spirit of carnival the constabulary acts only in cases of extreme provocation or to save some prominent citizen from self-destruction.

"People begin to arrive from Denver not long after the sun is up," wrote Ernie Pyle, who came to attend in 1941. "Opening night is a night of special privilege. Every big name in Colorado is there. The out-of-state guests are such people as the Delaware DuPonts.

"Almost everybody in Central City on opening day 'knows somebody' or holds an invitation to something. The stray tourists wander around looking hungry for somebody to speak to. Being an ex-social climber myself, there's nothing that delights me so much as to see tourists ogling us members of the upper classes. . . .

"I do not wish to give the impression that festival opening is a brawl, for it definitely is not. Much liquor is consumed, true, but it is spread around so many people, and there is so much more coming later, that the celebrators practice a certain degree of temperance. . . .

"Between noon and daylight next morning, I'm sure I must have met 300 people. The fishing was sure good. We just threw back such small fry as Congressmen and railroad presidents. We did keep governors, but didn't bother to weigh them.

"Around five in the afternoon, the hundreds of visitors in Central City disappear, and the town suddenly is silent and lonely. Where have the people all gone? They've gone to put on their evening clothes. . . . Finding a place to change your clothes is one of Central City's biggest problems. . . .

"Our hostess for this event was . . . a charming lady who was born right in her present house and still has the bed she was born in. It was she and her brothers who gave the old opera house to the Festival Association. Our hostess put the men in one set of rooms, the women in another. But it didn't make much difference. Right in the middle of my second shirt stud, a man knocked at the door and came prancing in with a lady who said she was in a hurry and this was her last chance to tell me she enjoyed reading these columns. It was the first time I have ever received the public formally without any pants on.

"When we got downstairs, a governor was there (he had pants on), so we exchanged a few political pleasantries and then dashed up the street to . . . a cocktail party consisting of a few thousand people.

"Suddenly it was getting dark, and word came that we had to hurry to the opera house. 'Way down below, the man in his ancient costume was ringing a handbell up and down the street; through the shadows, women in white gowns were picking their way down muddy lanes; a stillness came over the old town, and the great moment for the West's three weeks of grand opera among the tailing-pines was at hand, . . . one of America's really fine events."

All of this has wrought a change in the old Central that some of us knew years ago. Many "improvements" have been made, and more are contemplated. This may outrage a few diehards, but as recently observed by Thomas Hornsby Ferril of Denver, poet and shrewdest critic of the West, this is precisely what our pioneer fathers would be doing if they were alive today.

The Argonauts "would approve of the shining Cape Cod architecture on Eureka Street in Central," he writes. "Everything run-down is being reconverted and restored. Even the old calico house down by Blackhawk is going to be preserved 'just as it is,' plus whatever it takes to make it better. Hamburger joints are going in for neon signs. This is precisely what the Arcadians of Central would have done. It is all a living memorial to their booster spirit. . . . A superb antiquarianism is everywhere vibrant and progressive.

"There are, unfortunately, stuffy tourists who frankly admit that they are disappointed in Central City. They took it for a ghost town, but would you look at it! What the hell! This difficulty, I understand, will soon be corrected by spiritual zoning ordinances under which you can have every comfort of the electronic age in your home, provided—and this is important—provided the outside of your house preserves some flavor of dilapidated American gothic. In other words, the Victorian false front has turned face.

"Where the original Arcadian lived rather wretchedly inside and put up the false front outside, we are to have all the indoor comforts of an air-conditioned mausoleum, but try not to let on.

"As nearly as I can make out, there are two schools of thought: those who fear Central City will turn into some opiate thing like Williamsburg, Virginia, and those who insist that it must.

"Neither faction need worry. The resurgence of the pioneer spirit is taking care of everything. We are honoring the pioneer as we never did before: he is no longer a static zombie; he marches with us, arm in arm, under a neon torch! . . . The bonanza soul is again whacking out the blossom rock."

The play series is to be resumed for a three-weeks' season in July, 1946, with the presentation of Verdi's *La Traviata* and Mozart's *Seraglio,* which will be performed on alternate nights by a distinguished cast under the direction of Frank St. Leger, assistant general manager of the Metropolitan Opera of New York.

CHAPTER V

1. See Howard L. Conrad, *"Uncle Dick" Wootton* (Chicago, 1890).

2. Byers' partner, Thomas Gibson, soon withdrew from the enterprise and founded the *Rocky Mountain Herald,* Colorado's first daily newspaper, which is now a weekly, published and edited by Thomas Hornsby Ferril, one of America's great poets and one of the few authentic voices of the West in either verse or prose. For the spirit, color, and "feel" of the Pike's Peak country, see his books of verse, especially *High Passage* and *Westering.*

3. See J. E. Wharton, *History of the City of Denver from the Earliest Settlement to the Present Time* (Denver, 1866).

4. See the Reverend W. J. Howlett, *Life of the Right Reverend Joseph P. Machebeuf* (Pueblo, Colo., 1908); and "Bishop Machebeuf," in *The Colorado Magazine* (July, 1935). Born in France in 1812, at Riom, in the province of Auvergne, and educated there, Father

Machebeuf sailed for America in 1839, journeying first to Ohio, coming west in 1851. He appears in Willa Cather's *Death Comes for the Archbishop,* an eloquent novel based upon the life of Father Machebeuf's superior, Archbishop John B. Lamy of Santa Fe, New Mexico. Father Machebeuf was consecrated Bishop of Colorado in 1868, dying in Denver in 1889.

5. The Ute were of Shoshonean stock and apparently Colorado's only indigenous tribe. The Arapaho and Cheyenne, of Algonkian stock, had been pushed south and westward by the increasing pressure of white settlement. Both tribes were divided into northern and southern bands, and together commanded the territory along the mountains from the North Platte to the Arkansas. Other Indians on the neighboring Plains were the Comanche, of Shoshonean stock, and the even fiercer Kiowa, of unknown origin.

6. See Albert D. Richardson, *Beyond*

the Mississippi (New York, 1867) and his racy letters from Denver City at this time, in *Kansas Historical Quarterly* (1943), Vol. 12.

7. For the importance of the revolver in the conquest of the West, see Walter Prescott Webb, *The Great Plains* (Boston, 1931), pp. 167-79.

CHAPTER VI

1. I have a theory, open for discussion and subject to exploration by competent psychopathologists, that many of the "lone wolves" who came to the West in the wild and woolly days were schizophreniacs, driven to desperate adventure and often bloody violence by their own difficulties and deep-seated emotional conflicts. They sought in the free and unconventional ways of the Frontier a release from the maladjustments they suffered under the restraints imposed by established and more rigid social patterns at home. In a life of action and danger allowing them little time for introspection, they hoped to bury their own inner confusions and forget themselves, even lose their identity, as many of them did, cutting all ties with the past.

From reading the records and from other evidence it is obvious that many of them were sexually maladjusted to an acute degree. They suffered from what James Thurber has wittily but penetratingly called "pedestalism," which is a sort of virginity complex in reverse, as it were. In their minds they could not associate sex with a "decent" woman and stood in frightened, speechless awe of such remote and chilling goddesses. They were always unhappily ill at ease in their presence and at the first sign that a camp was about to become respectable and succumb to domesticity, the "bad men" and many a law-abiding old sourdough took to their heels and fled to the far frontier.

The obverse of this was the attitude that, as no "good" woman had anything to do with sex, those who frankly did—the women of the town—were scarcely human; indeed, were lower than animals, and to be treated accordingly, with all manner of brutality and perversion. Anyone who knows the mountains is well aware that the traditional old sourdough was celibate only in terms of respectable society, and those who have listened to his stories also know that the most blood-curdling tales of violence and sadism on the Frontier have never been printed, and never will be.

CHAPTER VII

1. Sutherland returned to the Pike's Peak country, it appears, and in 1865 was keeping a small hotel in the camp of Breckenridge, on the headwaters of the Blue, on the far side of the Continental Divide. Bayard Taylor, poet and novelist, later our ambassador at the Court of St. James's, came on a visit and was a guest at the hotel, reporting that Sutherland, "taking the bugle with which he blew the signal for the immortal Light Brigade charge at Balaclava, made the notes of 'Peas upon the Trencher' ring over the shanties of Breckenridge."

For many of the Colorado camps in '65, see Bayard Taylor, *Colorado: A Summer Trip* (New York, 1867).

2. Some of the type lost in the flood came to light in 1932, at the depth of the Depression, when some destitute old sourdoughs began panning the sands of Cherry Creek again to make a few dollars a day when they were lucky.

3. See Clark Wissler, *North American Indians of the Plains* (New York, 1920); also, Walter Prescott Webb, *The Great Plains* (*supra*), pp. 47-84, for an excellent summary of the horse culture of the Plains Indians.

4. This is not the present Fort Lyon, which lies some twenty miles upstream, built there in 1866 when Bent's fort at Big Timbers, the first Fort Lyon, threatened to fall into the Arkansas which was undermining the bank on which it stood.

5. Colonel William Bent had tried desperately to prevent the outbreak of hostilities, getting little encouragement and less cooperation from the local authorities. Five years later, in 1869, the greatest of the Plainsmen died at his daughter's ranch beside the Purgatoire River, a few miles from where his famous Old Fort had stood along the Arkansas, forcibly separated at last from the Cheyenne and Arapaho with whom he had lived at peace for more than forty years.

6. Three years later, in 1867, Hal Sayre became Adjutant-General of Colorado Territory, serving until 1872. After his first summer of unsuccessful prospecting, Sayre settled at Central City and opened an assaying and abstract office there. In later years he was president of a local bank and one of Senator Teller's partners in many mining ventures, dying in Denver in 1926, aged ninety-one.

7. For Jim Beckwourth, a Virginia mulatto, most fabulous of the Mountain Men, who early joined the powerful Crow (the Sparrowhawk people of the northern Plains) and rose to be a war-chief among them, see T. D. Bonner (ed.), *The Life and Adventures of James P. Beckwourth* (New York, 1856), reprinted in the American Deserta Series (New York, 1931), with notes and a splendid introduction by Bernard DeVoto.

In his narrative Beckwourth, known to the Crow as Bloody Arm, attributed to himself a great many of the extraordinary and often next-to-incredible exploits of the Mountain Men, being always the hero of his tall tales. But there was an innocent quality about Beckwourth's lying. A born storyteller, he knew the secret of personalizing a good yarn, partly to satisfy his own ego, quite as much to fascinate his audience with ostensibly a first-hand account of what happened, a literary device that all of us now and again indulge in to point up and sharpen a good story that has come to us second-hand.

Throughout, Beckwourth jumbles events and greatly magnifies them, to increase his stature and prowess, but the tales he tells are essentially true. The things he relates did happen, though not always quite as he describes them. His story is an authentic Odyssey of the Old West, a western Song of Roland, with all of the primitive "magic" of the plain and mountain country when first seen by the white man.

"Here is the West," as DeVoto rightly says, dismissing the pedants who have wasted their time pointing out the historical inaccuracies in the yarn. "From these pages, better than from any others that exist, can be recovered the era of the mountain trade. . . . Here one may find the American savage unretouched."

8. See George Bird Grinnell, *The Fighting Cheyenne* (New York, 1915), which contains a carefully documented and masterful account of the Indian troubles and the Sand Creek Massacre; and Howard M. Fast, *The Last Frontier* (New York, 1941), for the Cheyenne's final desperate dash for freedom, as heroic an episode as any in history.

9. See Harvey O'Connor, *Mellon's Millions* (New York, 1933), pp. 96-7. The Larimer and Mellon families had been friends for years, long before 1854, when Judge Thomas Mellon was named administrator of Larimer's affairs when the latter's bank crashed, with assets of $410,000 and liabilities of $758,000. At Leavenworth, in 1867, the General's daughter Rachel was married to the Judge's second son, James Ross Mellon, and their first-born, William Larimer Mellon, was for years (from Andrew Mellon's appointment as Secretary of the Treasury in 1921 to his own retirement in the late 1930's) the head of the far-flung Mellon empire of banks, trust

and insurance companies, aluminum, oil, coal, gas, electricity, railroads, railway equipment, and traction lines—which must have brought a wan smile of envy and admiration to the ghostly lips of the old General as he thought of his own cemetery and real estate enterprises in Denver.

CHAPTER VIII

1. Of Augusta Tabor's diary, obviously one of the most interesting and fascinating of its day, all that remains is this single page, now in the possession of the Colorado State Historical Society. How it got out of the diary is not known.

After Augusta's death the diary passed to her son, Maxcy Tabor, a banker, who kept it under lock and key for reasons that will be obvious. Presumably, it was among his effects when he died, but his wife declared that it could not be found, and it remains "lost." It may possibly have been destroyed, but one still hopes that it will turn up some day and be published as one of the great human documents of its day.

In later years Augusta Tabor granted many interviews and did some writing on the early days, contributing much to our knowledge of the period.

In his *Silver Dollar* (New York, 1932), David Karsner claims that Augusta's diary was made "available" to him by Mrs. Maxcy Tabor, shortly after her husband's death. If so, Karsner is the only one to have seen it. But there is certainly no slightest evidence of this in his book.

2. See "Father" J. L. Dyer, *The Snow-shoe Itinerant* (Cincinnati, 1890), a graphic and endearing account of the trials and tribulations, and the quiet heroism, of a boom-camp preacher.

3. See David J. Cook, *Hands Up: A Pioneer Detective in Colorado* (Denver, 1897); and William R. Collier and Edwin V. Westrate, *Dave Cook of the Rockies* (New York, 1936). As a youth of nineteen, Cook had joined the rush to Gregory Gulch at the height of the excitement there in '59; he died peacefully in his bed in Denver in 1907.

CHAPTER IX

1. This chapter and the three following are based largely upon the Leadville newspapers of the day, manuscripts, and pamphlet sources in the Colorado State Historical Society and the Denver Public Library.

2. See Harvey O'Connor, *The Guggenheims: The Making of an American*

Dynasty (New York, 1937).

3. The value of the grubstake was $17.50, according to some—$64.75, according to others.

4. For a different version of the discovery of the Crysolite, see Lewis C. Gandy, *The Tabors* (New York, 1934).

CHAPTER X

1. Mart Duggan appears as Chris McGrath in *Youth Rides West* (New York, 1925), by Will Irwin, who was born and grew up in Leadville.

2. See Frank Waters, *Midas of the Rockies* (New York, 1937).

3. See Evalyn Walsh McLean, *Father Struck It Rich* (Boston, 1936).

Commenting upon this passage, Mrs. McLean took exception to my statement: "Mother was the *most* refined woman I ever knew," she declared, "and she was not an isolated case even in the wildest days of Leadville."

The Walshes soon sold the Grand Hotel and moved up into Sowbelly Gulch, as the uninitiated persisted in calling it.

4. Having squandered his fortune, Rische ended his days as night watchman at the state capitol building in Denver. George Hook saved his money and left most of it to the Odd Fellows Orphanage at Canon City, a town which seems to have been wise beyond its years in its younger days. In 1868, when offered its choice of the contemplated state university or the established state penitentiary, it chose the latter on the ground that it was a going concern and likely to be better attended, which was a not unreasonable assumption at the time.

CHAPTER XI

1. See Mary Hallock Foote, *The Last Assembly Ball* (Boston, 1889) and her *Led-horse Claim* (Boston, 1882), which was the first of the romances laid in the Colorado mining camps.

2. "Powder House Billy," barkeeper at the Tabor Grand Hotel (now the Vendome, one of the gayest and pleasantest hostelries in the mountains), had his own way of dealing with anti-saloon cranks. When one of them came in, ordered a number of drinks, drank them all, and then refused to pay as a matter of principle, "Powder House Billy" came around from the back of the bar and knocked him cold, remarking that he did not wish to encourage intemperance.

3. For one of the greatest "con" men of the day, who got his start here in Leadville at this time, see William Ross Collier and Edwin V. Westrate, *The Reign of Soapy Smith: Monarch of Misrule in the Last Days of the Old West and the Klondike Gold Rush* (New York, 1935). Soapy met his end at the hands of vigilantes in 1898 at Skagway, Alaska, three days after leading a great Fourth of July parade.

4. See Robert Ross (ed.), *The Complete Works of Oscar Wilde* (New York, 1921).

5. One of the State Street girls, a "hostess" at the old Pioneer Saloon which opened in 1882 and has never closed its doors, not even during the Prohibition era, was interviewed by the *Rocky Mountain News* in 1935.

"These modern girls are a bunch of ninnies," Maude Deuel is reported to have said, "and the modern man is worse—a sissy of the first water. . . . In my day, you were either good or bad. These ninnies do everything that branded us as bad—and get away with it."

Just why they are "ninnies" is not so plain.

CHAPTER XII

1. For the much-maligned Molly Maguires, see Anthony Bimba, *The Molly Maguires* (New York, 1932).

2. The Miners' Co-operative Union, it has since transpired, was secretly chartered by the Knights of Labor, organized in 1869, America's first national labor organization. A year after the Leadville strike, in 1881, there was founded at Pittsburgh the organization that five years later became the American Federation of Labor.

3. For the frank aims of the exponents of "law and order," see Carlyle C. Davis, *Olden Times in Colorado* (Los Angeles, 1916).

4. For an objective "public interest" view of the strike, see David J. Cook, *Hands Up* (*supra*).

CHAPTER XIII

1. See Elmer Ellis, *Henry Moore Teller: Defender of the West* (Caldwell, Idaho, 1941). As already remarked, Teller was another of the "bright young men" who got their start in the early days at Central City, in the "Golden Kingdom of Gilpin," as local watchdogs of the mining and milling corporations with offices in New York.

2. Hundreds of stories have been told of this romance, many of them self-contradictory, some of them highly salacious, and neither Tabor nor his wife ever attempted to deny or contradict them. During her long life the second Mrs. Tabor shunned all interviews and explanations.

After her death, *True Story Magazine* (January-May, 1938) carried a series of articles entitled: "Silver Queen: Baby Doe's Life Story, as told to Sue Bonnie," which adds some new material that is probably true, for Sue Bonnie was Mrs. Tabor's most intimate friend in her last years.

In general, however, the series is a piece of patchwork. Whole paragraphs were lifted from the original edition of this book and from others without quotes or any acknowledgment. Throughout, the articles are gushy and "corny," tailored to fit the MacFadden "true story" formula. Nevertheless, I believe that many of the graphic personal details could have been supplied only by Mrs. Tabor, and for some there is corroborative evidence.

As Sue Bonnie reports the story, Harvey Doe and his wife quarreled at Central City, and he returned to Wisconsin, leaving her stranded. In her plight she was befriended by Jake Smith, a professional gambler, who ran a table at the Gold Boom Saloon on Eureka Street. It was he who made it possible for her to come to Leadville.

Arriving early in 1880, she first met Tabor a week or two later at the old Saddle Rock Café, opposite the Tabor Opera House on Harrison Avenue. She was sitting there alone one evening, sad and depressed, when Tabor and Bill Bush came in during the intermission at the theater for their usual refreshments —oysters and champagne. Baby Doe caught Tabor's eye, and he sent a waiter over with a penciled note scratched on the back of a theater program;

"Won't you join us at our table?"

The evening passed quickly and happily, particularly after Bill Bush had returned to the theater, and after the second or third bucket of champagne. Learning of her obligations to Jake Smith, Tabor insisted on paying off her indebtedness to him—about $1,000. Taking a pen from his pocket, he handed her a draft for $5,000.

"Just a grubstake," he said when she hesitated to accept it, "and you'll need some clothes and other things, too."

In a few days she was occupying a suite on the third floor of the Clarendon Hotel, which was connected with the Opera House by a bridge over the alley. Some months later both she and Tabor had suites at the Windsor Hotel in Denver, though she soon removed to the American House to quiet gossip.

CHAPTER XIV

1. On March 8, 1883, Secretary of the Interior Teller wrote Dawson, a friend and associate (see Elmer Ellis, *Henry Moore Teller*):

"Tabor has gone home. I thank God he was not elected for six years; thirty days nearly killed us. I humiliated myself to attend his wedding because he was Senator from Colorado—but Mrs. Teller would not. . . . Tabor is an honest man in money matters, and I believe he is truthful, but he made a great fool of himself with reference to that woman, and he ought now to retire and attend to his private affairs."

2. At this time *The Statesman* of

Bayonne, New Jersey, began booming Tabor for the presidency in an article widely quoted:

FOR PRESIDENT OF THE UNITED STATES

HORACE A. TABOR

Silver King of the Pacific Coast, Colorado's Citizen, Banker, and Senator of Sterling Worth and Purity of Character

AN INDEPENDENT STATESMAN UPHOLDING THE CONSTITUTION AND THE UNION

A Foe to Monopoly and Centralization of the Money Powers Endangering Liberty, Favoring a Gold and Silver Currency, and Protection of the Manufacturing of the Country. Champion of the Working Man. A New Light from the Ranks of the People.

In reprinting this, the *Rocky Mountain News* remarked that Tabor was probably as good as anyone the Republicans could find.

3. For Cripple Creek and neighboring camps, see (American Guide Series) *Colorado: A Guide to the Highest State* (New York, 1941), pp. 245-52.

4. For a fine biography of Stratton, the eccentric carpenter who became a great bonanza king, and for a lively account of the Cripple Creek gold field, "the $300,000,000 cow pasture," see Frank Waters, *Midas of the Rockies* (New York, 1937).

Upon striking it rich after twenty years of hardship, Stratton shocked all of the "better" people of Colorado Springs, his home, by not building a huge mansion but buying an old two-storied frame house, on the edge of the business district, which he himself had built some years before. On one occasion every laundress in the city received a bicycle from him so that all of them might ride to work. And a few years before his death in 1902, to show local "society" what he thought of it, he took out a card in the Carpenters' Union.

He also shocked the community by leaving most of his fortune to establish the Myron Stratton Home, an intelligently conceived and well managed institution which stands on the outskirts of the city, for the care of local residents physically incapable of earning a livelihood, young and old alike. Many loudly protested that it would merely attract tramps to "Little London," though the community now points to it with pride.

5. Rummaging through his papers a few years later, Stratton came upon Tabor's note and the deed to his Arizona mine, and returned them to him with this letter, one of the few acts of generosity toward the bewildered and beaten old man: (see Frank Waters, *Midas of the Rockies,* pp. 197-8).

September 24 1898

Hon. H. A. W. Tabor
Denver

Dear Sir:

Mr. W. S. Stratton wishes me to say that he never at any time contemplated the retention of your note and papers as an evidence of indebtedness to him on your part, and in going over his affairs he finds them still on hand contrary to his wishes and intentions. If they remain with him, he must list them with the assessor of taxes and in case of his demise they could not then be returned by his Executors. He therefore directs that they be returned to you at once and asks that you accept them back again as an expression of his best wishes and good will for your future success.

*Respectfully and sincerely yours,
William A. Ramsay
Secretary for W. S. Stratton*

For a preposterous version of this Stratton loan, see David Karsner, *Silver Dollar* (New York, 1932), a book brimming with incredible misinformation and uninformed surmise.

6. When the Matchless was about to be sold for $15,000 to satisfy a judgment, Stratton liquidated all claims

against it and secured the title in Mrs. Tabor's name—a generosity publicly applauded by the employees of the Denver post office and the miners of Cripple Creek and Leadville. See Frank Waters, *Midas of the Rockies (supra)*, pp. 231-32.

7. In 1928, a $14,000 mortgage on the Matchless was foreclosed by the Shorego Mining Company, owned by J. K. Mullens of Denver, one of Mrs. Tabor's wealthy benefactors. But the action was merely a technical one. It was taken, said Mrs. Tabor, "to prevent depredations and to prevent me from unfortunate business dealings. The Matchless has really been mine."

8. For my portrait of Mrs. Tabor at this time, I am chiefly indebted to the late Henry M. Butler, publisher and editor of the Leadville *Herald-Democrat,* one of her close friends during her late years. Though I saw her in the street from time to time, I never managed an occasion to meet and talk with Mrs. Tabor.

While I was in Leadville in 1930, gathering material, Butler suggested one noontime that we visit Mrs. Tabor at her cabin, saying that he would do most of the talking and, if things went well, I might have an opportunity to slip in a question or two. That summer her favorite brother, Phil, a professional gambler in his day, the only one of her family with whom she was friendly, was staying with Mrs. Tabor.

As Butler and I came up the slope into sight, the two of them were sitting in front of the old cabin on the dump of the Matchless. Spying us, Mrs. Tabor rose and went inside. Phil received us pleasantly and very courteously, and after some conversation Butler asked if he might see Mrs. Tabor, saying that he would vouch for me. Phil went inside the small one-room shack and finally came out to say, quite formally: "Mrs. Tabor is not at home."

9. Later, almost a score of trunks were found in a Denver warehouse, all filled with Tabor finery from the 1880's and 1890's, including the elaborate silk-and-lace dresses of "Baby" Tabor and the $7,000 gown worn by Mrs. Tabor when she was married at the Willard in Washington. These and other Tabor relics are on view in the Colorado State Museum, Denver.

10. As the news of Mrs. Tabor's death was flashed across the country, reporters set out to find her elder daughter, and finally succeeded. But the latter refused to be interviewed, saying that she had no comment to make on Mrs. Tabor and her tragic fate, even denying her relationship with her mother and father, saying that she was the daughter of Tabor's brother John, who had lived obscurely in Denver during his later years.

11. For the enterprising Mrs. James J. Brown, see Lewis Graham and Edwin Olmstead, *The Unsinkable Mrs. Jay* (New York, 1934).

The Campion fortune was the means of establishing another great Colorado industry and many more large bonanza fortunes, those of the Sugar Beet Kings, now the ruling dynasty. From the Little Johnny and others in the Ibex group of mines at Leadville came the gold that built the first sugar beet refinery in the state, at Grand Junction, in 1899.

More than twenty years before, in 1876, Peter Magnes, a farmer a few miles up the Platte from Denver, had written with clear-eyed prophecy, "If we had sugar beet factories in Colorado . . . I imagine Colorado farmers would produce more gold than all the miners in the mountains."

For years, the sugar beet has been the Pike's Peak country's largest single source of revenue.

As for hard-rock mining, it has been estimated by competent engineers that, as an industry, it does not pay for itself —that more money has been put into the ground than was ever taken out. A few of the more fortunate, of course, have made millions, but the industry's books as a whole do not balance.

12. The sale of the building and its probable demolition were reported by the Denver *Post* in October, 1945.

SELECTIVE BIBLIOGRAPHY

This list is for the general reader who may wish to get off the main track and into one or another special field.

Readable, authentic, and comprehensive, the best single volume on the Pike's Peak country, past and present, is (American Guide Series) *Colorado: A Guide to the Highest State* (New York, 1941).

Almost all of the books on this list can be found in any large library. Those marked with an asterisk (*) are fiction. They have been included not because they are particularly good, for the most part, but because they are all we have.

The list has been divided into three categories:

I. BEFORE THE GOLD RUSH

Bonner, T. D. (ed.), *The Life and Adventures of James P. Beckwourth.* New York, 1856. (See reprint, New York, 1931, with introduction by Bernard DeVoto.)

Chittenden, H. M. *The American Fur Trade of the Far West.* New York, 1906.

Conrad, Howard L. *"Uncle Dick" Wootton.* Chicago, 1890.

DeVoto, Bernard. *The Year of the Decision: 1846.* Boston, 1942.

Duffus, R. L. *The Santa Fe Trail.* New York, 1930.

Farnham, Thomas Jefferson. *Travels in the Great Western Prairies.* Poughkeepsie, N. Y., 1841.

*Fergusson, Harvey. *Wolf Song.* New York, 1927.
   Superb tale based upon deep knowledge and understanding of the life of the Mountain Men.

Garrard, Lewis Hector. *Wah-To-Yah, and the Taos Trail.* Cincinnati, Ohio, 1850.
   Best contemporary account of pre-Gold Rush days in the plain and mountain country.

Ghent, W. J. *The Road to Oregon.* New York, 1934.

Gregg, Josiah. *The Commerce of the Prairies, the Journal of a Santa Fe Trader.* New York. 1844.

Grinnell, George Bird. "Bent's Old Fort and Its Builders," in Kansas State Historical Society Collections, Vol. 15.

————. *The Cheyenne Indians: Their History and Ways of Life*. New Haven, Conn., 1923.

————. *The Fighting Cheyenne*. New York, 1915.

Hafen, LeRoy R., and Ghent, W. J. *Broken Hand*. Denver, 1931. Biography of Tom Fitzpatrick, perhaps the greatest of the Mountain Men.

Majors, Alexander. *Seventy Years on the Frontier*. New York, 1893.

Marcy, Col. R. B. *Thirty Years of Army Life on the Border*. New York, 1866.

Nevins, Allan. *Frémont: The World's Greatest Adventurer*. New York, 1928.

Oregon Trail (American Guide Series). New York, 1939.

Parkman, Francis. *The Oregon and California Trail*. New York, 1849.

Ruxton, George Frederick. *Adventures in Mexico and the Rocky Mountains*. London, 1847.

*————. *Life in the Far West*. London, 1849.

Sage, Rufus B. *Rocky Mountain Life*. Boston, 1857.

*Vestal, Stanley. *Dobe Walls*. Boston, 1929.

————. *Kit Carson*. Boston, 1928.

Webb, Walter Prescott. *The Great Plains*. Boston, 1931.

Wissler, Clark. *North American Indians of the Plains*. New York, 1920.

II. PIKE'S PEAK OR BUST

Davis, Herman S. (ed.), *Reminiscences of General William H. Larimer and of His Son William H. H. Larimer*. Lancaster, Pa., 1918.

Foreman, Grant. *Marcy and the Gold Hunters*. Norman, Okla. 1939.

Greeley, Horace. *An Overland Journey from New York to San Francisco in the Summer of 1859*. New York, 1860.

Hafen, LeRoy R. *Colorado Gold Rush: Contemporary Letters and Reports*. Glendale, Calif., 1941.

————. *Overland Routes to the Gold Fields: 1859*. Glendale, 1942.

————. *Pike's Peak Gold Rush Guide Books of 1859*, Glendale, 1941.

Richardson, Albert D. *Beyond the Mississippi*. New York, 1867.

————. "Letters from Denver City," etc., in *Kansas Historical Quarterly* (1943), Vol. 12.

Villard, Henry. *Past and Present of the Pike's Peak Region*. St. Louis, 1860.

III. AFTER THE GOLD RUSH

Bird, Isabella L. *A Lady's Life in the Rocky Mountains*. New York, 1875.

Breakenridge, William. *Helldorado*. Boston, 1928.

Collier, William R., and Westrate, Edwin V. *Dave Cook of the Rockies: Frontier General, Fighting Sheriff, and Leader of Men*. New York, 1936.

Cook, David J. *Hands Up: or Thirty-five Years of Detective Work in the Mountains and Plains*. Denver, 1897.

Davis, Carlyle C. *Olden Times in Colorado*. Los Angeles, 1916.

Dyer, "Father" J. L. *The Snow-Shoe Itinerant*. Cincinnati, 1890.

Ellis, Anne. *The Life of an Ordinary Woman*. Boston, 1929.
> An honest and extraordinarily vivid account of life in Bonanza, Cripple Creek, and other Pike's Peak mining camps—one of the great American autobiographies.

Ellis, Elmer. *Henry Moore Teller: Defender of the West*. Caldwell, Idaho, 1941.

Ferril, Thomas Hornsby. *High Passage*. New Haven, 1926; *Westering*. New Haven, 1934; and *Trial by Time*. New York, 1944.
> There is more of the Rocky Mountain West, past and present, in these three volumes of verse than in thirty volumes of conventional history.

*Foote, Mary Hallock. *The Led-Horse Claim*. Boston, 1882, and *The Last Assembly Ball*. Boston, 1889.
> Novels picturing life in Leadville during the boom.

Fowler, Gene. *Timberline*. New York, 1933.
> Story of the fabulous Denver *Post* and its owners, "Bon" and "Tam," who climaxed their career—as fantastic in its way as Tabor's—by muscling in on the Teapot Dome swindle and pocketing $1,000,000.

*Graham, Lewis, and Olmstead, Edwin. *The Unsinkable Mrs. Jay*. New York, 1934.
> Story of the "unsinkable" Mrs. James J. Brown, wife of one of the later bonanza kings of Leadville.

Howbert, Irving. *Memoirs of a Lifetime in the Pike's Peak Region*. New York, 1925.

*Irwin, Will. *Youth Rides West*. New York, 1925.

McLean, Mrs. Evalyn Walsh. *Father Struck It Rich*. Boston, 1936.

*Raine, William McLeod. *Highgrader*. New York, 1915, and *Colorado*. New York, 1928.

Good popular fiction.

*Sinclair, Upton. *Mountain City*. New York, 1930.

*Sublette, Clifford D. *Golden Chimney*. Boston, 1931.

Taylor, Bayard. *Colorado: A Summer Trip*. New York, 1867.

Waters, Frank. *Midas of the Rockies*. New York, 1937.

Spirited biography of the bonanza king, Winfield Scott Stratton, the eccentric ex-carpenter.

Wharton, J. E. *History of the City of Denver from the Earliest Settlement to the Present Time*. Denver, 1866.

INDEX